# CULTURESHOCK!

A Survival Guide to Customs and Etiquette

## FINLAND

Deborah Swallow

This edition published in 2008 by:
Marshall Cavendish Corporation
99 White Plains Road
Tarrytown, NY 10591-9001
www.marshallcavendish.us



Other Marshall Cavendish Offices:
Marshall Cavendish International (Asia) Private Limited. 1 New Industrial Road, Singapore 536196 ■ Marshall Cavendish Ltd. 5th Floor, 32–38 Saffron Hill, London EC1N 8FH, UK ■ Marshall Cavendish International (Thailand) Co Ltd. 253 Asoke, 12th Flr, Sukhumvit 21 Road, Klongtoey Nua, Wattana, Bangkok 10110, Thailand ■ Marshall Cavendish (Malaysia) Sdn Bhd, Times Subang, Lot 46, Subang Hi-Tech Industrial Park, Batu Tiga, 40000 Shah Alam, Selangor Darul Ehsan, Malaysia



ISBN 10: 0-7614-5506-1
ISBN 13: 978-0-7614-5506-6

Please contact the publisher for the Library of Congress catalog number

Printed in China by Everbest Printing Co Ltd

Photo Credits
All photos by the author except pages 86, 137, 147, 200 (courtesy of Finland Tourist Board, UK Office); pages 156–157, 196–197 (Photolibrary)
■ Cover photo: Photolibrary

All illustrations by TRIGG

# ABOUT THE SERIES

Culture shock is a state of disorientation that can come over anyone who has been thrust into unknown surroundings, away from one's comfort zone. *CultureShock!* is a series of trusted and reputed guides which has, for decades, been helping expatriates and long-term visitors to cushion the impact of culture shock whenever they move to a new country.

Written by people who have lived in the country and experienced culture shock themselves, the authors share all the information necessary for anyone to cope with these feelings of disorientation more effectively. The guides are written in a style that is easy to read and covers a range of topics that will arm readers with enough advice, hints and tips to make their lives as normal as possible again.

Each book is structured in the same manner. It begins with the first impressions that visitors will have of that city or country. To understand a culture, one must first understand the people—where they came from, who they are, the values and traditions they live by, as well as their customs and etiquette. This is covered in the first half of the book.

Then on with the practical aspects—how to settle in with the greatest of ease. Authors walk readers through topics such as how to find accommodation, get the utilities and telecommunications up and running, enrol the children in school and keep in the pink of health. But that's not all. Once the essentials are out of the way, venture out and try the food, enjoy more of the culture and travel to other areas. Then be immersed in the language of the country before discovering more about the business side of things.

To round off, snippets of basic information are offered before readers are 'tested' on customs and etiquette of the country. Useful words and phrases, a comprehensive resource guide and list of books for further research are also included for easy reference.

# CONTENTS

Preface vi
Acknowledgements ix
Map of Finland x

Chapter 1
First Impressions 1

Tranquility and Conformity 2
Mobile Phones 4
Technology 5
Cleanliness 6
Customer Care 7
Reverse Logic 9
Traffic 9
Daylight Hours 10
First Impressions for a Finn 11

Chapter 2
Land, History, Economy and Government 13

Finland: A Land For All Seasons 14
Geography 16
Climate 20
History 26
Finland Today 39
Top of the Class 40
The Economy 41
Government, Politics and the Judiciary 49
The Military 52

Chapter 3
The Finns 54

Population 55
Physical Characteristics 56
Bilingualism 57
The Finns 58
Finnish Values 60
Finnish Values in Action 64
A Classless Society 67
Personal Space 71
Environmental Consciousness 73
Religion 76
Education 79
The Woman's Role 80
Marriage, the Family and Divorce 85
Finland's First Woman President 89

Chapter 4
Socialising with the Finns 91

Dress Code 92
Clothing You Need 95
Tolerance 97
Scandal 100
Alternative Lifestyles 101
Silence 102
Humour 104
Flirting 106
How to be a Good Guest 107
Dancing 107
Alcohol and Smoking 108
What to do at a Sauna Party? 109
Regional Differences 113

Chapter 5
Settling In 115

Administrative Procedures to Enter and Live in Finland 116
Finding A Home 116
Inside a Finnish Home 118
Getting a Telephone and Internet Line 121
Domestic Help 121
The Education System 122
Medical Facilities and Health Information 126
Provision for Religious Groups 126
Transportation 127
Traffic Safety and Road Conditions 132
What You Can Import 133
Shopping 135

Chapter 6
Food and Entertainment 138

The Cuisine 140
Lappish Food 144
Typical Finnish Dishes 145
Special Occasions 149
Eating Out 150
Dining Out with a Finn 152
The Coffee Culture 153
Cafés 154
Restaurants 155
Buying Food 160

Chapter 7
Enjoying the Culture 163

Finnish Heros and Champions 164
They Call This Sport 169
Holidays 170
Seeing Santa Claus 175
Things To Do 180
Travel 186
Hotels and Lodgings 191
The Regions 195
The Towns 199

Chapter 8
The Language and the Literature 207

The Language 208
Learning the Language 213
The Literature 216
Finnish Folklore 219
Finnish Sayings 220

Chapter 9
Working in Finland 222

The Finnish Handshake 226
Getting Down to Business 227
Meetings and Appointments 229
Negotiations 230
Decisions and Actions 231
Consensus 232
Presentations 233
Letter and Emails 234
Customer Care 235
Payment Terms 238
Corruption 238
Money and Banking 239
Applying for a Work Permit 241
Finding a Job 242

Chapter 10
Fast Facts 244

Culture Quiz 256
Do's and Don'ts 262
Glossary 266
Resource Guide 270
Further Reading 296
About the Author 299
Index 300

# PREFACE

I first fell in love with Finland in the summer of 1997. It was my first trip to the country and I was travelling with my new boss who was Finnish. He spent the entire plane trip from London Heathrow to Helsinki enthusing about his country, telling me about the people and the geography. It was obvious he had such a love and a pride for Finland. Since then, I've been travelling to Finland at least once or twice every month and his enthusiasm and love for his country has spilled over to me. I now realise, of course, that this love and pride is not exclusive to Seppo, but is shared by the Finns as a race.

Indeed, this love and pride is well deserved. This small nation has made a substantial contribution to world civilisation out of all proportion to its size and the number of its population. Finland is not a major power and is not on the main road to anywhere, so few people really get to know anything about the country. Back in 1990, Finland was reckoned to be the most expensive country in the world. However, today it is far more affordable, especially compared with its Scandinavian neighbours. The Finns are currently more prosperous than all but a very few developed industrial countries, but they have a more peaceful life-style and live in a 'softer' society.

Finland, however, is a land full of contrasts and contradictions. The Finns often seem aloof or restrained but in contrast, once you get to know them, they have a great sense of humour (and can be very noisy!). Of course, the weather in the winter can be extremely cold, but that first summer I spent in Finland, the temperature was up in the thirties. The long winter nights are contrasted with the length of the wonderful summer sunshiny days. Over the years, both East and West have influenced Finland and, therefore, its culture is a surprising mixture of the two. Some of the old traditions of the East survive happily in their high tech world. The Finns love new and modern things, and always have the latest gadgets, but in stark contrast some of their customs have their roots in a bygone age.

It has been said that the Finns are very dour and solemn. But they do love to laugh and have a great sense of humour. They really are the first to joke about themselves and have a great sense of humility: "An American, a German and a Finn are looking at an elephant. The American wonders if the elephant would be good in a circus, the German wonders what price he would get if he sold it, and the Finn asks himself, 'I wonder what the elephant thinks of me?'"

Finland is a country where you can still get away from it all, enjoying picnics in pristine forests of pine, spruce and birch. Amongst these undisturbed forests, you'll discover crystal-clear lakes and huge quiet skies. Here you will encounter spiritual richness and plenty of recreational opportunities such as trekking or fishing. But when you've had enough of the peace and quiet, you can roll into town and enjoy the many activities going on. There are always festivals and concerts taking place and a town never misses out on its weekly dances!

I hope, as the reader, you will find this an informative book about Finland, but my main wish is to help you understand some of those things that have captivated, delighted, charmed and sometimes puzzled me about this country. Finns argue that they are extremely individualistic, although, to the outside world, they share a group mentality and dislike standing out in the crowd. My experiences in Finland and of the Finnish value-set have influenced me profoundly. They have changed my life, especially my attitudes to business, and have added richness in a way I would not have dreamed possible before I went.

This book is not meant to be the definitive tourists' guide; there are plenty of those. This book, written with love and admiration, has a different focus—it tries to paint a picture of Finnish life, as seen through my eyes and heard through my ears, and draws on Finnish history to explain its culture, traditions, behaviour, literature, music and mindset. This book is targeted at those wishing to have an insight into the character of the Finns and an understanding of how they have won more Olympic medals than any other nation, lead the world in competitiveness and are number one in the Environmental Sustainability Index. This book is definitely not intended to be just a tourists' one-stop book. Therefore, the reader will find in this book only brief descriptions of the regions and tourist centres.

For this new edition of *CultureShock! Finland*, I want to re-emphasise to you, the reader, that my experiences have been interpreted through the 'eyes and ears' of an English woman, brought up in an overpopulated part of south-east England, of English parents and with a British cultural background. My interpretation of Finnish life is, therefore, coloured by my own background, or 'spectacles' so to speak. However, I hope that I have been able to intertwine with my own thoughts the many stories and various experiences of foreign colleagues, friends and fellow travellers that I have met along the way. This edition has been enriched by the many Finns from all over the world who have written to me over the years after reading the first edition, giving me snippets of new information, little anecdotes and occasional corrections: "just because we want to get our story out!"

Finland is a highly industrialised and technology-driven nation with a deep-rooted sense of time-honoured values. In many respects, it has protected itself from the greed of individuals and has worked towards the common good. This is all part of the Finnish culture of 'striving for excellence' which you will come to know as you read on. Each decade creates its own standards for assessing the material well-being of its people. Until recently, the guiding principle has been continuous growth, but these days 'the good life' means spiritual harmony and a healthy environment. Aware companies pay increasing attention to work satisfaction, employee motivation, the work-leisure relationship and environmental issues. There has also been a revived interest in traditional and alternative methods of production.

In 1999, I wrote, 'I believe that I have been privileged to experience a gentle sort of society at the end of a violent, war-torn 20th century. Now poised at the beginning of a new millennium, one has to wonder how much Finland will change as it takes its rightful, prominent, place on the world's stage.' Now read on and make the discovery… Better still, go to Finland and widen your horizons because you will see and appreciate things from a very different angle.

*Tervetuloa*—Welcome—from Dr. Debby Swallow!

P.S. Summer 2007. CNN still haven't got Helsinki on their weather maps! Let's hope by the time the next edition comes out, with my help and yours, they will have discovered Finland.

# ACKNOWLEDGEMENTS



To my colleagues and fellow travellers whose shared stories and perceptions have given this book greater insight and richer stories—thank you for making Finland such a colourful place for us all to read about. To my dear friends (alphabetically): Hely Abondatti at the Finnish-British Chamber of Commerce (FBCC) in London; Seppo Hoffren in Kuopio and his staff; and Timo and Sari Holopainen in Helsinki—I hold you all warmly in my heart and thank you for giving me the gift of Finland that has changed my life immeasurably.

My thanks also to: Harry Mäkinen, my Finnish publisher from Yrityskirat, who gave me some of his short, humour-filled books on Finland that definitely gave me a very different view of the Finns; Roman Schatz (a German) whose totally irreverent view of the Finns had my sides splitting with laughter; Richard Lewis, whose deep insights into Finnish culture bring so much understanding; members of the Junior Chamber of Commerce in Finland from whom I always learn so much.

And, for the preparation of this book: Matti Sonck and Eeva Tulenheimo at the Helsinki City Tourist Information Office; Katariina Haarla-Heinonen and Jaana Hede at the FBCC who pulled out all the stops at the last minute to help me, Pirjo Pellinen at the Embassy of Finland in London; Annabel Battersby, an Australian who allowed me access to her blog about living in Finland; and, last but not least, Hannu Sivonen who kindly sent me a 12-page document, on reading my original book, to give me alternative insights and understandings, all of which have been included in this new edition.

Thank you.

# MAP OF FINLAND

# FIRST IMPRESSIONS

CHAPTER 1

'The voyage of discovery lies not in finding new landscapes, but in having new eyes.'
—Marcel Proust

YOUR FIRST IMPRESSIONS OF A COUNTRY stay with you all your life, and so has it has been for me and my experience of Finland. I would never have realised when I first arrived that I was about to fall in love with this country, its people and its values. Finland has completely changed my outlook on life, on the planet and on how we should conduct business. Perhaps you will come to understand some of this as you read this book. If you do, then my intention has been achieved. But let me not spoil the story by taking you straight to the destination. First you must enjoy the journey as I did—and experience those first impressions.

**Kevin's First Impressions**

Upon first moving to Finland, I went to visit my new Finnish in-laws at their house. We were all sitting around the kitchen table eating when the family dog walks into the room and my mother-in-law says to the dog, "*Pois*!" After we had eaten, we went to sit in the living room and the dog comes in again. I decide to pay the dog some attention, so I command the dog, "*Pois*! *Pois*!" My wife turns to me and asks, "I thought you liked dogs, why are you telling it to go away?" I had innocently guessed that '*pois*' meant sit and for the rest of the day whenever '*pois*' was said, everybody immediately sat down laughing. http://www.6d.fi/cultural_bemusion

## TRANQUILITY AND CONFORMITY

Your first impressions of Finland will probably be gleaned from arriving as a passenger at Helsinki airport. This sea of tranquillity is a foretaste of what greets the visitor in their travels around Finland. Helsinki airport really does have to be experienced to be believed. There is none of the hustle and bustle that greets you at most airports, nobody running around shouting and screaming at the top of their voices. If you arrive stressed out from travelling, Helsinki airport is a good place to 'chill out'. You will soon become calm and tranquil.

On my travels, I met up with two Armenian pilots who were on their fourth visit to Finland for flight simulation training. When I asked them what was the one thing that they liked best about Finland their answers were, "Calmness" and "Everyone is so civilised".

In fact, this peace and tranquillity transcends the whole country. You may well ask what is behind this tranquillity. Well, it has been said that the Finns must be the world's most obedient people. There seems to be a plethora of enforced rules and regulations that govern Finnish life. However as a visitor, you are not aware of the rules and regulations; you just realise that everybody conforms. This conformity can be seen in the décor in homes, the way people dress, the month they take their holidays, the newspapers and magazines they read, and, as I read, who they will vote for in the next election. The Finns themselves joke that of all the EU rules, they obey 120 per cent of them! Everyone, therefore, has an expectation of how everyone else is going to behave—and they usually do. Being loud is definitely frowned upon.

## MOBILE PHONES

The next thing that strikes the visitor is that everybody seems to be using a mobile phone. You wouldn't believe that the Finns are supposed to be the most silent, non-talkative nation in the world. Put a phone in their hands and they will talk away for hours! Even the Finns find this reversal of their national characteristic quite humorous and joke, "How do you get a Finn to talk? Put a phone in his hand!" A recent national advertising campaign in Finland for mobile phones conveyed the message, 'Helping Finns talk more'.

In 1991, Finland inaugurated the first Global System Mobile (GSM) network in the world; by 1999, 60 per cent of the population were mobile phone users; by 2006, 124 per cent of the population had a subscription (obviously some people have more than one). They are the highest per capita users of mobile phones in the world. Interestingly, Finland, as a nation, adopted the ordinary telephone faster than any other country. The Finns go for modern technology in a big way, and constantly look for ways of using it in their everyday lives. A mobile phone can be used to operate vending machines; the cost of the chocolate bar is added to the user's telephone bill. Even the smallest companies have all the latest technological gadgets.

I remember watching three gentlemen, in the quiet of a hotel breakfast-room, sitting at the same table having breakfast. None of them were taking much notice of the others for they were all too busy talking on their phones. It is extremely common to see people in a restaurant get up from the table, whilst answering their phone, and walk to a secluded spot to carry on their conversation. In Finnish society, it is considered good manners to excuse yourself from the company of others to conduct your conversation in private. So important is the mobile phone to a Finn that I concluded, shortly after I arrived in Finland, that the name 'coffee-break' was a misnomer and renamed it 'telephone time'.

**Phones Everywhere**

The invasiveness of the phone culture was brought home to my family in an amusing incident in Lapland. We had decided to spend a few days before Christmas experiencing the snow and the wilderness and went on a Reindeer safari. It was the first time any of us had ever been to this part of the world. Accompanied by only two reindeers, a dog and our guide, we set out across a frozen lake on our journey into nowhere. After half-an-hour, civilisation seemed thousands of miles away from us. Romantic notions of trekking in the wilderness were soon obliterated by a ringing in the jacket pocket of our guide—it was his mobile phone!

## TECHNOLOGY

Finland has a high-technology environment. She is commonly reputed to be the world's leading information society with an advanced communications infrastructure and with the highest penetration of mobile phones and Internet connections in the world. The Finns are also considered 'tech-savvy' and respond well to technological innovations, welcoming the benefits that they can bring to their working and domestic lives. It has been the rapid adoption of the new technologies by many industries, and especially financial institutions, that has made them world leaders in several sectors. It seems hardly surprising then that Finns always adapt to 'e-services' so quickly, as in online buying and bank services. You won't do anything the 'old-fashioned' way in Finland—if it can be done with new technology, it WILL be done with new technology, even down to paying for a chocolate bar with your mobile phone or a credit/debit card. It's almost a cashless society. You will notice gadgetry everywhere; technology must be used. Some of the ideas will blow your mind. Going to Finland is like stepping into the future. Well, at least it is for someone from Britain, as Britain seems to be about seven years behind the Finns in technology take-up.

## CLEANLINESS

The next thing a visitor will notice is the cleanliness that surrounds you. Again mentioning Helsinki airport, the floors positively shine, and the toilets and all facilities are immaculately clean. The Finns take a great pride in their environment and you will never see rubbish and litter lying around. It just isn't in the Finns' nature to dirty their environment, and you will soon be frowned upon if you are seen to be throwing rubbish around public places. Hotel rooms, restaurants, shops and even public transport will all appear clean and tidy to the foreign visitor. The focus on cleanliness is all part of the Finnish national pride.

One of the great things in Finland is that public conveniences are well equipped. There is always one toilet cubicle which is large and has a hand-held shower, washbasin, mirror and more than adequate space to manoeuvre. In addition, parent and baby rooms will have complimentary nappies, baby-changing mat and potty.

## CUSTOMER CARE

There is something that will strike the visitor to Finland as peculiarly odd. It is the Finns' attitude to customer care. They haven't got any, or so it seems. This may sound very harsh, but in truth, the Finns address customer care in a completely different way from the one that British, Asians or Americans would be used to. Herein lies the first real culture shock that most visitors to Finland will experience.

One evening, I was sitting with a colleague of mine in a hotel restaurant. I had ordered my evening meal from the menu and she had decided that she wanted just a plain ham sandwich. She went into some detail to explain to the waitress that all she required was two slices of bread, plain, with plain ham in the middle. She stipulated that she wanted 'no green stuff, no red stuff, no fruity bits either'; just a plain ham sandwich. My dinner arrived, her sandwich didn't. I had almost finished my meal when her sandwich eventually arrived. In all its glory, with all the greenery, the red bits and the fruity bits came her 'plain' ham sandwich. When my colleague quizzed the waitress, she was told this was how the sandwich was served, and if she didn't want all the other bits and pieces, she could take them out; they wouldn't mind.

It's also very difficult to get served in a Finnish restaurant once you've received your initial order. You can never seem to catch the waitress' eye, so you might well have to resort to gesticulating madly. This usually provokes a quick but dismissive nod, as the waitress walks off in the opposite direction. This leaves you wondering whether she will return. It is rare that anyone will come over to ask whether you would like another drink. I recall a time I called a waitress over to complain that my soup was not hot. She commiserated

## Jack Shannon's First Impressions

When I first got to the city, I was just starting out with my Finnish language. I used the Internet a lot, for working and to keep in contact with my friends back home. Usually, I would just find some Internet cafe and ask, in Finnish, for some time on the Internet. Unfortunately, I had never bothered to learn units of time, because seconds are *sekunnit*, minutes are *minuutit* and I just assumed that hours were...*houra*. For a month or more, I had been asking the girl at the counter for a coffee and a whore for the Internet; the worst thing was that for a month she never corrected me. (http://www.6d.fi/cultural_bemusion)

with me, said 'shame', and ran away quickly. There have been occasions when I have stood up to leave a restaurant, in order to get my bill, so that I could pay.

These incidents might lead the reader to think that the Finns really don't care, but nothing could be further from the truth. You have to understand the Finns' psyche in order to understand that they really do care. The first instance with the ham sandwich demonstrates the Finns ability to genuinely give you what they think you really ought to have—not what you've ordered. The first time I tried to buy a pair of boots, the assistant kept bringing me different models to try on rather than the ones I originally asked for.

In the second case, the Finns believe that it is an invasion of your privacy to have eye contact, so they leave you alone in silence and without any contact to enjoy your meal, and it's up to you to get hold of them. The Finns don't normally complain and they find it very difficult to handle a complaint. Therefore, when I mentioned about the soup, the waitress really didn't know what to do about it. I have since learnt, that if I have cold soup, I have to say, "Excuse me my soup is only warm would you please take it away and make it hot." This allows them to understand what I want. The Finns are not used to pushing themselves forward, and in a very egalitarian society, they are not used to being subservient. It is therefore down to you as the customer to make clear your wishes. In a restaurant, apart from asking about desserts, they will not come and ask you if you want anything else. In other words, you will not be 'sold to'. This will be seen as being an invasion of your privacy and an interruption of your personal silence.

**Mihalis Hatzis's First Impressions**

I am Greek and I am a large man. Here is my story. I first arrived in Finland one dark November evening and my brain was confused from a week of speaking English, French and Greek. It didn't get any easier walking the few freezing steps from the aircraft to the terminal. I hadn't recovered by the time I reached passport control where I presented my passport to a young quiet official. He examined it, checked his computer screen and returned my papers, with a hardy "*Kiitos*!" (thank you). I went red with anger because in my language, when somebody is very fat, we call them *kitos*, which means elephant! I want to apologise now for calling him a bloody bastard.

## REVERSE LOGIC

During the first occasion when I was trying to buy boots, it became obvious that my feet were too wide for some narrow-fitting Finnish shoes. The assistant told me that lots of people had the same problem and she wondered why there had not yet been devised an operation to cure wide feet. Never did it occur to her that they could make the shoes wider rather than us having to suffer the painful machinations of a surgical operation! Often I find the Finns coming at a situation from the opposite direction from me. Some foreigners regard this attitude as a form of arrogance, but I prefer to think of it as reverse logic—I do find it funny at times.

The Finns do not like to disappoint you or let you down and, as a result, they rarely make 'draft' timetables or 'pencilled in' dates. When they are confident that a meeting can be made, you will hear about it and are expected to jump. This is the one trait that most annoys the Brits who have diaries full of 'pencilled in' appointments!

## TRAFFIC

The next thing that strikes a visitor, especially from the more crowded parts of Europe, is the lack of traffic in Finland. I even think that the word 'traffic' is a misnomer when applied to the vehicles on Finnish roads. At certain hours of the day in Finnish towns, you really have to play a game of spot the car because, normally, the roads are very quiet. Generally speaking, Finnish families only have one car and children make their own way to school; so there are no school runs and rush hours as we have in Britain, for example. Junctions will normally clear in one turn of the traffic lights.

There was a bus strike in the town of Tampera just recently, and my Finnish colleague, Timo, experienced a few queues building up at each junction for the first time ever and was quite baffled as to the reason why. When he met me the next time, he told me that he had actually seen a 'traffic jam' in Finland and realised it had been caused by the bus strike. My French colleague Christine, who lives in Marseilles, said when she first came to Finland that she was absolutely 'stunned at seeing all these empty roads'.

## DAYLIGHT HOURS

The next thing that makes a big impact on visitors coming to Finland in the summer months is the length of the days. The memories I have of my first trip to Finland, in the summer of 1997 when the weather was gloriously hot, are of me sitting in the market square at 7:30 in the mornings, under the shade of an umbrella, drinking coffee and watching people on their way to work. The sun, already high in the sky, penetrated through the umbrella to warm my skin. It was quite warm even though it was still early in the day. In contrast, I have sat out late at night reading a book by the natural light in the sky. At 11:30 pm, it is only just beginning to become dusk. The Finns, of course, are quite used to light nights, but I can never resist going for a walk at midnight, by the shores of a lake, along the banks of a river, or in the town square.

My greatest memory, and the one that will stay with me all my life, is the moment I stepped off the plane at Kuopio—my first visit to Finland. It was half past midnight and the sun was just beginning to set. The sky was a beautiful colour of puce pink with purple clouds. It was just an absolutely unbelievable sight and birds were still flocking to make their way to their nests. Half an hour later, the sun was up and it was definitely dawn.

One thing that astounds me (and all the foreign colleagues I know) is that the Finns often close the blinds as soon as the sun shines, winter or summer. They cannot have a room too bright!

## FIRST IMPRESSIONS FOR A FINN

I recall one occasion when I was travelling by train from Helsinki to Joensuu. I met a lady Lutheran priest who had recently returned to Finland with her family having spent two years in Tenerife. We talked for a long while and she described to me how she was seeing the Finns through Spanish eyes, realising how much she and her family had changed their behaviour in the time they had been away. She said the things she most noticed were:

- An increase in the use of mobile phones.
- Everyone was drinking beer.
- Fewer people were drinking vodka, and wine was now very popular.
- At first they were very noisy in restaurants, until they noticed that no one else was!
- As a family they have had to learn to be quiet again.
- The Finns don't smile.
- They seemed not to be happy in comparison with the Spanish.

- The Finns are impatient and have to get things done quickly.
- The Finns are impatient in restaurants. They don't want to wait for good food to be cooked. They expect their meal quickly.
- The stillness, the silence and the calm.

# LAND, HISTORY, ECONOMY AND GOVERNMENT

## CHAPTER 2

'One cannot overestimate the importance of geographic conditions, including climate, and their influence on the development of the Finnish mindset. A question often asked is why the Finnish people chose this broad expanse of land...where winter darkness (kaamos) reigns for fifty-two consecutive days and where temperatures plummet to -40° C, one also asks why they stayed.'
—Richard D. Lewis, *Finland, Cultural Lone Wolf*

## FINLAND: A LAND FOR ALL SEASONS

Very few people know where Finland actually is. Everyone has heard of the place, but few can pinpoint it on a map. Most people associate it with Scandinavia, saying, "It's somewhere up there". I was one of those people. However, Finland is NOT part of Scandinavia, which is defined as incorporating Norway, Sweden and Denmark. It is a Nordic country and is referred to sometimes (but mistakenly) as one of the Baltic States; these being Estonia, Latvia and Lithuania. So, Finland stands on the shores of the Baltic, in its entirety above 60° North, separate and independent of its neighbours.

**Finland and the North**

Half of the world's population that live north of the 60th parallel (the level of Helsinki) live in Finland! This means that the populations of Norway, Sweden, Russia, Canada, Iceland, Greenland and Alaska, above the southernmost level of Finland, all put together, is very small; ergo—Finland really is up north!

And, it is this separateness that has shaped Finland. The Finns are unique. They are not Scandinavians, nor are they Slavs. Their language is totally different from other European languages and has no Indo-European roots. Their climate is said to be bleak and their geography isolated.

People usually go to Finland because they have a reason to, not because it is a convenient stop over. Finland has never been on the main road to anywhere. However, this has recently changed as the Japanese are now finding that the capital city, Helsinki, is a great place to stop on their way to the rest of Europe. Nowadays, the quickest transportation routes into the interior of Russia are through the southern part of Finland by rail or road, as there is only one border to cross.

**How Far in the North?**

For my first trip to Finland, in great excitement, I got out our big family world atlas. I turned to the pages for the Nordic countries and eagerly sought the town which I was visiting in Finland. To my absolute consternation, I found that Finland was well north of Moscow. I never thought that there was much north of Moscow. I found Kuopio, the town that I was visiting, was so far north that the only three towns that I recognised on the map north of there were Archangel, Reykjavik and Murmansk! I thought I was going to the North Pole. How wrong I was...

Although Finland has immense physical beauty, it is the people that make it memorable. Their traditions make it interesting; their love of all things modern makes it astonishing. Their language makes it impossible, and the influences from both East and West could be said to make Helsinki the 'Istanbul of the North'. Set on the Baltic, Finland's capital Helsinki is an intriguing mix of European, Scandinavian and Russian cultures. There are two official languages, Finnish and Swedish. In northern Finland lies the country of Lapland, home to about 6,500 Sami (Laps) who have their own language and culture.

Contradictions and contrasts are the two words that I constantly use when describing Finland:

- The stillness of the summer forests interrupted by mosquitoes and other pesky insects in June and July.
- The absolute quiet and silence of the countryside challenged by nightlife in the city.
- The glow of the long 'white nights' in mid-summer contrasted with the awesome silence of the snow-covered forests in mid-winter.

- Modern versus old traditions.
- The blue, blue spring skies which contradict the complete 'white outs' in winter.
- Traditions of Lapland versus cosmopolitan Helsinki.
- Vast uninterrupted forests which are actually managed.
- A well-ordered country that looks totally natural.

## GEOGRAPHY

Finland lays at the most eastern part of Europe and is, therefore, two hours ahead of GMT (Greenwich Mean Time). It is Europe's fifth largest country, covering 338,000 sq km (130,558 sq miles). About 70 per cent of the land is covered by forest (an area larger than the size of England), 10 per cent is under water, and only some 6 per cent of it's total land is used for agricultural purposes, with barley and oats the main crops. Finland is a country of considerable wilderness. There are vast areas of uninterrupted forests and woodlands, with tens of thousands of square kilometres of untouched terrain.

There are more lakes in Finland than in any other country in the world. The lake land area of the country is an immense tangle of lakes, inlets, islands and peninsulas. There are some 187,888 lakes, 5,100 rapids, 179,584 islands and although the Finns can't name them all, they are very proud to tell you how many there are. There are some 80,000 islands dotted around Finland's coasts, the rest are all in the inland lakes. The largest Finnish Lake system, greater Saimaa, is 4,400 sq km wide and has some 13,710 islands. Almost all Finnish municipalities have a lake, and some municipalities have more water than land in them.

Finland is often called the Land of a Thousand Lakes. Most of these were catalogued by an engineer called Toivo Virkkala, who spent his holidays charting the waters. He started in the mid-1930s and by 1956 had managed to catalogue 1,500 lakes. There are slightly more than 30,000 persons whose surname is Jarvinen, meaning 'Lake Person'.

To enjoy the unique beauty of this natural environment, you really do need to behave like a Finn for a while. Finns regularly take a walk in the woods in search of wild mushrooms or go berry picking. It is a part of their way of life. The people of this country, from early childhood, have become used to living in close harmony with their rich natural surroundings. These people have a respect for this priceless and irreplaceable gift, and believe it is the only way to enjoy a real relationship with the environment in which they live. The Finns have a great love of fishing, whether it is from the shores of a lake in summer, or from holes in the two-foot deep ice of a frozen lake, in the middle of winter. Whatever you are doing, it will take place in a silence that is broken only by the twittering of birds.

The best way to discover Finland and the quiet beauty of this unspoiled natural environment is either on foot or by bicycle. However, it is said that the best way to see Finland is to see it from an aeroplane, as there are so few mountains or tall hills from which you can gaze out over these wondrous landscapes. Because there are no hills to interrupt the view in many parts of the country, the sky seems enormous and on fine days, in summer or winter, the blue of the sky seems to go on forever. In the south, the gentle rolling farmland slips into the vast forests and lakes of central Finland, and these gradually transform into the peat and tundra of Lapland in the north.

Relaxing on a riverboat cruise is a wonderful way to spend a long summer evening after a hard day at work. These mini-cruise boats offer dinner dances, partying or just a quiet evening on the water.

Virtually the whole of the country is accessible because of the hard work of the Finns in opening up remote areas. Sound Finnish engineering, in the form of good railways and road systems, has criss-crossed the forests and traversed the lakes. Endless roads run through tall trees of pine, spruce and birch. The natural barrier of thousands of lakes, which form the largest expanse of inland water in the world, have been overcome.

Nearly one-third of the country of Finland lies north of the Arctic Circle and here the real beauty of Lapland can be found. The semi-domesticated herds of reindeer roam freely and the remoteness of each farm makes the land seem immense. In summer, this is the land of the midnight sun; and during the awesome silence of the snow-covered winter, the *aurora borealis* (northern lights) can be seen. Here in Lapland, one experiences 52 consecutive days of 24-hour daytime and 60 days of continuous winter darkness. The highest hills of Finland, *tunturi*, are located in Lapland, with Halti as the highest point. However, Halti, in the north-west corner of Finland, is only 1,328 m (4,357 ft) high.

**Aurora Borealis**

The *aurora borealis*, the northern lights, is the celestial phenomenon of bands, curtains or streams of coloured lights that appear in the sky on cold, winter nights near the Artic. In Finnish Lapland, the number of aurora displays is around 200 a year. In southern Finland, the number is generally fewer than 20. The beautiful blaze can manifest at any time of year when the conditions are right, but unfortunately won't be seen in the summer months due to Finland's long, light evenings.

Folklore abounds with explanations of the origins of the spellbinding celestial lights. In Finnish they are called *revontulet*, which means 'fox fires', a name derived from an ancient fable of the arctic fox starting fires or spraying up snow with its brush-like tail.

For further information and predictions/forecasts go to: http://virtual.finland.fi/finfo/English/aurora_borealis.html or http://www.laplandfinland.com

Finland has borders with three countries. The border with Russia lies to the east and is 1,269 km (788.5 miles) long. To the far north, Lapland has 727 km (451.7 miles) of border with Norway, whilst the west of the country has a 586 km (364.1 miles) border with Sweden. The Gulf of Finland separates southern Finland from Estonia. The Southern-most point, Hanko, is on the same latitude as Oslo in Norway and Anchorage in Alaska; while Joensuu, in the East, is nearly as far east as Istanbul.

The landscape looks idyllic. Unfortunately, the pristine lakes are not as clean as they appear. The 1997 survey of Finland's lakes and ocean waters showed them to be some of the most polluted in the EU, failing to meet even EU minimum standards of cleanliness. This has been caused by massive pollution through paper and pulp factories and agriculture. This pollution is the main topic of environmental debate and is a hot political issue. However, much has been done in recent years to make amends and Finland is now quite proud of its efforts to mitigate previous pollution.

Wildlife in Finland is rich and abundant. There are about 120,000 elks; Karelia, in the East, has a bear population of

The Finns are taking great efforts to preserve their natural environment and to prevent pollution.

Near Oulu, in the north-west of Finland, can be found one of Europe's most treasured wildlife sanctuaries, Liminganlahti. It was here, in just one week of the summer of 2000, that 300 different species of birds were recorded arriving in the spring.

240; reindeer are plentiful, with around 200,00 roaming freely in Lapland. Along with these, the animal kingdom includes the fox, lynx, weasels, hares, wolf and wolverine. There are around 65 species of mammals. There are also 400 species of birds, including black grouse, whooper swans, osprey, black woodpeckers chaffinches and sparrows, along with eagles and owls. And, of course, we must not forget to mention the fish. Finland has an abundance of different fish including, perch, pike, cod, flounder, whitefish, pikeperch, rainbow and brown trout, sea trout and salmon.

## CLIMATE

Finland enjoys four distinct seasons. March heralds spring, when the days are becoming longer. In fact, by mid March the length of the day is longer than that in the UK. After 21 March, week by week, Finland steals a march on the rest of Europe by gaining many more hours of daylight. By the end of the month, it easily experiences 14 hours of daylight between sun up and sun down. These are the first days of spring. Although the days are longer and can be full of sunshine, the snow can still be knee deep! But with the sunshine, everything seems brighter and whiter and the promise of summer lies ahead.

April sees the days lengthen from 5:30 am to 10:00 pm. By May, the snow has disappeared. The days are long, but everywhere is still brown. There are no leaves on the trees and the grass is still dead, but the forests are filled with the first flowers of the year: a small white flower like our snowdrop. Everything is awaiting the new summer growth which will start appearing towards the end of the month. The length of the day has stretched to 19 hours.

**Warm Weather in Finland**

I think it was the climate that gave me the greatest surprise when I went to Finland. It wasn't at all how I thought it would be. We all seem to have a perception of long dark days in the middle of winter and Finland being so very, very cold. And yes, Finland is like that. But, the surprising thing is that it can be so very, very hot. I have always been used to Mediterranean countries, where the heat of the day dies down and becomes a warm and refreshing evening. In Finland this does not happen, and this was my greatest surprise. As I mentioned before, on my first visit to Finland, they were experiencing a heat wave. When I woke up in the morning, it was already very warm and humid. Naturally, I thought that in the evening the temperature would drop substantially. This didn't happen, and the temperature at 8:00 in the evening, was very similar to what it had been at mid-day. In fact, the temperature may only drop two or three degrees over night. The reason for this is the sun never goes down, so the temperature doesn't either! Until you experience this, you have no concept of it. However, during bad weather, in the summer the nights can be cool!

In the far north of Finland, from mid May until late July, there is continual daylight. This is the land of the midnight sun. In Rovaniemi, on the Arctic Circle, the midnight sun lasts from 20 May until 20 of July. This means there is continual daylight because the sun is forever above the horizon. In central and southern Finland, 'officially' there is no midnight sun because the sun does dip just below the horizon. However, the night never really grows dark. It is just dusk for an hour and a half. At this time, the sky will take on the most beautiful hues. To you and me, this is the midnight sun and the experience is truly awe inspiring. Breathtaking. Unbelievable.

**More about Finland's Climate**

Overall, Finland's climate is quite moderate without the extremes, when compared with other regions so far north. It is the northernmost country where wheat is grown. It is the second coldest country in the world with average mean temperature across the whole country and whole year of 1.5°C/34.7°F (Russia is the coldest with -5°C/23°F)

In June the leaves are out and the grass is green. Rhododendrons blossom and whither quickly, followed in quick succession by a multitude of different blooms. Window boxes are full of geraniums, bizzie lizzies and numerous other colourful flowers. As the days become ever longer, the richness and vibrancy of Finland's slumbering beauty burst upon the landscape, accompanied by those skittish sorts of days I remember as a child in England.

During my first summer in Finland, I was so surprised to see the variety of flowering plants growing in tubs and gardens. Soon afterwards, I realised my surprise was due to the fact that in England I never see all these plants flowering at the same time—our season is much longer. Therefore, the balconies and marketplaces in Finland all looked like mini-flower festivals.

Compared with Siberia, Greenland and Alaska (with their extremes), the Finnish climate is relatively warm. This is due to the warming effect of the Baltic Sea and the winds from the Gulf Stream. In summer, you can experience hot spells, around 28°C (82.4°F) or 30°C (86°F). However, the temperature can be as low as 10°C (50°F) at times. When the weather is hot, it is, of course, very humid. The weather is very unstable in Finland and, rather like the UK, you can never tell from one day to the next what the weather will be like. Therefore, it is always advisable to have raincoats and cardigans with you.

By mid August, the days are already beginning to be noticeably shorter. No longer does the evening twilight merge straight into the half-light of morning. By the beginning of September, the leaves are already turning. Autumn arrives early in Finland, but the temperature is quite similar to autumn in England. When I first visited Finland in the autumn, the beautiful colourings of the trees in the vast forests astounded me. Of course, the best view came from the aeroplane in which I sat. It wasn't until I experienced this sight that I realised that Finland wasn't full of just pine trees, but in fact had many birch trees which gave life to these wonderful colours: red, yellow, orange, gold. This special period is called *Ruska*. The autumn equinox takes place on 23 September, and from then on the days are getting significantly shorter, week by week.

Autumn is the time for cloudberries and mushrooms, walking in the forests and picking nature's fruits. You have the right to pick the fruits of the forest and sell them tax-free.

With the longer, darker nights come darker and drab days. The first snow that appears in October is a welcome sight. Everyone rejoices. The whiteness and brightness of the snow adds lucidity to the days, and winter can truly be said to have arrived. It will snow now until the end of March, with every fresh fall layering upon the previous until the snow is immeasurably deep. In Lapland, the snow may arrive in September and stay until late June. In Helsinki, in the south, some of the snow will melt away before another fresh layer falls. The winters are cold and the temperature can rise or fall dramatically from one day to the next.

I was in Rovaniemi just before Christmas and was fortunate to experience quite a warm spell. It was around -7°C (19.4°F). However, on the day I was leaving, the temperature had fallen to -32°C (-25.6°F) overnight. Although by any measurement the temperature is cold, the climate is very dry and, provided you are wrapped up warmly, the cold doesn't penetrate into your bones like the cold and damp in England. The cold is so dry that you continually have to apply cream to your hands, lips and face. This dryness is the cause of a great amount of static electricity. Your hair will stand on end, even with a

My daughter on holiday in Lapland in December. She is pointing to a thermometer that reads -17°C (1.4°F) at midday. Two days later, the temperature dropped to -32°C (-25.6°F)!

good dose of hair conditioner, and you will forever receive little electric shocks. After experiencing a few winter weeks, I begin to dread pressing the button for the lift or reaching for a door handle!

But winter is a magical time in Finland. The snow is absolutely beautiful. When the temperature falls to -10°C (14°F), each flake of snow freezes as an individual entity. The light from the street lamps, shining down, makes it look as if you are walking through a field full of sparkling diamonds. Each snowflake twinkles in its own way, with its own colour, and as you walk you can hear the crisp sound of crunching under your feet. For anyone who hasn't experienced this, it is as though you were walking on glass crystals and crushing them under foot.

In the far north of Finland, from 22 November to 20 January, the half-light of morning seeps immediately into the twilight of the evening. This is known as the polar night. In Rovaniemi on the Arctic Circle, there will be about two hours of daylight. By about 1:30, whatever daylight there has been slips into a twilight called blue time. In December in southern Finland, daylight comes about 9:30 and begins to retreat at 3:00. However, by the end of January, the days are noticeably drawing out.

The coldest temperature, -50°C (-58°F), was measured in Salla, Lapland, in 1985. The highest temperature was recorded in Turku in 1914, which was 36°C (96.8°F).

One of my Finnish friends wrote to me: 'In fact, just as you have noticed, we Finns think we have a wonderful secret here: The country is very pleasant to live in, but most

## The Magic of Winter

I don't think I will ever lose the excitement I feel when I fly into Finland and see the first winter snows. When the landing lights from the aeroplane reflect on each individual frozen snowflake, making them sparkle, I automatically think to myself, "Here are my acres of diamonds!"

The Kuopio city centre in mid-winter. The roads are well maintained despite the abundance of snow during the Finnish winter.

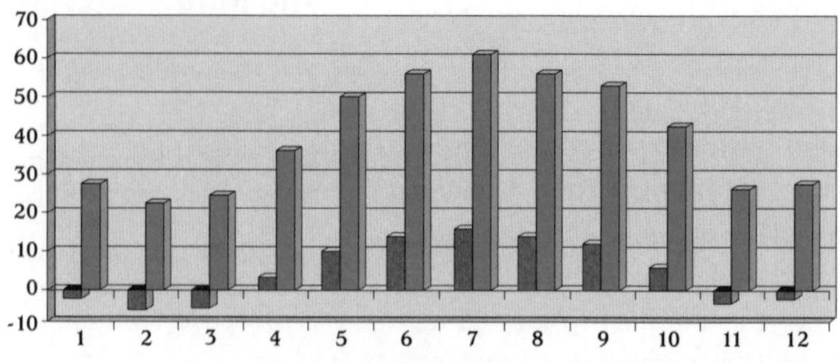


**Mean Monthly Temperatures in Helsinki**



foreigners don't know it. They think it is an impossible place because of its far northern position. Instead, Finland has an astonishingly mild climate with no real extremes (compared to USA, Canada, Asia, Africa: no earthquakes, no hurricanes, practically no heavy snowstorms, no real heat), a climate better than UK or Ireland because of the true seasons, wonderful summer, lots of space, water and nature.'

## HISTORY

Many people are surprised to learn that the country we know as Finland today is a very young country—just 90 years old. For almost seven centuries the Finns were under Swedish rule and then, for over a century, under Russian rule. Perhaps this is the reason that the Finns are so enormously proud of their country and nationhood, seemingly more patriotic than many other nations. Also, this might explain why, as foreigners, no one really knows much about the country although we have all heard of it.

### Origins

Much of Finnish history before the 12th century has been passed on through folklore with very few written records concerning the Finns and their country. In 98 AD, Tacitus mentions a people called the Fenni in the Germania, which is how the population of present-day south-west Finland came to be known. The inhabitants of the interior were called Hamme people, a name derived from an old Baltic word meaning 'an inhabitant of the interior'.

It is generally accepted that the first settlers came to Finland about 9,000 BC as antler carvings have been found that evidence the first records of mankind in this region. They occupied the coastal lowlands of southern Finland and lived by hunting elk and by fishing in the Baltic Sea, which was then a fresh-water lake. The land was no more than a bleak, tundra-like terrain without its present-day characteristics. Around 6,000 years ago, the Sami arrived from the east.

There are many competing theories as to the origins of the Finns, but it seems that the south-western part of Finland was settled by boat people from western Europe and the eastern part by nomadic tribes from Russia. These people came from the surrounding areas of the Ural Mountains and the River Volga and settled to become the Finns, Estonians and Karelians of today. From them developed the Finno-Ugrian language. These peoples displaced the Sami who migrated further north to Lapland and are today's Laps (Sami in Finnish).

Two distinct cultures evolved influenced from both the east and the west. The two Finnish tribes, the Hamenites in the west and the Karelians in the east, constantly warred with each other. Trading links were set up with the Estonians and the Swedish Vikings. After about 800 AD, the Vikings began spreading eastwards through the Åland Islands, Finland and into Russia, ruling Novgorod and eventually reaching Kiev in 862 AD. The Karelians traded with Novgorod, supplying them with furs and skins. This contact influenced the Karelian culture enormously. Their craftsmen adopted Byzantine motifs for use in art and jewellery designs and these can still be seen today as 'traditional Finnish' designs. The Karelians acquired their Orthodox form of Christianity through contact with the east and Russian monks later travelled north to convert the Laps. In the meantime, Sweden brought Catholicism to the tribes in the west of Finland.

An English missionary, Bishop Henry of Uppsala, was the person charged with bringing Christianity to this region.

He was murdered by a man called Lalli, who opposed his teachings. Bishop Henry is the patron saint of Finland.

## Being Ruled

In the 11th and 12th centuries, Finland became a buffer between many rival powers. Sweden had established a strong monarchy and became a sustained medieval power. Novgorod had become a powerful military base. The expanding Danish kingdom was successfully resisting Swedish supremacy and founded the city of Tallin, in Estonia, in 1219. To the east, the Teutonic knights were encroaching on the lands south of the Gulf of Finland and were busy warring with the Danes as they tried to take hold of the lands along the Baltic coast. The Finns had not joined together as one nation state of their own and were subjected to influences from all these sources. In fact, they were divided into three main groups: the Suomalaiset (as the Finns call themselves today), the Hamalaiset (the Hamenites) and the Karjalaiset (the Karelians).

In the middle of the 12th century, the Swedish throne was occupied by King Erik. The Pope had issued instructions that the position of the Church in Scandinavia needed to be strengthened. As a Catholic, Erik led a crusade to convert the Finns to Christianity. He was accompanied by Bishop Henry who was later left in Finland to consolidate the gains of Erik's crusade while Erik returned to Sweden. Although not the first, it was this crusade that established the beginnings of an organised Finnish Church. The first cathedral was built in Turku in 1229 and dedicated to St. Erik and St. Henry. The bones of St. Henry were laid to rest there in 1290.

In spite of the fact that the Finnish Church was under the supervision of a Danish See, it was the Swedes who ultimately dominated south and west Finland. Eastern Finland was still heavily influenced by the Byzantine Empire through Kiev and Novgorod. Turku, in south-west Finland, became the centre of both religious and civil authority in Finland. Swedish occupation began in earnest in 1249. A number of incentives were devised to attract Swedish settlers to Finland. Large estates were created. Tax concessions were given. Soon the upper layer of Finnish society comprised

Catholic Bishops and Swedish nobility. Many privileges were granted to Swedish soldiers of the Royal Army to entice them to settle. The Swedish settlers began to colonise the coastal regions of south-west Finland and along the Gulf of Finland. They brought with them their language which established Swedish as a major language in Finland.

From a Finnish reader, Hannu Sivonen: 'We are proud to mention that a Finn, Olavi Maununpoika (alias Olaf Magnusson, Olavus Magni, Olave le Grant) was the headmaster of the Sorbonne University in Paris in 1435.'

The next hundred years saw conflict and skirmishes between the Swedes and the rulers of Novgorod, as each tried to snatch land away from the other. Eventually in 1323, a Peace was signed which established the border between the two countries as running in a north-westerly direction from a place near today's St. Petersburg in Russia to Oulu in north-west Finland. This brought about a period of relative calm and, as a result, Swedish influence gained strength in the south-western half of Finland. This influence brought about contact with Western Europe and Roman Catholicism. Over the next three centuries, Finland became firmly part of the Swedish Kingdom, adopting their laws and administrative practices. There was little friction between the Swedes and the Finns. The Swedes settled along the coastal lands whilst the Finns lived, for the most part, in the interior. They shared religious, judicial and administrative practices and co-existed peacefully. In the meantime, the north-eastern half of Finland was dominated by cultural links with the East and the Eastern Orthodox Church.

In 1527, King Gustav Vasa of Sweden adopted the Lutheran faith and this set Sweden and Finland firmly on the road to establishing Lutheranism as the official state religion. Wanting to expand his territories, he enticed his Finnish subjects to push forward the boundaries set down in the treaty with Russia and encroach upon the Savo and Kainuu areas. Turku became firmly established as the capital of Finland (as a 'Duchy' or province) from where the Governor General presided from his castle.

During the 'Golden Age' of Sweden in the 17th century, Finland was considered an integral part of Sweden, and the Finns were considered loyal subjects of the Swedish monarch. The official language was Swedish, Stockholm was the capital (Turku being a 'Duchy' capital), and by Swedish decree Finland began to grow and prosper. Schools and churches were established, ironworks built, transport systems created and a chain of castle defences built to protect against Russian attack. The Turku Academy was founded in 1640 as the first university in Finland and linked the city to the time-honoured family of universities on the continent. Trade increased but the 'burgher' class was predominantly Swedish as few Finns made a living from business. The ethnic Finns were largely peasant farmers. A small minority rented their land and worked for the mansion to pay their rent, but the vast majority were free landowning farmers in the fashion of the free farmer concept based on the legacy of the Vikings. The Swedish medieval society did not have a feudal system like the rest of western Europe. The farmers of Finland took part in the political life in Stockholm, just as any farmer in the western half of Sweden proper, by sending their representatives to the 'Diet of Four Estates'. This was a legislative body made up of the 'Estates' of Nobility, Clergy, Burgess and (free landowning) Farmers.

The 1700s saw Finland fought over and occupied on numerous occasions. The Russians, under Peter the Great, seized much of Finland and even conquered the west coast. In trying to regain its lost territories, Sweden warred with Russia for the best part of one hundred years. The Great Northern War (the Big Hate in Finnish) saw Sweden regain some territory through peace negotiations which had to be later ceded to Russia. Then came the Napoleonic Wars which were to have a lasting impact on Finland. After Tsar Alexandra I and Napoleon signed the Treaty of Tilsit, Russia attacked Finland in 1808. Sweden ceded Finland to Russia in 1809 and the Swedish king, Gustav IV Adolf, lost his crown to Napoleon. One of Napoleon's Marshall, Bernadotte, was subsequently invited to become the new Sovereign and his descendants still reign today, warmly loved by both Swedes and Finns.

Finland became an autonomous Grand Duchy of the Russian Empire with the Tsar of Russia being the Grand Duke of Finland. This period of Russian rule lasted for 108 years. Tsar Alexander I was a liberal and treated the Finns and their institutions with respect. Swedish laws remained in force, the Lutheran church left untouched, he recalled the Diet of Finland (after a 50-year pause), and power was given to its own senate with only major decisions having to be approved by the Tsar. Russia encouraged Finland to develop as a country, made free basic education available to all, established universities and transferred the capital from Turku to Helsinki in 1812. In the mid-1800s, Finland issued its own postage stamps, had its own customs office and gained its own currency, the markka. Equal official status was given to the Finnish language, alongside Swedish. Railroads were built and institutions created. Finland began to benefit greatly from this annexation. Russia benefited by having Finland as a buffer state between itself and Sweden.

The creation of institutions, the distancing of the capital from Sweden, the recognition of their own language, the development of its own money and stamps, and a conscript Finnish Army, lead to a strengthening of the Finnish sense of national identity. Thus, the Finnish independence movement gathered momentum. One of the first to encourage independence was Al Arwardisson, who stated: "Swedes we are not, Russians we will not be, so let us be Finns". Around this time, Elias Lonnrot published his work *The Kalevala*, which was an epic poem based on the spoken folklore of the many Finnish 'tribes' around the country. This proved to be a lynch pin in the swell of the independence movement because it came at a time when the Finns were beginning to think about who they were as a nation. For the first time ever, their own history and culture were written down and all could learn what it really meant to be Finnish.

The 1860s are referred to as 'The Hunger Years', when almost one-third of the population died from starvation. Many rural advisory centres were established to help farmers manage their farms more efficiently and effectively so they could increase food production. Farmers Associations started and the 'seeds of knowledge' were passed on in schools.

## 20th Century History

In 1906, a new single-house parliament, the *Eduskunta*, was created. Men and women alike from all stations in life were given full voting rights. Finland in one stroke changed overnight into a modern state. Finland was the first European country to grant women full political rights—universal and equal suffrage, meaning they had the right to vote AND the right to stand for election to Parliament. Indeed in the first election of *Eduskunta* of Finland in 1907, there were 19 women elected. So the women really exercised their right.

In spite of the many advances that Finland had enjoyed under the Russians, the Finns still felt oppressed. They had had a hundred years of ruling themselves as an autonomous Grand Duchy and during the turbulent years of the 19th century, they remained loyal to Russia. Then Tsar Nicholas II attempted to turn Finland into a mere Russian Province and his 'Russification' methods caused an outcry. Finnish intellectuals and artists were stirred by this greater oppression and helped create a surge of nationalism. Jean Sibelius composed his masterpiece *Finlandia* and Akseli Gallen-Kallela painted scenes from the *Kalevala*. This provided a core around which a new nation could rally. The Finns became emotionally ripe for independence. The Russian Revolution of 1917 resulted in the seizing of power by the Communists and the ousting of the Tsar. As a result, with their customary speed and efficiency, the Finnish senate declared independence on 6 December 1917. While they were prepared to stay 'loyal' to a Tsar, they were not prepared to be loyal to a mob in Moscow and Leningrad. Just one month

From Finnish readers: The people were so outraged by Nicholas II's Russification attempts that they instigated a peaceful demonstration at the statue of Tsar Alexander II in the Senate Square in Helsinki. Here the demonstrators brought thousands of flowers in honour of Alexander's birthday; Nicholas II could not arrest anyone for respecting his grandfather! In every town, there used to be an Alexander or Nicholas Street. After independence, only Alexander Streets remained.

later, Finland was recognised as an independent state by the Russians themselves.

## Independence

One of the perplexing questions for the new nation was whether it should become a republic or a monarchy. The Finnish Left, 'The Reds', comprising the working classes, aspired to a Russian-style socialist independent nation. The Whites, comprising the newly established government, favoured the option of becoming a monarchy based on the German model. Vladimir Lenin, however, recognising he would need support in the ongoing World War I, decided to give the Finnish Reds 10,000 guns and lend them troops to attack the Finnish Civil Guards (The Whites) in Vyborg. This forced the senate to flee Vaasa and a civil war ensued.

The poor harvest of 1917 meant the Finns were once again facing starvation. The widespread devastation of Russia meant that no food supplies would come from there. Aid committees were set up in Sweden, Britain and US to send food for distribution by the government, but the dilemma arose for these countries as to whom it should be sent. The White Government appeared to be in alliance with the Germans, then the enemy of Europe, and the Reds were supported by Russia, who had just exacted a bloody revolution.

On 28 January 1918, the Civil War started in earnest. It was fought on two fronts: the Reds, supported by the Russians, strove for revolution in Helsinki; the Government Troops (The Whites) fought Russian forces near Vaasa, were commanded by Mannerheim, who had spent most of his military career in the Russian Imperial Army, and were supported by the Germans. This new nation was divided. The Reds claimed the South whilst the Whites stood their ground in the North. The Civil War lasted 108 days and claimed the lives of 30,000 Finns. The Whites eventually became the victors under the military prowess of Mannerheim.

The Civil War ended on 16 May 1918. The Prince of Hessen, Friedrich Karl, was asked to become king of Finland by the *Eduskunta* on 9 October 1918 and accepted. However just one month later, Germany was defeated in World War I and the

Prince of Hessen resigned his kingship and the political model Finland wanted to adopt became discredited (the crown and throne still exist). Finland then chose a republican state model and Professor K J Stahlberg, a liberal-minded constitutional lawyer, became the first president (1919–1925).

The Whites extracted a bloody vengeance on their defeated enemies. Reds and their families were captured and locked up in prison camps where thousands died through starvation and neglect. An estimated 10,000 people died in these camps. By 1924, the problem of political prisoners was gone, though bitterness lingered on through another generation.

The Constitution of 1919, whose main architect was Stahlberg, retained the single-house parliament that was established in 1905. It also stated that Finnish and Swedish would be the national languages of the new republic and established the right of citizens to use their mother tongue before the law courts and administrative authorities. Records and documents were to be written in the mother tongue and this would be guaranteed by law. Regions would be unilingual unless a minority group existed which represented over 10 per cent of the local population. This would be reviewed statistically every ten years. Helsinki and Turku were to be bilingual. At the time, Swede-Finns accounted for only 11 per cent of the total population. The government recognised that toleration and accommodation of this minority would best serve the interest of the country as a whole. Shortly afterwards, Finland was admitted to The League of Nations and was, therefore, recognised by all as a new independent country.

The 1930s saw the fledgling nation at a low ebb. Civil war skirmishes continued with Right- and Left-wing extremists battering and bruising political life. Attempts were made to outlaw Marxism, which resulted in Fascism being made illegal. Fighting broke out between university students of the two language groups and a bitter language war ensued which shook the administration, universities and cultural circles. Finland developed close ties with Germany partly in response to the threat of their predatory giant neighbour, the USSR.

Before World War I, the Finns were said to be the most sober people in Europe. The consumption of liquor in Finland was decreasing year by year. In June 1919, the government introduced prohibition which was generally recognised as a sound strategic policy by the vast majority of the nation. By 1931, the law was repealed. It had turned out to be an economic disaster, creating a lucrative black economy. The State Alcohol Corporation was established having the right to sell liquor. Thus the importation and distribution of alcohol became state owned and state directed.

During the time between the two world wars, this new struggling nation gained an international reputation for bravery, honesty, integrity and hard-work. In spite of the fact that the economy was still agrarian based and two-thirds of the population worked on farms, Finland became the only country to pay its debts to the United States. Towards the end of the 1920s, the country's industrial production was increasing and there was an export boom in forest-related products which provided much needed foreign currency. At the same time, Finland began to shine in athletics with its sporting hero Paavo Nurmi (the Flying Finn) winning seven gold medals in three Olympics. Continuing success in athletics led to Helsinki being chosen as the venue for the 1940 Olympic Games, which were eventually held in 1952 due to the interruption of World War II.

With war clouds gathering over Europe, the Soviet and German Foreign Ministers signed a pact of non-aggression on 23 August 1939. The pact laid the way for Germany to have a free hand in Lithuania whilst the Soviet Union could move against Finland, Estonia and Latvia; Poland would be divided between the two powers. The Finns hoped to escape the conflict by declaring their neutrality. However, 1939 saw the outbreak of war in Europe into which Finland was reluctantly dragged on 30 November when the Red Army (the USSR) invaded, arguing that its security needed south-eastern Karelia and some other military areas by the sea. Also, the USSR had become insecure and suspicious of its near neighbour creating ties with the West.

The 'Winter War', as it became known, was especially tragic as temperatures during an extremely harsh winter fell to -40°C (-40°F) and soldiers on both sides died in their thousands. In spite of inflicting enormous losses on the Russian troops, after 100 days, the Finns had to sue for peace; the south-eastern part of Karelia (10 per cent of its land) was ceded to the Russians and Finland had to find home for 450,000 fleeing refugees. It was this episode that taught the Finns that they would never be safe from their giant neighbour and that they were unlikely ever to vanquish them—therefore, in future, they needed to tread very warily. Also, Finland learned that no other nation would come to its rescue.

The Soviet Union stepped up their efforts to wrest more land from the Finns and in desperation Finland turned to Germany for help. Although there was never any formal agreement between the two countries, German troops were allowed right of passage through Finland to Norway. When hostilities between Germany and Russia broke out in June 1941, the 'Continuation War' between Finland and the Soviet Union began. The valiant struggle of the small Finnish Army resulted in them repossessing Karelia and even land they had lost in the 18th century. However, in the summer of 1944, the Russians overwhelmed the Finns. Mannerheim negotiated an armistice with the Soviets and, as a result, then began to oust 200,000 German troops from Lapland. This struggle lasted until the general surrender in the spring of 1945.

The Finns are proud to quote: 'Of those countries that participated in the war in Europe, only three capitals were left unoccupied by the enemy at any time of the war: London, Moscow and Helsinki. Of the same countries, only UK and Finland retained a democratic system of government all through the 1930s and the wartime.'

The nation's struggle for independence, and the heroic and successful fight to retain that independence during World War II against immense odds (2 million vs 300,000), came with a price. In such a tiny population, 90,000 Finnish men lost their lives and 158,000 more had been injured. Finland had been truly unlucky—the Germans razed Lapland to the ground on their way out and the Soviet Union wrested territory and inflicted heavy war reparations. Finland, like Poland and the Baltic States, had been in the firing line as Stalin and Hitler played out their power games. However, unlike them, she did not have to cede her sovereignty and remained independent. The Finnish Army was never routed.

From a Finnish reader, Hannu Sivonen: 'You mention that Finns are proud of their war achievements... The Finns did not lose the war, but arrived at goal 'as good second' as they say.'

## Post-War Finland

Dreams of a 'Greater Finland', which had been the aspiration of a whole generation, were discarded as the nation faced up to the massive burden of trying to repay its debts. The reparations to the USSR amounted to US$ 300,000,000: 70 per cent heavy engineering (machinery, ships, locomotives, etc) and metal products; 30 per cent wood products, textiles and shoes. The schedule of payments was impossible and, with the USSR controlling the exchange rate, the debt doubled. Once again there was a shortage of food, everything was rationed and poverty was widespread. When America offered Marshall Plan aid, Finland refused, preferring to keep its independence. The government taxed heavily and invested in plant and machinery. Finland went through the fastest process of industrialisation and urbanisation, the like of which has not been seen until today in China. However, the war reparations were finally paid off in 1952.

In 1948, the Treaty of Friendship, Co-operation and Mutual Assistance was signed which bound the two countries in a semi-military agreement. Finland still laid claim to its neutrality but the shadow of its giant neighbour meant that Finland still had to bow to the wishes of the Soviet Union, even in terms of its own domestic politics.

Urho Kekkonen, the Finnish president from 1956 to 1981, was a master diplomat and became one of the great leaders of his time. He managed to grasp the nettle in the difficult relationship with the Soviet Union, cautiously walking a tightrope. He gained fame abroad as host of the initial meeting of the 'Conference on Security and Co-operation in Europe', held in Helsinki in 1975. He led Finland as a founding member of the Nordic Council. As a result, they enjoyed the same benefits as Scandinavia: free movement of labour, a passport-free zone, joint research and educational programmes and pursuit of the same type of welfare programme.

Finland was accepted into the United Nations in 1955 and joined EFTA (the European Free Trade Association) in 1961. She managed to conclude a comprehensive customs agreement in 1973 with the European Economic Union and made a similar agreement with COMECON of the Eastern bloc countries. The Soviet Union still exercised a great deal of influence over Finland up until the late 1980s, blocking its membership of the European Community and minimalising any influence from the United States. In 1989, Finland became a member of the Council of Europe. By choosing a path of neutrality, Finland opted out of the arms race.

The 1970s and 1980s were boom times in Finland. Free at last from war reparations, Finland's advance in industry, farming, trade, commerce and the professions was driven by sheer profit. However, from the outset, this drive was not aimed at the gain of the individual citizen but at the welfare of the nation as a whole. Taxation remained high. Through the 20th century, increasing attention was paid to finding solutions to social and economic problems through legislation and public expenditure: 'The interests of the people as a whole should be the active concern of enlightened citizenship.'

During the 1960s, many people migrated to the south and large urban areas grew up around Helsinki. Many areas in the north and east lost a large percentage of their young people. Self-sufficiency in food was reached by 1960 with bigger farms and more productive techniques to increase the food supply. This in itself created new problems: what to do with overproduction and how to employ everyone. The food industry became focused on quality and environmental aspects:

- Animal husbandry
- Diary farming

- Organic farming
- Crop cultivation
- Berry production
- Fishery centres
- Regional centres for country women and homemakers

Fortunately for Finland, the Soviet Union was so dependent on its products that Finland kept supplying them in exchange for oil and other raw materials. Finland's economy began to boom.

**The Strength of Finland**

'Finland's greatest contribution to the 20th century lies simply in the fact that it has survived intact as a nation state, dedicated to the principles of parliamentary democracy, and that it has been able to maintain a welfare state, rising living standards, despite the battering it has taken from a hostile world during the brief period of its national independence. A small weak nation learned to live alongside a predatory giant neighbour—without losing its sense of national identity.'

—Fred Singleton, *A Short History of Finland*

## FINLAND TODAY

Finland suffered more than most European nations during the recession of the early 1990s. The Soviet Union broke up leaving debts unpaid, the markka was devalued, many companies closed, unemployment rose from 3 per cent to 20 per cent, and the tax burden increased alarmingly. With far less hesitation than the Swedes, the Finns voted the country into the European Union by referendum in 1994, and joined in 1995. The economy took a turn for the better: food instantly became cheaper and the country received considerable financial aid through EU assistance with regional development grants. However, the traditional market place for Finnish goods, the Soviet Union, has not been restored and Finland has had to find new markets from all over the world. In 1999 and 2006, Finland took over the EU Presidency. In 2000, Helsinki became one of the Cultural Capitals of Europe and elected its first woman president and woman

Speaker of Parliament. In 2002, the Euro was introduced as its currency.

The break-up of the Soviet Union into several smaller states has considerably changed the balance of power within the Baltic region. Finland still vigorously pursues its policy of strict neutrality. It has retained commercial ties with the new republics and has offered its technological know-how in environmental matters and financial assistance to buy food supplies.

## TOP OF THE CLASS

The country is dark and cold in the winter and has some of the highest taxes in Europe. But that doesn't get in the way of Finns' overall happiness. Finland ranks 6th in the world in the happiness stakes in a 2006 survey of life satisfaction undertaken by Britain's University of Leicester (Denmark was 1st, US 23rd; UK 41st; China 82nd; India 125th; Russia 167th; Zimbabwe last). So, why do they score so highly? Because Finland is a small country with greater social cohesion and a stronger sense of national identity. But happiness isn't the only thing that they top the class in...

Finland has become a champion of civil liberties. Where freedom of expression and freedom of speech are concerned, Finland ranks among the top countries in the world, according to a 2007 report by the Reporters Without Borders (RSF) organisation. Other top countries include Iceland, Ireland and the Netherlands; France was 35th and USA 53rd. In their surveys on the degree of freedom experienced by citizens in various countries, Amnesty International always has Finland appearing near the top list. In a 1998 survey by the United Nations, Finland was rated fifth in the world in terms of quality of life. This survey measured education, income, health and life expectancy. They came first in an Organisation for Economic Cooperation and Development (OECD) survey of European standards of reading, mathematical and scientific literacy in 2003.

In 1999 and 2007, Finnish children were deemed to be the healthiest in Europe along with the Swedes. They are in the top two countries in the economic creativity index and are

well ahead of the US in terms of research and development spending as a percentage of GDP. The Finns are fourth in the world for filing successful patents. They easily beat all other countries to the number one position in The Economist's Environmental Sustainability Index (2004) and top the league in the Corruption Free Index of 2002 by Transparency International. Finland has adopted a zero-tolerance policy towards animal diseases and is the only EU country to have a disease-free status. And, more surprisingly than anything else, Finland has won more Olympic medals per capita than any other nation!

All this has been achieved by a population of only five million people. How far this small nation has come in 90 years!

## THE ECONOMY

Among the OECD countries, Finland is one of the late industrialising ones. Up until the 1950s, it was still a predominantly agrarian society. The industrialisation process really took off in the latter part of the 19th century, but the income per capita level remained roughly one half of that of Great Britain—the leading economy at that time. The loss of 10 per cent of its territory, including Viipuri (now Vyborg) and the manufacturing centres of Karelia, during World War II deprived Finland of a substantial amount of its resources. One-third of its hydro electricity, one-quarter of its chemical pulp production, 12 per cent of its productive forests and 9 per cent of its arable land were ceded to the Soviet Union. By the end of World War II, the Finnish economy had virtually collapsed. The reparations schedule imposed on Finland by the Soviets was to be paid in metal goods, heavy engineering products, ships and electrical cables. An intensive programme of investment, much state financed, was undertaken to bring Finland up to the level where it could begin to make reparations. Unlike some other countries devastated by the war, Finland received no foreign aid to help rebuild its broken economy.

The transformation from a rural society to an urban industrialised country had to be quick. Driven by the need to meet the Soviet's reparations, industrialisation made great strides. The reparations schedule eventually ended in 1952. For the next two decades after this, Finland began to prosper. The country recognised that it could not compete in the world of mass production along with countries like the USA and Britain. However, it has become among the top ten industrialised nations of the world, specialising in products in which skill, design, originality and flair account for more than bulk, volume and mass production. Finnish scientists help keep Finland at the cutting edge of new technologies in the fields of electronics and timber products. Production is concentrated on high-value technology orientated products, computer-controlled mechanical systems, special types of vehicles, mobile phones and shipping.

Timber is still the raw material of greatest economic value and it is fascinating to see the enormously long trucks, loaded with freshly felled logs, driving across the country. Finland is the most heavily wooded country in Europe, covering 72 per cent of its lands. 63 per cent of the forests are in the hands of private owners, which equates to one in five families being owners. Sixty-six per cent

**Finnish Expertise**

Finland sells its expertise all over the world. Amongst other projects, the Finns designed and built the roads in Tanzania.

of the total output of the forestry industry is exported. Timber, furniture, paper, pulp, cellulose and various chemicals are its products and Finnish scientists lead the way in finding innovative new ways to use wood and its derivatives. Finland has the largest copper mines in Europe, exports zinc and nickel, but has to import all its oil and coal. Today's top exports are: first, electronics and telecommunications; second, paper, pulp wood and board; third, metal exports, advance machinery and equipment.

Today, Finland is not only one of the most open economies in the world, but also one of the leading knowledge-based economies. Research and development expenditure in relation to GDP is one of the highest in the world—about 3.5 per cent. Higher education enrollment is well above the OECD average; number of researchers in relation to population is higher than in any other country. During the 1990s, the economy oriented heavily towards ICT (information and communication technologies) and by the end of the decade, the country was the most ICT specialised economy in the world. Finland has been ranked top in virtually all international comparisons measuring competitiveness, or knowledge economy developments—including the World Bank Knowledge Economy Index and OECD's Student Assessment tests (the so called PISA studies).

This transition to a knowledge economy is quite remarkable, especially when considering Finland's economic situation in the early 1990s. Finland went through one of the worst recessions of any experienced by the Western economies in 1990s, characterised by a major banking crisis and the accumulation of government debt from modest levels to over 60 per cent, and approaching international lending limits. The Soviet Union had accounted for 25 per cent of all Finnish exports and its demise cost the country dearly. Once the most expensive country in world (1990), Finland soon became one of the cheapest. From almost full employment, 500,000 jobs disappeared in two years. Finland suffered 20 per cent unemployment, the second highest in Europe. This proved to be an unimaginable burden on the state and in an effort to reduce the deficit the government imposed heavy spending cuts.

However, spending on education and grants for private research and development were actually increased. By 1995, Finland had become a net exporter of know-how and high-tech products. By the end of 1999, industrial production had grown by record-breaking figures. The biggest increase took place in the electronics and electro-technical industry, where the growth rate accelerated to 40 per cent. The primary factor boosting growth in industrial production is exports. The Trade Unions, who are a powerful force in the Finnish economy with 83 per cent of the work force, allowed salaries to be pegged at 1.7 per cent over two years, thus helping to keep inflation down. There are strict rules governing working hours and holidays, as Finland pursues a very generous social welfare programme. Finland was one of 11 countries whose economy qualified to begin using the new Euro currency at the beginning of 1999. (Their strict alcohol laws have been relaxed since joining the EU.) By the end of the decade, the country's macroeconomic performance was among the strongest in Europe.

| Main Destinations of Export 2005 | |
|---|---|
| Russia | 11 per cent |
| Sweden | 10.8 per cent |
| Germany | 10.6 per cent |
| UK | 6.7 per cent |
| US | 5.8 per cent |
| Netherlands | 4.8 per cent |

| Main Origin of Imports 2005 | |
|---|---|
| Germany | 14.9 per cent |
| Russia | 13.9 per cent |
| Sweden | 10.6 per cent |
| China | 6.0 per cent |
| UK | 4.5 per cent |
| US | 4.2 per cent |

Exports are now about 40 per cent of GDP with IT technology having the highest share of exports today. In

1900, 85 per cent of all exports were forestry related; now they account for only one-third. Finland is the second largest exporter of paper in the world. Nokia is the world's largest manufacturer of mobile phones. Metal mining, technology and engineering together make up exports almost as large as paper. The service and construction industries are playing an increasingly important part in the Finnish economy. There are very close links between Finland and Estonia and the opening up of the Baltic States with a population of 40 million has proved to offer Finland a great competitive advantage. Unemployment is down to 7.7 per cent (April 2007) and inflation, which has consistently hovered between 1 to 2 per cent annually, is 2.6 per cent (April 2007).

The Finnish experience shows that it is possible to make a dramatic recovery in GDP, undertake a major restructuring, and turn a crisis into an opportunity in a short time, as long as there is a real sense of urgency, supporting institutions and political consensus of what needs to be done. The Finnish case is not unique in this respect. Korea turned its major 1997 financial crisis into an opportunity and undertook a major reform of its economic incentive and institutional regimes. The Finnish transformation to a knowledge-based economy was, no doubt, to a large extent a business driven process, but policies and institutions played a role too. There was a clear shift in policy making in Finland in the 1990s. High priority was given to sound macroeconomic policies to overcome the recession, but at the same time there was a gradual shift to microeconomic policies, i.e. innovation, technology and education policies. It was recognised that, after all, the competitive edge of an economy is created at micro level: in firms, innovation and policy organisations, and educational institutions.

The Finnish experience confirms what the recent economics literature emphasises—institutions and organisations play an even more important role in economic growth than we have thought so far. In the case of Finland, two key elements are worth mentioning: education system and consensus building mechanisms.

**Finns and Technology**

Figures released at the end of 1999 showed that 67 per cent of the Finnish population had mobile phone subscriptions. By the end of 2005, this had risen to 102.5 per cent! Innovations by small technology companies have brought Finland to the forefront of development in the field of health care, in which the need to improve service efficiency grows as the population ages. One service creates better conditions for diabetes patients to care for themselves by allowing them, via mobile phone and the Internet, to give information on blood glucose measurements, dosage of insulin used, meals and exercise to a database, thus eliminating the need for patients in sparsely populated areas to travel long distances to see a specialist.

In 1999 I wrote: 'Finland is poised in a strong position to become one of the world's most successful economies.' At the outset of 2000, the Finnish Telephone Giant, Nokia, was Europe's biggest company by capitalisation. In 2003, Finland outranked all other countries in global competitiveness, reflecting the country's ability to sustain its high rates of growth based on 259 criteria, including openness of the economy, technology, government policies, and integration into trade blocks. Currently, Finland leads the world in The Economist's Environmental Sustainability Rating. This is based on five broad, durable areas: environmental systems, the reduction of environmental stress, the reduction of human vulnerability, social and institutional capacity and global stewardship. Finland is also the world leader in the management of water resources, and it was back in 1896 that she passed a law forbidding the wasteful use of forest resources and the compulsory planting of new trees to replace any felled to create sustainability. Finland is unrivalled in various fields of technology and number one in the world for network readiness for ICT. No wonder *The Economist* and the *Financial Times* in the UK recently stated that "The Future is Finnish".

Nearly 20 years ago, Finland was a closed society. Foreigners were unable to work in the country unless they had an exceedingly specialist job. Those who married a Finn found that the formalities took forever to grant them the right to live and work there. Finland was like a fortress. Foreigners were not allowed to own land or property without a special dispensation at ministerial level and they were not allowed to hold the majority of shares in any business. Today Finland is open, has more immigrants than emigrants and Helsinki has turned into a very cosmopolitan city.

During the past five years, immigration into Finland from other EU countries has been higher than emigration from Finland to other EU countries. In 2006, Finland had a migration gain of 3,300 persons from other EU countries. Immigration into Finland from other EU countries has been growing since 1997. Emigration from Finland into other EU countries has remained stable during the past few years. However, although Finland seems very welcoming to foreigners, especially foreign scholars and technical experts, the number granted residency is very low: just 0.4 per cent of the population.

| From the Economist Intelligence Unit | 2002 | 2003 | 2004 | 2005 | 2006 |
|---|---|---|---|---|---|
| GDP at market prices (bn) | 144.0 | 145.9 | 151.9 | 157.4 | 172.9 |
| GDP (US$ bn) | 136.0 | 165.0 | 188.9 | 196.1 | 217.1 |
| Real GDP growth (%) | 1.6 | 1.9 | 3.3 | 3.0 | 5.2 |
| Consumer price inflation (av; %) | 1.6 | 0.9 | 0.2 | 0.8 | 1.6 |
| Population (m) | 5.2 | 5.2 | 5.2 | 5.2 | 5.2 |
| Exports of goods fob (US$ bn) | 44.9 | 52.7 | 61.1 | 65.5 | 86.5 |
| Imports of goods fob (US$ bn) | 32.0 | 39.8 | 48.4 | 55.9 | 74.7 |
| Current-account balance (US$ bn) | 13.9 | 10.7 | 14.8 | 9.5 | 12.0 |

| | | | | | |
|---|---|---|---|---|---|
| Foreign-exchange reserves excl gold (US$ bn) | 9.3 | 10.5 | 12.2 | 10.5 | – |
| Exchange rate US$: (av) | 0.94 | 1.13 | 1.24 | 1.25 | 1.26 |

## GOVERNMENT, POLITICS AND THE JUDICIARY

In 1906, the 'Diet of 4 Estates' (the legislative body that was inherited intact from Swedish times) became a parliament of 200 seats called the *Eduskunta*. The new parliament was elected by equal and universal suffrage in a secret vote, which included women, with everyone having the right to stand for election. After having been ruled by two powerful neighbours for about 800 years, Finland finally achieved independence in 1917. The Finnish Constitution came into effect in 1919 and guarantees equality, freedom of expression, freedom of conscience, freedom of assembly, freedom of movement and the freedom to choose one's own residence. The voting age at present is 18.

The Finns are governed by means of a presidential republic. The executive government comprises the president, in council with the prime minister and the cabinet. The office of president used to have substantial powers but recently this has been reduced to a more figure-head role, although a powerful one! The president has great influence over foreign policy. The Council of State is made up of 13 different ministries and 17 ministers, plus the prime minister. The president is elected for a six-year term, while the prime minister is elected every four years by the 200-member *Eduskunta* (parliament). *Eduskunta* members serve a four-year term and are elected from 14 national districts. The parliament is a single chamber—unicameral. The Åland Islands are self-governing and have their own parliament (*Landsting*).

Finland's proportional representation system encourages a

I found fascinating the fact that in the March 1999 election, one politician thought it would be wise to visit southern Spain and canvass for votes there, because there were so many Finns living in that part of the world.

multitude of political parties. Many Finns are floating voters and easily have ten different political parties to choose between, although there are three main political parties that have long been the major players: the Social Democrats (the largest political party—left of right, but right of left), the Agrarian Center Party (rural urbanites) and the Conservative National Coalition Party. There are also the left-wing Alliance, the Greens, the Swedish People's Party and the Christian Union. The government often becomes a coalition usually consisting of two or three of the largest parties, with one or more smaller parties.

Nearly 4.3 million people were eligible to vote in the elections of March 2007, and the turnout was 69.7 per cent of the electorate. Altogether, 2,004 candidates were nominated, 799 of whom were women. About three-quarters of the candidates were nominated by parties currently represented in parliament. The number of female MPs rose as 84 women were elected (formerly 75), now representing a record 42 per cent of the 200 MPs. Election themes included a reduction of income tax and VAT on food. A proposal for a minimum income has been propsed by a few parties. Because of high economic growth in recent years, the government will probably have extra money to use on the welfare state.

The date of the 2007 Finnish election was near to the 100th anniversary of the first Finnish parliamentary elections, which were held on the 15 and 16 of March 1907 and were the first elections held under universal suffrage in Europe.

The elections were a major victory for the opposition National Coalition Party under Jyrki Katainen. It gained ten seats and took over the position of the second-largest party in Finland. The main government partners, the Centre Party and the Social Democrats, both lost ground. With the Left Alliance also losing seats, the labour parties received the worst result in the 100 year history of Finnish democracy. For the Social Democrats, the result is the worst since 1962, while the Left Alliance has lost seats in every election since 1999. The Centre Party, despite the loss, maintained its position as the biggest party in parliament, with one seat more than the National Coalition. It is also the only time, except for the parliamentary election of 1930, that the Centre Party and the National Coalition Party together have an absolute majority in parliament. The outcome could lead to the formation of a new centre-right government and leave out the left-leaning Social Democrats in opposition for the first time since 1995. In the general election, the Centre Party won 51 seats, compared with the National Coalition Party's 50 and the Social Democrats' 45 in the 200-strong Parliament.

The parliamentary factions are expected to authorise Matti Vanhanen, the prime minister of the caretaker government (as party leader of the Centre Party), to start formal coalition negotiations and establish the other parties' stands on issues he considers key during the 2007-11 legislative period. Mr Vanhanen is expected to pose questions on services, taxation, energy and climate to the factions and ask what issues they consider important enough to prevent them from joining a coalition. This means that the new government coalition will likely be centre-right.

**Foreign Vote**

There are almost 200,000 people with foreign backgrounds living in Finland, but there is not a single immigrant representative in Parliament. There are estimated 65,000–70,000 immigrants from more than 150 different countries who have received Finnish nationality and are, therefore, eligible to vote, with the Russians forming the largest segment (almost 10,000). There are also 3,258 Somalis, 3,104 Estonians and about 2,000 Vietnamese.

Local government is divided into provinces (*laani*) with each headed by a prefect. The functions of local government include regional planning, transport, health and education. These are administered by rural and municipal communes.

Holding the EU presidency for the final six months of the 20th century helped raise the international profile of Finland. During this time, policies concerned with the 'Northern Dimension' were passed. One decision which was taken was to extend the European Investment Bank's coverage to Russia, allowing for the planning of a road bypass of St. Petersburg. A road link between St. Petersburg and the Finnish border is now under construction. As this was the first time that Finland had presided over the EU, many of their diplomats and civil servants undertook training sessions on small talk to enable them to appear more sociable.

The judicial branch of government is independent of the executive and legislature. The judiciary consists of two systems, regular courts and administrative courts. Administrative courts process cases where official decisions are contested. The president appoints the judges at one of three levels. The three levels of court in the civil and criminal cases are: the general courts, the Court of Appeal and the Supreme Court. Cases are not decided by juries but by magistrates and judges. The barristers (lawyers) deliver a factual appeal (in line with Finnish culture) with much less emotion than may be familiar to some through American TV programmes. Speed and efficiency are the main characteristics of the Finnish system when compared with other countries' judicial systems. Payouts in lawsuits are generally kept to realistic levels—those in the UK would find them modest and those in America intolerable.

## THE MILITARY

Finland has a very small 'professional' standing army but has a large reserve force. Young men of 18 are expected to do their national service. They have a choice of either doing military service, with or without arms, or community service. This can be for a period of six, nine or 12 months (11 months for officers and non-commissioned officers in reserves). Since 1995, women have been allowed to volunteer for national service. Some people can opt to do national service when they are older. For men, reserve duty continues until at least the age of 50. Conscientious objectors have the right to choose non-military forms of national service.

Defence spending is low relative to other European countries at 1.5 per cent of GDP and 5.5 per cent of the total government budget. The Finnish army has some Swedish-only units. The most notable role that the Finnish army plays is in peacekeeping activities for the United Nations and they serve all over the world.

Finland remains a relatively safe environment. All forms of public transportation are considered safe. Street crimes, such as mugging and pick-pocketing, remain relatively uncommon, but do occur. Due to the low crime rate, Finland has one of the smallest police forces of any European nation. Outside of key urban centres, they rarely project a visible presence. Finnish police services are excellent.

Police are part of national government and operate under the control of the Ministry of the Interior. Local police are supervised by provincial authorities and organised into town police departments and rural police districts. These manage routine police work. The mobile police assist local police where necessary, but they are responsible for traffic safety and riot control and operate at a national level. The security police are there to prevent subversion and espionage. The central criminal police maintain centralised criminal files, mount extensive investigations and keep contact with foreign police forces. The coast guards and border police are charged with the security of the border areas and would have a military role in times of war.

**In Case of Emergency**

The telephone number for police and other emergency services throughout Finland is 112.

Finland has a programme to provide financial compensation to victims who suffer serious criminal injuries. According to existing regulations, the victim must report the incident to the police and file an application for compensation within ten years of the date of the crime. Finnish police routinely inform victims of serious crime of their right to seek compensation. The relevant forms and further information can be obtained from http://www.valtiokonttori.fi/insurance/.

# THE FINNS

## CHAPTER 3

'All good people agree,
And all good people say,
All nice people, like us, are We
And everyone else is They.
But if you cross over the sea,
Instead of over the way,
You may end by (think of it!)
Looking on We
As only a sort of They.'
—Rudyard Kipling, *We and They*

## POPULATION

As with most European nations, the population in Finland is ageing. Only about 19 per cent of the population is less than 15 years of age, and the middle-aged groups predominate with the average age as 39.4 years old. Nowadays, the average household size is 2.2 people, although it would not have been uncommon to find families with ten children in them around the time of World War II. Of Finnish households, 54 per cent of households live in single-family houses and 43 per cent in apartment blocks, with 77 per cent of the nation being urban dwellers.

**Finland's Population**

The population of Finland is currently just over five million people, giving a density of 17 per sq km. One million people, 22 per cent of the population, live in the greater Helsinki area. Over half the population lives in the three south-western provinces around Helsinki, Turku and Tampere.

Around 6 per cent of the nation is of Swedish stock. There are 6,500 Sami (Laps) who live in the north of Finland, Lapland. The first Romanies (gypsies) arrived in the 16th century during Swedish rule, and they now number around 6,000. They live in the southern half of the country in tribes called *cherhas* that are divided into extended families. The majority

Finland has the world's longest regularly collected population statistics. Regular collection and compilation of population statistics was begun in the kingdom of Sweden-Finland as early as 1749, though regular publication did not start until the 1870s.

of refugees are Vietnamese, Somalis or Kurds. Finland has the lowest percentage of any European country of resident foreigners, around 200,000, comprising 10,000 Russians and 3,000 Estonians.

## PHYSICAL CHARACTERISTICS

The Finns genetic make-up is 75 per cent the same as the Swedes. However, the Finnish people are not a homogeneous race. They are the descendants of no less than five different ethnic groups, these being the Hame people, the Karelians, Savo people, Ostro Bothnians and the Laps (Sami). These people came to Finland by different routes after the last Ice Age. They journeyed from the east, south and west, over a process lasting for several thousand years. These Finno-Ugarians were nomadic tribes people who inhabited much of northern Russia. Recent research, however, has demonstrated that much of the original populations came from the south, moving northwards as the ice retreated. A substantial Indo-European influence over the years has affected the population of Finland also. As Finland was owned by the Swedes for 600 years, many Finns, especially in the south-western part of Finland, now look very Swedish.

The light colouring of the Finns reflects their long history of inhabiting northern Europe. North Europeans are the lightest coloured people of the world because they have lived in northern latitudes the longest. Therefore, natural selection has had the longest time to produce the light skin colour adapted to low levels of ultraviolet radiation. The Finns could be said to be the 'darkest' of the Nordic races. Some Finns are descended from the Swedes, and tend to be taller, slimmer, fairer, blonde-haired with pale blue or grey eyes. Other Finns are descended from the eastern Europeans and tend to be shorter, stockier, dark-haired and brown-eyed. Mix these two very difference races together and you get multiple variations on the two themes. There have been few refugees and immigrants, so Finnish stock has been little diluted by other influences since the 'original mix'.

There definitely is a typical Finnish look, which I cannot describe. There are strong themes in their physical make up which can be recognised, but more probably because you know someone that resembles the stranger you are currently looking at. A national trait I can distinguish is that the Finns have extremely baby-fine hair (apparently this is very difficult for hairdressers from other parts of the world to cut) so many Finns wear their hair short. They have finely pronounced cheekbones, may be heavy browed and a tendency for small eyes, generally blue or slate-grey in colour. They have pale, fine skin. On the whole, the Finns are either slim or of medium build. It is very rare to see anyone who is obese and only a few are overweight. Heart disease is reckoned to be a problem in Finland, especially in the eastern region called Karelia, where a lot of their traditional food contains cream, butter or milk. Even there, obesity is a rare sight.

## BILINGUALISM

Finland has a 5 per cent Swedish-speaking minority and is officially a bilingual country, so maps nearly always bear both the Finnish and Swedish names for cities and towns. For example, Turku (Finnish) and Åbo (Swedish) are the same city, even though the names differ totally. Many other things also bear two names, such as streets, roads and suburbs. Roads, for example, can be especially confusing—what first appears on a map to be a road that changes its name is, in most cases, one road with two names. This is common in the Swedish-speaking areas on the southern and western coasts, whereas inland Swedish names are far less common. In the far north in Lapland, you'll almost never see Swedish, but you will occasionally see signage in Sámi instead.

There is just one place in the whole of Finland where the official language is Swedish alone. This place is the Åland Islands, the largest archipelago of 6,500 islands, and lies off the south-west coast between Finland and Sweden. It has been an autonomous, de-militarised region since 1921, has

26,000 inhabitants, its own provincial government and flag, own radio and TV station, and exquisite stamps.

**One Language Only!**

From a Finnish reader, Hannu Sivonen: 'My lady cousin took a trip to Åland. In a taxi there, she gave the address to the driver in Finnish. The man turned back and answered in Swedish: "There's only one language on this island." My cousin, being Canadian and not knowing Swedish much, gave the same request in English. Now the driver turned again and said with a little raised voice: "As I said, there's only one language on this island." So my cousin stepped out and tried another taxi.'

For the Finnish speakers, Swedish is not viewed as a foreign language, but as the second domestic language. Those with Swedish as their mother tongue must learn Finnish by the same token. Therefore, from a young age Finns are brought up speaking both languages. Children start learning a foreign language in the third grade, and this is most often English. Nowadays, Russian is very seldom chosen, with French being slightly more popular but seldom taken up. German comes second to the choice of English. There is no obligation to learn more foreign languages, but many do. Youngsters hate the compulsory Swedish, but the fact is that a great majority of Finns can speak Swedish if they have to, some clumsily maybe, some more fluently. However, getting to grips with Swedish does allow the Finns a more streamlined introduction to the main European languages as they derive from the same Indo-European basis.

## THE FINNS

Meeting a Finn is definitely good for a stressed-out soul, especially if you come from a nation of money-oriented achievers, celebrity fixations, and the latest 'must have' status items. As a whole, the Finns definitely to do not 'do' this status thing, nor do they vie for one-upmanship. They are unpretentious, warm, and friendly—but like their solitude. Although they may appear taciturn, they have a genuine natural affection, are hospitable and easy to get along with. They are tolerant but distrust and despise people who gossip, are melodramatic and overemotional. Being overconfident and over-opinionated is frowned upon. They do not boast, brag or show-off and definitely recoil from the foreigners that do—for in this land only a foreigner would behave like that. In many respects, the Finns have protected themselves from the greed of individuals, as greed and excess are cultural taboos—society works towards the common good. They have a robust self-esteem (in terms of self-reliance), a deep-rooted sense of time-honoured values and a healthy sense of irony!

It has been said that a characteristic of the Finns is their sameness. They do not like to stand out in a crowd and their mode of dress is very similar to everyone else's. The Finns, of course, disagree with this overgeneralisation and consider themselves very individualistic. However, an example which illustrates this trait is they do not celebrate people's achievements much. Whilst births and marriages may be news on the office grapevine, outstanding achievements in professional life, educational examinations or industry awards seem to be swept under the carpet. Their culture does not accept outright propaganda. Any open broadcast would be seen as bragging or showing off, which isn't good. Being humble is regarded as a plus.

The Finns have had a long struggle for emancipation and a continuing struggle to survive once independence was won. This brave country has had to fight so many times for its freedom. This fact alone has seemingly strengthened the resolve in each and every Finn. They have a built-in resilience to survive prolonged hardship. This Finnish trait is called *sisu*, meaning guts, toughness, stamina, courage, stubbornness. Even if all looks lost, a Finn with *sisu* will fight on valiantly until final defeat, and then he still won't give up. *Sisu* is a quality that is central to their being—a tough independent personality—engendering self-reliance and cool pragmatism. What *sisu* is really all about is

*Sisu* is the ability to endure hardship and adversity. The Finns reckon that it is this trait that helped them fight off the Russian Army in World War II. Although heavily outnumbered (300,000 against 2 million), they could fight as self-reliant, free-thinking individuals, using guerrilla tactics, against a trained army and incredible odds.

Timo H: 'The older generation believe that the young, globetrotting MTV generation don't have as much *sisu* as they have; life has been too cushy for them. So, they have not such an attitude to tough times and making do.

doing things until they're done, not because they're important but because they need to get done, somebody's got to do it, and you just don't leave anything unfinished. It's not about what the 'neighbours might think'—it's about what you think about yourself.

The Finns do not consider themselves Scandinavian, nor do they like to admit that any part of them may be Russian. However, Finnish traditions owe something to both cultures. In spite of being very modern, very technologically driven and 'Western' in outlook, old traditions bind people together.

## FINNISH VALUES

Values are borne of a cultural mindset, developed through taught and learned national concepts which become core beliefs. Generally speaking, culture is the total of the inherited ideas, beliefs, values and knowledge which constitute the shared bases of social action. It is the ideas of a group with shared traditions and the tastes valued by that group.

**Understanding Culture**

Culture is a social and psychological prism: 'We think we perceive the world as it is. In fact the world is mediated through our dominant assumptions, values, and beliefs. Our cultural prism determines how we understand and know ourselves, others, and the world. Each of our cultural prisms is built out of a history of our group, our religions and other belief systems, economies, educational and legal systems, aesthetics, language, and to some extent our geography.'

—Terence Brake, *The Global Leader*, 1997

Culture is not simply about outward gestures, the do's and don'ts and the taboos. It is the embedded psychological reality of a group and how it affects thoughts, feelings and behaviours. It is a group reality that has evolved over many years. Studies highlight that every culture distinguishes itself from others by the way they react to certain situations. Of the many ways to analyse culture, the following gives a shortened overview:

- **Individual or community spirited**
  All Anglo-Saxon cultures are driven by the spirit of individuality. Mainstream America chases the 'American Dream', believing that one's own effort alone can make the dream come true. Asian and African cultures believe that everyone has to pull together for the good of society. In Japan, individual thinking is a sign of immaturity, demonstrating that a person has not grown up enough to put societal values first!

  The Finns lie between these two extremes, being very individualistic but having a social conscience, thus they have heavy taxation to provide first-class social/health benefits free for all. They perceive themselves as fiercely individualistic, but (as we say in English) they won't rock the boat because of what the neighbours might say, as this will make them stand out from the crowd.
- **Sticking to the rules or bending rules**
  This is the degree to which a society allows and expects rules to be universally applied. All Nordic countries believe rules should be strictly adhered to. In Britain, we believe rules create a level playing field (but do bend them occasionally to suit ourselves, British saying: 'rules are meant to be broken'). Other cultures (the Arabs and Latins) believe that relationships are more important than any rules, which can be discarded or overlooked—some people may be beyond the law.

  The Finns lie at the 'sticking to the rule' extreme. This has engendered a comparatively safe and crime-free country, where people behave predictably because they all adhere to the same code of conduct. They are inherently honest and cannot understand other cultures' mental and moral elasticity—it totally confuses them. And, (as above) they hate rocking the boat etc.

- **Given status versus achievement**

  This is the degree to which a society gives recognition for attributes such as age or birth right, versus recognition for one's own personal and individual achievements. Generally speaking, community societies such as Japan and China respect age, wisdom and grey hairs. In Individualistic societies, respect is given to those who achieve (achieving is defined by the value set of the society: climbing corporate ladder, money, celebrity status, education, entrepreneurship, etc.). Britain and Spain, having been class driven societies, lie between the two extremes, but they are both achievement oriented, with Britain more so.

  The Finns are definitely achievement oriented, respecting those who achieve through hard work. They are industrious, tenacious and have a solid work-ethic. Achievement in this engineer-filled land is defined as academic achievement, innovation and entrepreneurship. Very little credence is given to celebrities.
- **Equality versus hierarchy**

  The Nordic countries all have an equality ethos—no one is thought of as being superior to anyone else for any reason whatsoever. They respect hard-work and achievements (as above) but that does not give anyone the right to believe they are superior. There are no hierarchies in institutions, organisations or the small firm—everyone can talk to the boss. This applies to some extent to all the Anglo-Saxon nations. Those in authority are respected, but not thought to be superior—a modern phenomenon. Most other cultures have a hierarchical structure to a greater or lesser extent. In India, there are so many levels that everyone jealously guards each trapping that signifies their status.

  The Finns believe in total equality, with everyone having the right to voice their opinion. They are therefore very tolerant and seemingly patient. However, the boss is still the boss and will make the decisions to speed up any inefficiencies.

- **Cool and calm versus emotional behaviour**
  This is the degree to which a society tolerates the expression and use of emotion (especially in decision-making and business). When an Italian is in love, the whole world knows—likewise when s/he is angry. In Italy, it is quiet acceptable to demonstrate how you feel, but not in other countries where assuming the disposition of a rational human being is highly prized. The Chinese, of course, are inscrutable.

  The Finns, to foreigners coming from emotive cultures, seem 'closed' and often withdrawn. They are suspicious of melodrama, which confuses them, and secretly believe that people showing this disposition are untrustworthy. They admire coolness and calm judgement. As emotion has no place in their daily, operational lives—FACTS do! Facts, evidence and truth are believed to produce the best outcome, and truth is very black and white in Finland—there are absolutely no shades of grey. When you tell Finns this, they insist that greyness does have its place (after all they are pragmatists), but their greyness is very black to the likes of you and me!
- **Attitudes to time**
  This is the degree to which time is elastic. Is a culture run by the clock with people clock-watching the entire day, or do things happen when they happen? Does *mañana* really mean tomorrow or not today?

  The Finns love time–it keeps their society well-ordered! Trains and buses leave on time, everyone pays their bills within 24 days, and people arrive punctually for appointments.
- **Environmental consciousness**
  This is the degree to which people either abuse their environment, versus being a part of the cosmos system and ecologically aware.

  The Finns are surrounded by nature and forests cover 72 per cent of the land. They are a forest people at heart. One of their core beliefs is about looking after the environment. Laws, dating back to 1886, promote well-managed, sustainable forestry and these are updated constantly with new and pertinent regulations. This is just one incidence of how long the Finns have been 'green' in their outlook. To a large extent, their climate, nature and geography has shaped the Finnish mindset. They perceive themselves at a distance from other cultures, apart and separate—but inextricably mixed with their forests and lakes.

The Finns have developed a strong national identity, an ancestral love of their land and a national pride that envelopes them, instilled in them from birth and through good education. They remain a forest people at heart. They are naturally reserved, especially towards foreigners, and are likely to seem very formal and aloof. In a culture where silence is a virtue, extreme chattiness is viewed with surprise or suspicion. In a culture where personal space is a right and not a privilege, a handshake is always appropriate, but a hug and kissing is not.

## FINNISH VALUES IN ACTION

The Finns are an extremely conscientious and industrious race. It seems to be part of their national pride that they work hard and study seriously. On the whole, they have a very great respect for education and training and are always working towards long-term good, rather than short-term gain. These people are not lazy or indolent. If there is a job to be done, they just get on and do it with no small talk to interrupt.

I know a management trainer who has worked in various parts of the world. He always claims that the Finns are the only people he knows where he can give them an exercise to do, return in 15 minutes, and find that the exercise will be completed.

### Integrity and Honesty

The Finns are extremely law-abiding; they are honest and have integrity. You will not be cheated out of any change. Similarly, they do not expect you to cheat them. You don't have to wear your handbag padlocked to your side, and if you were to leave your wallet in a restaurant, it would, more than likely, be returned intact. This relatively safe-from-robbery environment does not mean to say that the Finns take this for granted. They do secure their personal belongings and lock their doors. On the whole, Finland is a country where you can walk safely at night. There seems to be a sort of invisible authority that rules the lives of the Finns. It is certainly not a heavy-handed police presence, as one French friend of mine said about Finland, "I don't think I've ever seen a policeman in Finland, so I couldn't describe one".

Integrity and honesty in action: no one will check before you leave if you have drunk anything from a hotel mini-bar. I queried this once and the lady receptionist just turned and said to me, "We trust you."

This national trait of obeying the rules means that their moral and ethical code is very black and white, without the elasticity of other nations. The Finns have only been in the EU for a few short years, and yet they are already discovering that if they want to survive, they are going to have to learn to bend the rules, just like everyone else. However, this does not sit happily with them. The Finns have a highly developed civic sense. As individuals, they act as they wish, as long as it is not against the common good. They are self-sufficient and independent, and keenly respect the rights of others to be independent. They intensely value their freedom and their personal space. However, they all realise that they have to take responsibility for this total freedom.

Interestingly, one Finnish political party suggested that should they be elected to power, they would reduce the tax burden on the ordinary Finnish citizen. This has not proved to be a popular and winning election policy, as the majority of the Finns believe this will increase the gap between the 'haves' and the 'have nots'. Their deep-rooted sense of fairness and their belief in looking after those who are less fortunate than themselves means Finland is a country where few have too much and fewer have too little.

## Hatred of Debt

Since the beginning of the 1990s, there has been a rapid build-up of household debt in the Euro area, both in terms of ratio of debt to disposable income and debt to GDP. The ratio of household debt to disposable income rose by more than 50 per cent, reaching a ratio of 86 per cent by the end of 2004. Finland's ratio, however, stood at 35 per cent, meaning it is one of the lowest debt-ridden countries in the EU (and industrialised nations). Also, Finns are the least likely to fall into arrears with any debt. Finns abhor debt at a personal level, refusing to buy on credit cards as a means to get what they want. They will, of course, take out loans for their homes. At the business level, a recent European survey showed the Finns pay faster than any other country, within a month of receiving them: 24 days on average. At government level, debt has continued its clear downward trend.

The chart below shows the EMU deficit (-) and debt of Finnish general government, per cent of GDP, as reported in August 2005 by Statistics Finland. The EMU debt describes general government debt to other sectors of the economy and to the rest of the world, and it is influenced by changes in both gross debt and internal debts of the general government.

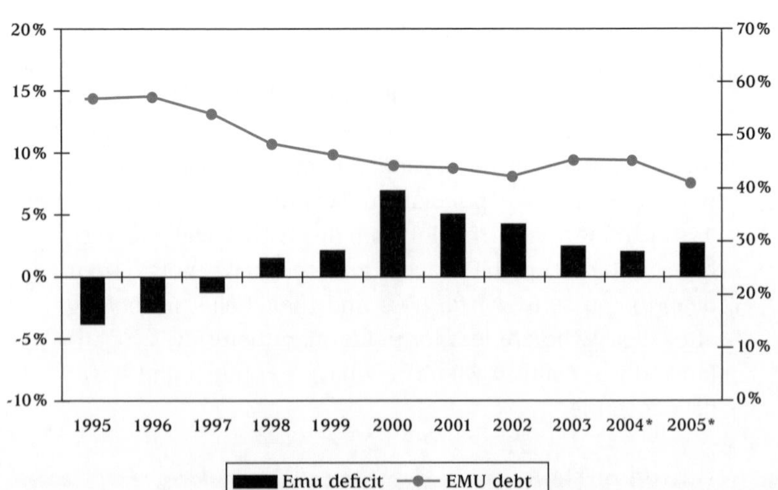

### Reliability

Deriving from the values of honesty, integrity and hatred of debt comes the other solid characteristic the Finns value—reliability. You keep to time, deliver on deadline, and to the highest quality possible. Your reliability is defined by your competence and the fact that you never promise what you cannot deliver or do. You must never let the Finns down, and they will never let you down either. In Finland, your word is your bond—a statement is like a promise. A handshake on a deal is as good as a written contract. You say EXACTLY what you mean, and mean EXACTLY what you say. This means the Finns direct communication approach can seem rather rude to other cultures used to 'softening' their approach. The Finns will never tell you what you want to hear and are confused by foreigners who seem to 'lie'—this makes them mad. I never realised how 'polite' the English were, or how much 'greyness' they put into their communication, until my Finnish boss asked me to accompany him to a meeting, in spite of his good English, stating, "I never understand when a 'Yes' is a 'Yes' in England—and what does 'that sounds interesting' mean?" All this is set to confuse a Finn. Chattiness is a sign of empty-headedness and should be avoided at all costs!

**Qualities of a Finnish Prime Minister**

'Paavo Lipponen, the prime minister at cross-century, was voted the least charismatic Finnish politician; he shunned hype and small talk, preferring to do his job seriously. What country other than Finland would have fired the following prime minister, Anneli Jäätteenmäki, because she was guilty of a questionable untruth in her remarks to Parliament?'

—Richard Lewis, *The Cultural Lone Wolf*, 2005

## A CLASSLESS SOCIETY

Finland is a society where few have too much and even fewer have too little. One thing that particularly strikes visitors to Finland is the apparent absence of class distinctions in education, in everyday social life and in the protocols

Being virtually classless has really prevailed since the 1980s. As Finland has turned into a knowledge society, few people work in the classical sense of labouring—most of them work with their heads. Industry concerns itself with controlling automated machines, and labour jobs have been transferred to China or Estonia.

of public life. It has been said that without the existence of an overseas empire, or a native monarchy and aristocracy, there has been no opportunity for racial, social or class superiority to take root.

The relative absence of invisible social barriers in their own society has led the Finns to be very well liked and accepted in many parts of the globe. The Finns have been very successful missionaries in Africa because they were seen to be of European stock, but without the taint of white supremacy and colonial attitude. No one resents the Finns when they arrive abroad. There are many foreign aid programmes and development programmes supported by Finland, especially in East Africa. The roads in Tanzania were built with Finnish support. The Finnish are particularly well accepted in their UN peace-keeping roles and many political summits are held in Helsinki as Finland is seen as a country with 'no axe to grind' and no historical alliances.

One Finnish friend told me, "We have no social class. It is very impolite to admit or think in terms of social classes". Of course, Finnish society is not without snobbery, but it is said that it harks back to the days of Swedish nobility and German barons. Some say there exists elitism in some of the minority of Swede-Finns. Some speak little or no Finnish, by speaking Swedish at home and by attending Swedish-speaking schools and universities. Although they have a Finnish passport, they see themselves as superior and refuse to integrate in Finnish society or speak Finnish. Also, they have no wish for their children to be bilingual. The majority of Finns do not witness this, though an English friend of mine who works in Helsinki knows a small 'clique' who keep themselves very separate.

One American lady I met who had worked for a Finnish company in the States for over 20 years spoke about the Finnish 'old guard' as being very arrogant and superior. Nowadays, she explained, the Finns are quite changed and really very hospitable.

An Englishman I encountered, who is married to a Finn and has been living in Finland for ten years, told me that when he first came to Finland, he was treated as a second-class citizen. "Things changed," he said, "when they joined the EU". He added that before Finland joined the EU, there were many who suffered paranoia that the rest of Europe would come and take away their lands and everything they had worked hard to build up. This, of course, could give rise to resentment of refugees arriving. However, the Finns have given homes to Vietnamese boat people and Kurds, who integrated well into their society because they learned the language, became better educated and worked hard—all of which the Finns admired. In record time, they turned themselves into entrepreneurs because their livelihood depended on it.

There is a new hierarchy of wealth. The 'Nouveau-riche' is a new phenomenon in Finland. These are people who have earned money quickly, usually through share options in some of the companies that have become large and successful, such as Nokia. Increasing wealth is being generated by the IT companies who lead the world in leading-edge technologies. Some of these people like to show off their wealth. They buy expensive things because they can afford to do so. This is typically un-Finnish, whose culture values modesty, humility and keeping a low profile. Until recently, all Finns believed that if you had something you didn't show it off, because it wasn't good to do so.

I keep hearing little stories about Finnish jealousy from the Finns, and I'm told that they are a jealous people, "In the west they try and keep up with the Jones' and in the east they try to take away what people have got!" They must do it in secret though, as it is definitely not overt and would be frowned upon if known.

In a recent survey, it was shown that people who won the lottery, tended to keep quiet about it. All they did was change their car for a slightly better one. They repaired their houses and they travelled a little more—but nothing that was ostentatious. Another survey of 50 countries shows that the Finnish and New Zealand males are the least susceptible to flattery. Humility, modesty and shyness are valued characteristics.

Although the Finns have built for themselves a sort of classless society, it would be unfair to say that there are no prejudices at all. Indeed, people in the north and rural areas feel that those who live in the big city of Helsinki look down on them. It has only been in very recent years that the Sami people and their culture have begun to emerge from under Finnish 'suppression'. These hardworking people from Lapland, who endure the most extremes of weather that this earth can give, have long been regarded as a slightly inferior race. Also, there is a small population of gypsies who live in Finland. These Romany people number about 6,000. They have their own language, culture and dress. These people have long been despised (unusually for the tolerant Finns) probably because they do not try to integrate into mainstream society.

**The Finns and Foreigners**

Back in 1990, there were only 9,000 foreigners in the whole of Finland, which included 1,000 refugees. However, nowadays there are reckoned to be around 200,000 foreigners in the country. Think of the shock to a nation that has had few visitors from the outside world.

Roman Schatz: When Finns encounter a foreigner, 'their heart rate rises and sweat appears on their brows!' (*From Finland With Love*, 2006)

Their passion for equality means they have built for themselves a sort of classless society where living standards are high and with relatively little difference between high and low salaries. High levels of taxation gives Finland one of the most comprehensive welfare systems in western Europe, and all this has been achieved by gradual consensus over a long period of time. Employment law is quite rigid and very much favours workers' rights. The owner of a small engineering company explained that his workers were only allowed to work 40 hours a week and 300 hours overtime in any year and have six weeks holiday, plus all the bank holidays. Thus, to get the work done, he and the family had to work all hours! It is extremely difficult to un-employ someone when they have started working for you.

Interestingly, the law in Finland requires all major employers to provide a 'Nuclear' Bunker, stocked with provisions, water and blankets at their premises for the protection of their workforce in case of an emergency.

## PERSONAL SPACE

To understand the Finns' need for personal space, you have to realise that until modern recent history, most Finns lived a simple life by fishing, hunting and cultivating the land. With so few people and such an expanse of land, this life was very lonely and often the only contact with people were with the family that lived with them. The vast majority of the Finns live in towns and cities these days, but they still remain a 'forest people'. They love to be in close harmony with nature, and it has to be understood that sometimes Finns just like to be alone. They have no personal need for constant socialising, have a great respect for each others personal space, and can regard any unnecessary and irrelevant small talk as an invasion and intrusive. (Read about silence in Chapter Four: Socialising with the Finns).

From a Finnish Reader, Hannu Sivonen: 'In a Spanish discussion group in Helsinki, the leader was Jorge from Mexico. One time, suiting the context at the time, I just gently wanted to inform him about the feelings that are raised in me (as an example of Finnish culture) when my (first or second) name is repeatedly mentioned when someone talks to me. I explicitly said that this is a habit of especially American (US) salesmen. I feel pushed and my personal space violated. Jorge dramatised it and asked desperately, how should he then address me, with "you, yes you over there or what?" He seemed to be genuinely somewhat embarrassed and insulted. Later I have talked about this with my countrymen and they perfectly joined in my opinion about the Finnish feeling.'

Indeed on a number of times I have travelled on an aeroplane and seen two Finns sitting next to each other. They might nod to each other on arriving and they will nod as they leave, but during the two- or three-hour flight they won't talk at all. Above all, the Finns appreciate a calm, ordered society where each individual is accorded space and privacy.

**The Finnish Manner**

From Maria, a Finnish reader: 'The idea of personal space is very different here... Once I had a huge tulip painted on my face (long story). The tulip's blossom was my lips but the stem went all the way up my nose and onto the forehead. I also had quite sizeable green leaves painted on my cheeks. I had to go home using several modes of public transport but no one batted an eyelid. There was one drunk guy who looked at me twice, but I think it was because he must have thought he was seeing things. It was only when I came home that my family erupted in laughter after seeing my face.'

A quarter of the population of Finland owns a summer cottage—there are about 400,000 of them. The majority of Finns have access to one, either through the company they work for or their families. This is where the average Finn goes to get away from it all. The summer cottage or *mokki* is ideally located on the shores of a lake, surrounded by forest and in the middle of nowhere. These log cabins usually only provide the very basic of amenities. Normally there is no electricity or running water, but the two things that a *mokki*

A typical Lappish wooden cabin is your journey's end after the reindeer safari. The cabins are surprisingly warm and well insulated, thanks to a central fire that is used for heating and cooking. Your nearest neighbour will be a long way away.

has to have are a sauna and a rowing boat. Most Finns don't travel abroad for their summer holiday; instead they spend the time in their lonely log cabins by the edge of the lake. Some people will spend just two or three weeks at the summer cottage, but many will take their family for a long stay, and mum and dad will commute to work (children have 11 weeks holiday in the summer). This return to nature is a family affair. The love of the natural environment is common to all Finns of all ages, whether city dwellers or not.

From a Finnish reader: I spent two months in England to learn the language when I was 17. The place was not a big city, but even so I felt very clear distress when I realised that there is never a place or a moment when I can be alone. In the parks and beaches and everywhere, there is always a bigger or smaller crowd around me. The feeling grew worse as time progressed. Otherwise I was very happy in England.

## ENVIRONMENTAL CONSCIOUSNESS

I cannot emphasise enough that the hearts of the Finnish people lie in the lakes and the forests. As a race, the Finns really do care about their environment and the defence of nature, especially the lakes which are high on their political agenda. There is an ongoing battle to save the country's greatest assets: their lakes and their forests. As early as 1886, the Forestry Act was passed and was intended to curb the wasteful use of forests. In the early days of independence, the republic introduced legal protection for the forests and threatened species. Nowadays, there are strict conservation laws and everyone is encouraged to take individual responsibility for the protection of their wild life. Green policies are part of everyday life in Finland. There is ongoing research to improve house insulation. Recycling schemes are the norm and not the exception, and the government is committed to ever better public transport.

The Finns have recognised that they are living with a fragile harmony. Their will to preserve what they cherish above all else is almost without parallel. Their concern to do right by their natural environment is deeply anchored in their beliefs. Recently, the Finns have become aware of the detrimental effect the salt that they sprinkle on the roads in winter is having on the water-courses. Research for a better substitute is now underway.

Forests cover 72 per cent of the total land area of Finland. These forests have always been an extremely important source of the wealth of Finland. This is the country's largest resource and a major export. Potentially, forestry, timber processing and mining can do the greatest environmental damage. However, these industries add up to a considerable portion of the country's income.

About three-quarters of the forests in Finland are owned by ordinary private families. All forest owners are under legal obligation to replace anything they cut down. So it is in everybody's interest to maintain healthy forests, and trees are carefully managed and harvested. Sustainable forestry is high on the political agenda. Protected zones now account for one-third of the area of Lapland and there are 30 national parks and nature reserves. These

## Every Man's Right

Forests are also an important source of recreation in Finland. There is a law called 'Every Man's Right' which means that anyone is allowed to pick berries and wild mushrooms in any forest, private or public. It is also a right of access and is an important part of Finnish traditions as the picking of berries and harvesting of mushrooms is a national summer/autumn pastime.

areas have been created to encourage natural forestry; this means there is no extensive tree felling, few roads and natural regeneration.

To the outside world, Finland still represents a supremely unspoiled environment, with 350 types of birds and about 65 different species of mammals. However, Finland has its problems. It was the first Western country to notice the disastrous affects of the Chernobyl catastrophe. This meant that hundreds of reindeer had to be slaughtered. It suffers from air and water pollution arising from the activities of its Russian neighbour. Poland and East Germany are contributing to the pollution of the Baltic Sea. By comparison with some areas in Europe which are really polluted, Finland is relatively unspoilt. However, the country is aggressively pursuing energy conservation policies, trying to limit the despoliation of its natural landscape and trying to create new and environmentally-friendly waste management systems. All these initiatives have meant that the Finns have developed a great deal of expertise in environmental matters. They have offered their technological know-how and clean air and clean water industrial technology to their neighbours, Russia and Eastern Europe, in the hopes of slowing down the pollution process.

Even the national anthem and the blue and white flag of Finland are linked to the people's love of their landscape: the national anthem was written to celebrate the country's summer landscape; the flag is supposed to represent the white of the snow and the blue lakes of summer. (See Chapter Seven: Enjoying the Culture for Flag Raising Days). Literature, fine art, design and architecture are all expressed in terms of their environment.

Good design is a passion for the Finns. Although their design can be put under our generic term of 'Scandinavian' or 'minimalist', the Finns have created their own style. This style has had many threads of influence. From the original Byzantine designs that came with eastern invaders, the geometric designs of Chorale have developed. From Sweden came designs originating from the west. There has been a strong heritage handed down from traditional textile art which can often been seen on their pottery, textiles or in interior decoration. On the whole, Finns prefer natural products, but they bring together both natural and artificial products in a way which stamps modern Finnish products with a unique character. Whether creating a product for glassware or textiles or industrial design, the Finns pursue their obsession for things to be of aesthetic beauty. The Finns long ago discovered that good design was not only something that was aesthetically satisfying, but also commercially profitable.

## RELIGION

There are two official churches of Finland: the Lutheran Church and the Orthodox Church. They still collect taxes and register births. Nine out of ten Finns belong to the national Lutheran Church. This Church has about 4.5 million members in 600 communities, and is the third largest in the world. Christianity came to Finland in the 12th century from both the east and the west. Hence Finland has an Orthodox Church of which there are around 55,000 members (about 1 per cent of the population).

The sparkling white Helsinki Cathedral stands on a hill and is clearly visible even from far out at sea.

There are less than 4,000 Catholics and some 13,000 Jehovah Witnesses. Judaism arrived during the 19th century with Jewish merchants and men working for the Imperial Russian Army. Today, there are around 1,300 living in the Helsinki and Turku areas (south and south-west Finland). Muslims were introduced into Finland with the Russian army at the end of the 19th century. The number of Muslims has increased from 1,000 in 1990 (the long-established Tartar Muslims) to about 15,000 at cross-century (brought about by Somali refugees). The emergence of the immigrant religions in the 1990s is one of the most striking changes in the Finnish religious field since the spread of new religious movements to this country in the 1970s. The number of foreign citizens, including refugees, has rapidly risen since the late 1980s. Consequently, numerous new religious immigrant communities have taken root in Finland, most of which, however, profess Islam. Around 10 per cent of the population have no religious calling, and therefore belong to the civil register.

The Reformation of Martin Luther gradually displaced the Catholic Church encouraged by the conversion of the Swedish king to Lutheranism. The first complete Bible in the Finnish language was written in 1642. Nowadays, there are women Lutheran Priests, and the Church is seen to be quite progressive and building for the future. The Church has become very much more popular in recent years and plays an important role in baptisms, funerals and confirmations. Over 90 per cent of Finnish youth attend confirmation camp. The church employs its own social, youth and daycare workers. They help the aged, the disabled, drugs addicts, alcoholics, and counselling is given to those families with financial and social problems. As such, the church is an active participant in the community and plays an important role. The Finns do not necessarily

In the town of Nokia, every Thursday evening the church is so full you cannot get more people in it. People are turning to the Church for security and as a way to help them cope with the enormous changes that are taking place in their lives. There are three well-known fashion models who tour the country giving speeches and the Church is especially giving its attention to young people.

consider themselves religious, but they feel comfortable belonging to an organised church. Although only a few Finns attend church on a weekly basis, it is appropriate to comment that nearly everyone will attend church several times in a year. They are privately reverent and do not suffer a need to attend regularly.

**Foreign Culture and Religion**

'It has been argued, both by researchers and by Muslims themselves, that Muslims are discriminated, for instance in Britain and France, not only because of their skin colour or ethnicity, but because of their religion. A similar kind of atmosphere was apparent in Finland in the beginning of 1990s when there was an influx of Somali refugees. It has been said that their arrival in this country constituted a shock for Finns. Certainly, these new arrivals kindled a heated discussion in respect of foreigners in Finland and, in particular, about the different cultural habits that they brought with them to this country. Very often these habits were (and are) associated with women and, at times falsely, with Islam. In this regard, one need only mention women's veiling and the circumcision of girls. Interestingly enough, it was only with the arrival of these recent Islamic immigrants that such customs as the circumcision of baby boys and particular ways of slaughtering animals became issues for dispute, even though similar customs had prevailed in Finland for over a century among Jews and the long-established Tatar Muslims.'

**—Academy of Finland, SYREENI project**

It wouldn't be right to finish the chapter on religion without mentioning the rich tradition of folklore and the mention of the old Finnish gods. The ancient Finns had their own indigenous religious traditions. Their gods included: Ukko, god of growth, rain and thunderstorms was the supreme god, married to Rauni; Ilmarinen, god of winds and storms; Ahti, god of waters and fish; Tapio, god of forests. There were also: Kratti, guardian of wealth; Tonttu, guardian of the home; Kekri, the god of celebrating.

**Resources for Other Religions**

The website of 'The Islamic Society of Finland' provides information such as prayer timetables for the year, contact information and numerous other resources. The website is available in Finnish, English and Arabic. The website can be viewed at: http://www.rabita.fi.

For a list of Buddhist groups in Finland, see: http://www.buddha-dharma.info/ihmisia.htm.

## EDUCATION

Finns are probably some of the best informed people in the world on global current affairs. Their newspapers are very objective, placing emphasis on fact and evidence far more than on emotive headlines. A large proportion of television programmes are highly educational (or focus on the national obsession of sport). The Finns are world leaders in literacy, mathematics and science.

Finland has repeatedly been rated top of the class in international comparisons of educational standards, even though spending on education is low and Finnish children spend much less time in school than children in other countries. In terms of average PISA scores (organised by the Organisation for Economic Co-operation and Development to compare educational standards), Finland rates highest overall among a group of well-performing countries, including the other Nordic countries, Japan, Korea, Belgium, Holland, Canada, Australia and New Zealand.

Foreign educationalists are particularly interested because Finland's success does not seem to be related to money: OECD statistics show that Finland spends just 6.1 per cent of its gross domestic product on education, significantly below the OECD average of 6.3 per cent, and well below spending levels in many similarly wealthy countries. A surprising factor is the amount of time children spend in the classroom. Finnish children move on from the kindergarten playtime to primary school at age seven. Their schooldays remain short, often ending as early as 12:00 or 1:00 pm. They have a

10–11 week summer holiday, which surely must be the envy of children all over the world. Also, Finnish pupils spend an OECD record low total of some 5,523 hours at their desks, compared to an average of 6,847 hours. In Holland, children spend 8,000 hours in the classroom. Surveys also suggest that Finnish children spend less time doing homework than schoolchildren in many other countries.

The results of Finland's brightest students are not significantly above those from other successful countries, but where Finland really shines is in the scores of the lowest performing students. This means that very few Finnish schoolchildren are falling foul of the educational system. The Finnish system is designed along egalitarian principles, with few fee-paying private schools and very little streaming of pupils into different schools or classes according to their exam results. Schools were originally set up as part of efforts to form an autonomous Finnish nation, with no regard for any social class system. The whole of society participated in building the schools, including villagers and farmers, and public schools have always been equally intended for everybody. This kind of equality is perpetuated by the homogeneity of Finnish society and the absence of any major immigrant communities or socially deprived groups who could easily be marginalised educationally. It is true that children from better-off socio-economic backgrounds generally do better at school than children from poorer families, as is found in other countries, but such differences are not very pronounced in Finland.

## THE WOMAN'S ROLE

It may seem strange to focus on the role of women in this book, especially as Finland is an industrialised society, but it would be all too easy for one to mistakenly assume that Finnish women have the same role as most other women in Western society. I found that there was such a remarkable difference compared with what I am used to—it was so tangible you could hit me with it! I am, of course, talking about equality. Personally, I find that a woman's place outwardly is as near to ideal as can be found in any developed industrial society.

The Finns acknowledge that as a small nation, the role of women has been important in both agriculture and industry in supporting both the family and the nation. Thus Finland has had a long history in the emancipation of women. Traditionally in the 19th century, when boys had acquired the elementary skills of reading and writing, they were taken out of school and were put into farm work. Girls, however, stayed on to be further educated. Finland has long had equal opportunities as a 'trademark', and has continually updated their laws.

The history of the legal emancipation of women began in the 1860s.

- 1864: Single women attain legal majority at the age of 25 and the right to dispose of their own income from the age 15, and their own property from the age of 21, provided they notify a court of law.
- 1864: Marriage laws improved.
- 1868: Divorce made easier.
- 1871: Rights to enter university.
- 1878: First women physicians licensed.
- 1878: Inheritance laws amended to inherit equally with men.

- 1880: Emancipation movement began.
- 1890: Women allowed to teach in educational establishments.
- 1906: Universal suffrage, the first women in the world to vote along with New Zealand. First in the world to be allowed to stand for public office.
- 1907: First women elected to the *Eduskunta*—19 out of 200 MPs.
- 1916: Equal pay for women in schools and permitted to become university teachers.
- 1919: The new republic embodied the principles of full equality for the sexes.
- 1921: Compulsory general education decreed by law.
- 1922: Married women granted independent right to enter into Contracts of Employment.
- 1922: Formal establishment of the rights of unmarried mothers and their children.
- 1922: Father's obligation to support children until 17 years of age and the right of illegitimate offspring to inherit equally with legitimate children.
- 1926: Complete equality for women within the civil service. This covered issues such as competence requirement, salaries and pensions.
- 1930: Marriage Act granting legal equality of spouses.
- 1947: Central Association of Women Entrepreneurs founded.
- 1970: Grounds for abortion extended to include social considerations.
- 1970: Ratification of UN Convention on banning all discrimination against women.
- By 1981: 64 per cent of students taking university exams were women.
- 1986: New Surname Act passed, permitting spouses to take the surname of either party.
- 1988: Women permitted to enter the clergy of the Evangelical Lutheran Church.
- 1990: Elisabeth Rehn becomes first woman Minister of Defence in the World.
- 1994: Voluntary military service made available to women.

- 1994: Riitta Uosukainen becomes first woman Speaker of the Finnish Parliament.
- 1995: Stipulation of a 40 per cent quota of women in municipal select boards, municipal administration and government committees.
- 1996: Cabinet's Equal Opportunity Programme (1996–99).
- 2000: Tarja Halonen becomes first woman elected as president of Finland.
- 2005: Revised Act on Equality—requirement for gender equality planning at workplaces.

Finnish women are very proud of being among the first women voters in the world and they are well represented in the Finnish parliament. The part that women play in Finnish public life is far more important than can be seen in other countries.

There is a long tradition of women at work in Finland, with almost equal numbers of men and women working. The overwhelming majority of women (71 per cent) are in full-time employment whilst bringing up their children and looking after the family home. Women do less part-time work in Finland than anywhere else in Europe. There are many women in business, in forestry, in engineering and in the chemicals industry. There is no culture of traditional 'women's jobs', as there is, for example, in the UK in welfare and the caring services. Legally, women's pay is equal, but on the whole, women earn around 80 per cent of men's earnings. For Finnish women, financial independence is the basis of equal opportunities, and this explains the importance for them of working. Surveys show that 58 per cent of women regard work to be significantly important in becoming self-fulfilled. After 1945, Finnish women bore a heavy responsibility as breadwinners and equalled the men in their struggle to make reparations to Russia after the war. Until very recently, it was quite common for women to remain in agriculture and continue to maintain the family smallholding, whilst the men became the major wage earners.

The Rural Advisory Centres play an important role in supporting women's efforts in creating businesses. In many rural regions, women work from home—in isolation—and the centres have helped developed networks, mentoring programmes and an interactive Internet network. One bank in Finland offers reduced bank rates for women entrepreneurs. About 30 per cent of entrepreneurs are women and there are many government funded bodies helping to develop their skills through mentoring and training programmes.

In terms of breaking the 'glass ceiling', Finnish women can be said to be one generation ahead of those in the UK. Whilst many women in Western society got married and stayed at home to look after the children, however well educated they were, in Finland this did not happen. There are many women in Finland in their mid-fifties who have well-paid and powerful jobs.

There are those who have built businesses and sold them on successfully, there are those that have climbed quite high on the corporate ladder, and there are those who have become government ministers. In this respect, Finnish women can be seen as pioneers in working life. According to Statistics Finland, Finnish women are better educated than the men, which allows them opportunities for similar job status. Women also consider the workplace to be a good environment to learn new things and gain training. They have a great desire for self-development.

The nation as a whole is trying to encourage women to become more prominent at the highest level. In 1998, only 2 per cent of senior managers were women (four women in the top 200 companies). In 2005, 22 per cent of the highest management positions in public administration were held by women. In the private sector, just over a quarter of all managers were women. Some 17 per cent of the board members in the hundred biggest private companies were women in 2005. A third of Finns have a woman as their immediate boss, more than elsewhere in Europe.

Women are seen as popular and successful in their role as a boss. They are said to be more supportive and encouraging than

> Finland is 'a potential paradise for stressed males who hate to make decisions! ... After all, they [women] run the place.'
>
> —Roman Schatz, *From Finland with Love*, 2006.

their male counterparts, though, apparently, words of thanks and praise are just as few from the female boss! One of my clients from Kuopio, a man in his late twenties, voiced this opinion in public a couple of years before she was voted in. "The future belongs to women. They're good leaders". If women in Western societies want any role models, we need look no further than Finland to find them.

Finland is one of the safest countries in Europe for single women to travel. However, it is not usual to see a single woman in a pub, and she may therefore attract some unwanted attention.

## MARRIAGE, THE FAMILY AND DIVORCE

As with many Western societies, women are putting off getting married until an older age, but marriage, when it is undertaken, is more like a partnership between equal people. Most families have no more than two children, and again the women are putting off having children until later. Although the total responsibility of the family and the home lies on the shoulders of the women, men of all ages share the responsibility of looking after the children (and a few chores). It is quite common to hear even fairly elderly men talking about cooking or cleaning and looking after children or grandchildren because their wives are working. The Finnish housewife still does more of the chores than the man and just under one-third of couples share housework equally. Of women that work, 27 per cent feel that they are neglecting their home because of work.

A young Finnish student I met, who had spent several months in the United States staying with an American family, told me how 'different' life was there. Family mealtime was something that was a real culture shock for her. She was used to her mother cooking everyday and the whole family eating together. "At home," she explains, "I'll go to McDonald's twice a year. When there ... twice a week". She found the habit of TV meals and never eating together very strange, and remarked that the American Mum only cooked twice in the whole time of her stay. This is backed up by a recent survey by UNICEF, demonstrating that the USA was close to last when it comes to children eating and talking frequently

National dancing performances during a mid-summer festival. Finns value their traditions and family ties and such celebrations are opportunities for them to spend together.

with their families. In Finland, families still try to eat together, especially at weekends, when traditionally the meal of the day will be served at 2:00 pm.

Family ties and family values are very strong in Finland and this nation has a worldwide reputation for excellence in welfare. There is an intensive pre and post natal care service for mother and child, and Finland has the world's lowest infant mortality rate. The state guarantees ten months of fully paid maternity leave for either the mother and/or the father. This maternity leave can be split between them. In deed, Prime Minister Lipponen took two weeks off work when his wife had their child (and in the British press there was speculation whether Prime Minister Blair would copy him when his wife Cherie gave birth). There are modern state-subsidised childcare centres for children until the age of six, when they go to school. In recent years, the state has taken on more and more responsibility for family welfare, and currently it

It is still common to see women leaving babies in prams in the street while they pop quickly into a shop. Children make their own way to and from school. They walk, cycle or take the public transport. They certainly experience a degree of freedom that is no longer known in the UK. How good it feels to be in a society without the fear of baby snatchers and child abductors!

is one of the most generous systems of payment for mother and childcare in the world.

In the 1960s, Finnish men had the world's highest death rate from heart disease. Twenty years ago, it had reduced slightly, but heart disease was a problem all over Finland. As a nation, they decided to tackle the problem. A national project was launched to reduce the risk factors for heart disease and further reduce the number of deaths from cardiovascular disease. The 'North Karelia Project' took its name from the province in which it was launched (and which had the highest incidence). It was going to act as a pilot study for the rest of Finland. With good education and local medical centres giving advice, Finland has significantly reduced its national health problem.

An English friend, who works in the Health Care System in Britain, said the Finns brought about this change because each person took responsibility for their own health and that of their families. "It is a different culture," she explained. "They didn't want to be seen to be irresponsible. They didn't want to be a burden to the rest of society. That would have appeared selfish—and that is one thing the Finns are not". There has been a remarkable decline in heart disease in North Karelia and in Finland as a whole. There has also been a reduction in cancer deaths. Finland has reduced its incidence of heart attacks by 75 per cent since the early 1970s.

**Healthiest Children in Europe**

Along with Swedish children, recent surveys found Finnish children to be the healthiest in all of Europe. Also, in 2007, UNICEF's report on the well-being of children in industrialised nations found Finland fourth in ranking, after the Netherlands, Sweden and Denmark, when comparing six categories: material well-being, health, education, relationships, behaviours and risks, and young people's own sense of happiness. The worst, in descending order, were Portugal, Austria, Hungary, USA, and last Britain. The highest ranking countries have a greater family awareness, a better work-life balance and do not usually have such a 'dog-eat-dog' competition in their jobs.

### A Note on Hairdressers

Just a note—it seems very difficult to get an appointment at the hairdressers. You definitely cannot walk in off the street and have your hair done (which is what I tend to do in the UK and Mediterranean countries). Maybe this comes from their orderly mentality which I am disrupting. Anyway, hairdressers seem to be booked up ages in advance!

Medical care for the elderly is good and care for the aged is one of the Finns built-in values. Pensioners are well off financially even though there are 40 per cent more pensioners than there are adults of working age. Social security payments for the unemployed are relatively generous and include paying for television license, newspapers and telephone, as these are all seen to be essential to the education and well-being of a whole person.

As with many Nordic countries, the divorce rate in Finland is high—50 per cent. According to Finnish female friends, Finnish men are not demonstrative at all. They complain their men folk 'don't talk and they don't kiss'. However, very recently things have begun to change and talking about feelings and personal problems, for both men and women, is not such a taboo. What brought about this change has been the publication of two books. The first was written by the wife of former President Koivisto in which she describes her battle against depression—she 'went public'. The second was written by a man, a British author famous in Finland for writing TV scripts, named Neil Hardwick. He wrote about the effects on his life and family of the 'burnout' he suffered, how it made him drop out of his career and living, and the long slow journey to recovery.

Finnish divorce settlements are usually 'clean-cut'. As most women work and may well be paid better than their husbands, men need only help pay for the children and assets are split 50-50.

## Distribution of the Property of Divorcing Spouses

**Example 1: Short marriage without children, no marriage settlement.**

- Matti and Maija conclude marriage. After the marriage has lasted two years, the spouses are granted a divorce. Matti has property worth € 600,000 and Maija has a flat worth € 200,000. Both are gainfully employed and there are no children. Under the main rules applicable to the distribution of matrimonial property, the property of the spouses (€ 800,000) would be divided equally so that Matti would have to give € 200,000 of his assets to Maija. Under the rules on the adjustment of the distribution of matrimonial assets, it can, however, be decided that each shall keep his/her own property, because otherwise Maija would receive an unjust financial benefit after a short marriage.

**Example 2: Long marriage—marriage settlement.**

- Antti and Raija are granted a divorce after a marriage of 16 years. The spouses have children aged 14 and 12 from the marriage. Antti's monthly income is € 4,000 and Raija's € 2,000. Raija has been at home for ten years taking care of the home and the children. The only property of the spouses is a flat worth € 400,000 in Antti's name; the spouses have no debts. Under the marriage settlement concluded by Antti and Raija, neither has a matrimonial right to the property of the other, which means that upon the distribution of property, Antti would keep the flat in his name and Raija would obtain no property at all. Under the rules on the adjustment of the distribution of matrimonial assets, the stipulations of the marriage settlement may be disregarded and the property (€ 400,000) can be divided equally between the spouses, because compliance with the marriage settlement would lead to an unreasonable end result taking into consideration the duration of the marriage, the financial position of the spouses and Raija's activities for the common household. In this case each will obtain property worth € 200,000.

(Source: Brochures of the Ministry of Justice—http://www.om.fi/Etusivu/Julkaisut/Esitteet/Avioliittolaki/Puolisoidenomaisuudenjako?lang = en)

## FINLAND'S FIRST WOMAN PRESIDENT

Tarja Halonen was voted in as president at the beginning of 2000. She is described in political terms as a Social Democrat, with an intellectual humanist approach to life and the desire to find practical means to improve the society around her. She is called a 'pragmatic idealist'. She is probably the most left-wing head of state the nation has ever seen.

She was born and bred in Helsinki, though she lived on the 'wrong side of the tracks' in an area that is considered to be very working class. As a girl she suffered a serious speech impediment, which still affects her slightly even today. She grew up learning to be tolerant and sensitive to the 'differences' of others—especially those less fortunate than herself. She has always had a life-long interest in human rights and minority issues, and has played an active role in many civil rights associations. She is viewed as kind, tolerant, successful but slightly bohemian! She is extremely competent and very ambitious, and can be impatient and occasionally displays a flash of temper.

Tarja Halonen began her career as a trade union lawyer, was appointed as a parliamentary private secretary in 1974 and then accepted a junior ministerial position in the 1980s. She became Foreign Minister in the Government of Prime Minister Paavo Lipponen. Her traditional leftist views are in stark contrast to those of Prime Minister Lipponen, whose political ideology leans more towards a market-led social democracy. When elected president at the beginning of the year 2000, as is customary in Finnish politics, she resigned her party membership.

The president was the mother of a 21-year-old daughter, studying in England, at the time of her election. She has a 'companion' as the Finns say, of long-standing whom she recently married. Although they had separate flats in the same building because of 'differing views on housekeeping', they both moved into the presidential residence of Mantyniemi. Finland easily got used to having such an unusual 'first family'.

# SOCIALISING WITH THE FINNS

## CHAPTER 4

'The essence of effective cross-cultural communication has more to do with releasing the right responses than with sending the 'right' message.'
—Edward Hall, *Understanding Cultural Differences*

ON THE WHOLE, FINNISH SOCIETY is very conservative and gentle. No one disrupts the peace and harmony of their surroundings. No one talks loudly, gives a belly laugh or argues (that you know of) in public. Everyone makes a conscious effort NOT to disturb their neighbour, but to respect their personal space. Also, you need to remember that Finns don't like standing out in a crowd, so they will not behave in any way that draws attention to themselves. They will not smile at you as you pass in the street. They will not look you in the eye as they serve you in a shop. They will not cross the road until the 'green' man appears. In fact, they will all appear to behave in exactly the same way—calm, quiet introverts.

**Un-Finnish Earrings**

One early morning, I was arriving by train at Iisalmi to be met by a couple of Finns whom I had not met before. As soon as I stepped on to the platform, along with other passengers, they recognised me as the English consultant they were expecting. I was dressed in a completely Finnish-bought outfit (dress, bag, shoes, coat slung over my arm) and wondered how they noticed I wasn't Finnish. Apparently, my earrings had been the 'giveaway'—they were too ostentatious for a Finn!

## DRESS CODE

The Finns are very casual about dress code. If you see a Finn wearing a dark suit, white shirt and a coloured tie, he is probably not Finnish, or he is Finnish, but in another country! Finnish managers may wear slacks, jacket, shirt (and tie) for work. This is what they call in their terms, 'city wear'. A suit is for 'Sunday best', for big family occasions or business visits in foreign countries. A large proportion of men will wear jeans and a jumper. In winter, it is quite acceptable for managers to wear roll-neck sweaters under their jackets and be accepted as smart. There are no hard and fast rules about what you should wear. In summer, Finnish men tend to wear lovat-coloured jackets; although these are colourful, they are not bright. However, their blend of colours is unique to Finnish fashion. Women dress casually too. It is more usual to see women wearing trousers than a skirt. Topped with a jumper, this is quite acceptable for work and is far more casual than you will find in the UK. In summer, a cool cotton summer dress works fine. On the whole, Finnish women wear very little makeup, hardly ever wear coloured nail varnish, and jewellery is discreet.

There can only be few places in Finland to visit where you feel the need to look ultra smart or particularly glamorous. The Finns will accept you however you are dressed, and judge you little by your appearance. A French colleague of mine felt quite insecure when she first came to Finland. The Finns would avert their gaze from her, and she was quite sure that something disastrous had happened to her appearance. Nothing of the sort had taken place. It was just that the Finns rarely engage in eye contact, and even more rarely express an opinion about somebody's appearance. It is very unusual for anybody to pass comment on a pair of earrings, or a dress, or a nice pair of shoes. This tends to make you think that they just don't notice. However, I think it all boils down to the fact that Finns don't engage in small talk, and probably feel it would be very intrusive to make personal remarks. Anyway, the Finns are very pragmatic; they take you for who you are, not for how you dress.

It does seem that the vast majority of Finns conform in their manner of dress, which emphasises their national trait of not wanting to stand out from the crowd. However, there are a very few 'odd balls' about. It is possible to see

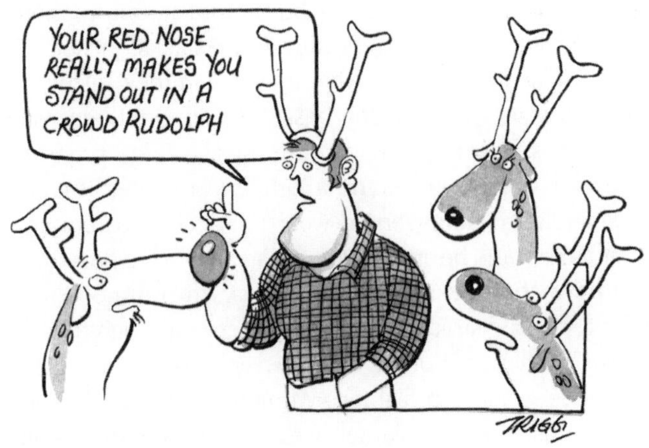


men with long hair and wearing a ponytail. You might see someone wearing an outrageously coloured outfit, or even the odd hippie walking the streets. However, these are very rare phenomena. In Helsinki, you may see women who are beautifully made-up and wearing designer outfits. However, I get the impression that there is no pressure to compete. For the handful of women who are dressed like this, there are hundreds that are not. Generally speaking, clothing for the Finns is practical; it's what they use to cover themselves up and keep themselves warm.

If you are visiting very good friends in the summertime, it will be quite normal to find your hosts in swimwear and a shirt. If you are visiting someone that you do not know very well, you are still expected to dress informally, but there will be a fairly smart element to this. It seems that jeans would be perfectly acceptable and expected at an informal gathering. If you are visiting a restaurant with family or friends, then smart casual or jacket and tie would be required. Suits are rarely worn. But whatever the choice of attire, it should reflect 'calmly-dressed'.

So, what happens when people go out at night? I have been to a few informal occasions, such as barbecues, and have found the Finnish men rather formally dressed compared with what I would expect to find in Britain. I am told that open-necked tee shirts or polo shirts would be the norm, but I haven't seen them being worn. Although very few restaurants insist on men wearing ties, the majority of times I've been to a restaurant, men have been wearing them. However, I do make a distinction here between restaurants and fast-food or chain restaurants. Women especially like to dress up, and I have seen some ladies turn up in wonderful eveningwear for special occasions. (They've had their boots on when arriving and their best shoes in a bag, and changed on arrival.) The local mid-week dance is a time when everyone tries to look smart—without 'dressing up'.

The overwhelming impression I have of a Finnish dress code is that people dress to suit themselves. This tends to be very pragmatic and sensible with nothing making themselves stand out from the crowd. Jewellery is minimal, though exquisitely designed.

## CLOTHING YOU NEED

So if you're travelling to Finland, what sort of clothes do you need to take with you? Layers of clothing work best at any time of year. As I was advised when visiting Lapland in mid-winter, you really need nothing more than your normal city/town wear. A layer of underwear provided in the form of vest or even long-johns is needed for the wintertime. Never forget that the Finns have very efficient central heating systems, so the need to dress warmly when you're indoors is not a necessity. One Finnish friend said she has piles of woollen jumpers in her cupboards given to her from foreign friends. Unfortunately, unless she travels to the Mediterranean in the winter time, she says she never has occasion to wear them in Finland—it is too warm! If you wear a jumper, you might find that you are too warm when you work indoors all day. However, danger time comes when you step outside.

Never underestimate how cold it can be. If you know that you are going to spend any length of time outdoors, ensure that you have warm underwear on, thick trousers and a thick sweater—for starters! To top this, an extra sweater comes in handy, but a must is a very thick and long winter coat. A scarf, woollen cap and mittens or lined gloves are also essential.

Whether in modern-day gear or traditional Lappish costume, the way to keep warm in Lapland is to clothe yourself in plenty of layers. A warm hat, lined gloves and good footwear are essential for your well-being.

However, for those who spend little time outside and are just going from home or office, jumping in the car or a taxi, normal city wear is what most people tend to wear. This is topped by their very warm, thick winter coat and, as always, a woollen cap, scarf, mittens and good shoes!

One of the most essential items that you will require when you go to Finland is a pair of lined and waterproof boots. If you are going to spend any length of time in Finland, or indeed visit Finland quite regularly, I would recommend that you buy your boots in Finland. The boots are made to withstand their weather. They are usually thick-soled to prevent the cold coming up through your feet. They also have good grips to prevent you from slipping on the ice. They are lined to stop your feet from getting cold from above when you step into snow, and most importantly they're waterproof. The boots are far less expensive than in many European cities and are tailor-made for the purpose. Winter boots and shoes with clever Finnish design mean that they can be extremely smart and appear very chic; you would never realise that these are such practical footwear.

The summer can be hot. If it's hot, it is humid! Cool cotton summer-wear is a must. However, warm clothes and a waterproof and windproof jacket can also be essential. In Britain, we say that we can experience four seasons in any one day. Finland isn't any different! Just as good waterproof shoes/boots are an essential part of winter life in Finland, very good sunglasses are an essential part of summer in Finland. Even in Finland, on a sunny day, 22 hours of sunshine can make your eyes very tired. From March onwards, sunglasses are needed. The spring sunshine reflecting off the snow means that the day can be unbelievably bright.

It's very usual in Finland to have outdoor shoes and indoor shoes. In winter, most people wear their boots and come to work carrying their indoor shoes in a bag. Open-toed sandals worn with or without socks are always in vogue. One of the things I have noticed is people often take their shoes off indoors and in public. On the aeroplane, in training rooms or even in business meetings, shoes will be slipped off without any self-consciousness. Obviously, this seems to be acceptable behaviour—don't try it in Britain!

## TOLERANCE

The Finns are a very tolerant people. This is derived from their value-set of leaving people alone and respecting people's privacy. They fiercely defend their right to live life in a way that suits each individual, as long as it does not disturb or harm anyone else. This manifests itself in the way they treat people—there are absolutely no value judgements in the Finns' psyche. People from other cultures find this confusing as they pass no comment on unusual behaviour, people's dress sense or the colour of someone's skin—it's as though they are blind. However, they will not tolerate lateness—of anything.

From Maria, a Finnish reader: 'In the States, an elderly women saw me sitting on a bench and said to me "Your shoes are so cute!" I was taken aback and thought she was so rude. Why should this complete stranger have the right to make value judgements about my dress, and why should she think I'd care? After all, I liked my shoes (that's why I was wearing them) and why should anyone else's comments matter to me? With time, I have softened up a bit, and will compliment strangers myself.'

Foreigners are still a pretty rare commodity in Finland, and rather than being viewed with suspicion, they are viewed with interest. They are welcomed warmly because the Finns are basically pretty tolerant of odd and different people and strange habits. The Finns are very open to new ideas, and will soon adopt, adapt and improve any concept or thing imported from abroad. Finland has become known as a very accommodating and profitable place to do business.

The Olympic Games held in Helsinki in 1952 was the first time that many people in Finland saw the different races of the world. Although the Finns have a very great ability to accept people for what they are and judge them later, their attitude and treatment of people of colour can seem fairly racist to people used to multi-cultural societies. I notice that whenever I go through customs, anyone with a non-European look always spends more time at the customs desk. A black British colleague found she was often the object of attention and suspicion. According to one Finnish psychologist, the refugee situation is now becoming quite a problem in Finland with racism becoming a real issue. It never seemed to exist before because there were so few foreigners. Until recently, many people, seeing a person of colour in the street, would make the assumption that he or she was probably a refugee; it never occurred to them that the person could be a professor or a businessman.

**Making Room For Others**

There can be very few other industrialised nations of the world that have so few ethnic minorities. Finland, as previously mentioned, gave a home to many 'desirable' refugees. With backing and sponsorship from the Red Cross, for the most part, these people were well-received and cared for. However in 1990, a real problem arose when a group of Somalis turned up at the Soviet/Finnish border, uninvited, unsponsored and unexpected. Most Finns did not want them to stay. This was little to do with racism but more to do with the psychological difficulty the Finns have with making room for other people and to share the fruits of their hard labour.

Things have changed enormously during the 1990s—especially since 2000—as the younger generation has become more worldly and well travelled, and Helsinki very much more cosmopolitan, with a multi-cultural society. The whole society has opened up a lot compared with 20 years ago, and everyone seems to have accepted that Finland needs a workforce from abroad because the 'baby boomers' are all retiring (retirement age is 65).

Some Finns still find it difficult to share or set up partnerships; this is due mainly to the fact that the Finns like to be independent and self-sufficient. They can view with suspicion partnerships and co-operations where they believe others may try and take away their hard-earned gains. Some people were extremely suspicious of joining the EU precisely for this reason. If you work for a Finnish firm and you are not Finnish, don't expect promotion; it seems very difficult for the Finns to give that to a foreigner. However, things are changing, especially in this new millennium. Some of the large international firms in Finland are beginning to learn that they need to bring in foreign advisors and different international expertise. They have recognised that in this international and global economy, they must embrace their foreign workers as valued, trusted and permanent members of their companies. This is not the easiest thing for them to do; after all, they have been isolated for such a long time through geography, language and the Soviet Union.

One consultant I met was working on a project for a newly merged Finnish/Anglo/German company. She was doing an audit of the skills and qualifications of the workforce. She soon found that a number of foreigners were leaving after reaching middle management because they were not native speakers of Finnish and perceived they had reached a 'glass ceiling'. When the Board were confronted, their response was, "After all, we are a Finnish company."

The small town of Jarvenpaa, the home of Sibelius, has 35 different nationalities and about 50 different languages or dialects. They have an Orthodox church, a mosque and a Lutheran church and are well used to many visitors. But the rest of Finland is not like this. When you travel into rural areas, you will find that as a foreigner you will be the object of fascination. The locals will take the opportunity to take short stares when they think you're not looking. For them, foreigners are what you see on the TV!

**Not All Good News**

October 2006: Finland's Supreme Administrative Court ruled that a Gambian man who had been sentenced for an aggravated narcotics offence in 2003 would be deported from Finland upon release from prison in 2007. The court weighed the man's offence against his family connections and lengthy stay in Finland. He had received a residency permit in 1998. The Helsinki Administrative Court had previously considered the fact that the man was married to a Finnish citizen and had a child by her to be weighty arguments against deportation. However the Supreme Administrative Court upheld a decision made by the Directorate of Immigration in 2004 and ruled in favour of deportation.

## SCANDAL

Just a note on scandal—the Finns don't 'do scandal'. Not at all! Because the Finnish view of what is considered normal in life is quite broad, there seems very little to gossip about. The key to whether your story is accepted is whether you are deceitful or not. Being deceitful is frowned upon, and children are taught that it is a real sin. (Remember the Finnish values of honesty and integrity).

Finns will give you quite a lot of information that, in other cultures, may be considered embarrassing or private, as these things are just considered normal things that people experience in life. Finnish logic tells them it is therefore not embarrassing or particularly private; your parents' divorce, illness in the family, breaking up, having difficulty deciding career path etc., are very openly talked about. If you feel uncomfortable, you can always say, "I'd prefer not to talk about that" and the conversation will continue without any interruption. In some cultures (as in the UK), what is deemed acceptable is defined by the person asking the question and s/he should not pose questions that the other person may feel uncomfortable with. In Finland, the responsibility of defining what can be talked about lies with the answerer.

There are few taboos, the main one is perhaps physical abuse within families. It is discussed on a general level but few people experiencing it will talk about it openly. They will say something like "my dad is very difficult".

From a Finnish reader: If you're from your father's 5th marriage, most Finns would say "Wow... that's interesting" meaning it's interesting that your father has had so many marriages and that your family situation must be quite complicated and therefore interestingly different. They are, however, not making any kind of value judgment about your father who could not commit. They are just genuinely interested.

From Maria, a Finnish reader: When Elisabeth Rehn ran for the president's office, it turned out that both she and her husband had had affairs during their 30 years of marriage. Elisabeth Rehn went on television and said in an interview that she's not proud about it but it's tough staying faithful for decades and they've gotten past the affairs and are still happy about it. Her popularity shot like a rocket as everyone thought she had a point: it is tough staying faithful for 30 years.

Finns traditionally don't have a celebrity culture, though with the advent of the MTV generation, things are changing slowly. Therefore, they don't have a target for curiosity and fascination. (And, they don't have a target because they like to leave people alone). The former president of Finland went to belly dancing lessons for several years, but the media didn't try to make a big four-week-long story about it. It was just accepted—she has a right to her privacy. For non-British readers, I can assure you if Cherie Blair did the same, the British newspapers would have made so much hype out of the 'story'.

## ALTERNATIVE LIFESTYLES

The younger Finns are even more informal and tolerant than their parents—everything is accepted. They have usually travelled quite extensively, and as a result are becoming more individualised and recognise that people may have different lifestyles from those they have been accustomed to. This is the globe-trotting MTV generation, with technology-based know-how and a high quality of life. There is a national trend towards acceptance of gay and lesbian cultures, with gay bars being openly advertised and no longer hidden. Swingers (couples who swap partners) were definitely not tolerated ten years ago, however this practice seems to be accepted.

SETA or *Seksuaalinen tasavertaisuus* (Sexual Equality) is the national human rights organisation in the field of legal equality and social justice for sexual and gender minorities such as lesbians, gay men, bisexuals and trans-people in Finland. SETA strives to change the Finnish society and legislation in such a manner that all members of the society would be treated equally irrespective of sexual orientation, form of family, gender identity or gender expression. They hold regular meetings.

- SETA's offices
  Mannerheimintie 170, A4 00300, Helsinki
  Phone: (9) 681-2580
  Email: info@seta.fi
  Website: http://www.seta.fi

## SILENCE

I mentioned earlier that extreme chattiness is viewed with suspicion or surprise by the Finns. This is because it is in their nature to be very silent. The Finns don't feel at all uncomfortable with silence. They don't babble or chat. They joke they are good at being silent in two languages—Finnish and Swedish. Indeed they find no need to fill gaps in conversation with small talk, and have an intense dislike for the noisiness of southern Europeans and are suspicious of strangers who smile at them in the street. They never look you in the eyes, as this is seen as being intrusive. The Finns only speak when they have something to say, and this is usually said in a very quiet, calm and succinct way. They always answer questions with minimal information without expanding on the answer. Many foreigners take this abruptness as an affront, especially as the answer usually comes without a smile!

The Finns have come to realise that they are probably the odd ones out in this respect, and they are learning that they have to develop more social skills when trying to deal internationally. The Finns themselves understand that they can have a disturbing affect on foreigners, especially when they are abroad.

A Finnish client of mine went with her sister on holiday to Rhodes, and while they were there, people in restaurants kept asking them whether they were all right, and whether they were angry. It turned out that the constant questioning was because neither of the girls seemed to be happy or smiling. Compared with the Greeks, they seemed suicidal.

Interestingly, the *Helsingin Sanomat*, one of Finland's premier newspapers, published an article in May 1999. The article explained how Finland was going to be taking over presidency of the EU, and that civil servants had had to be trained in small talk. This adds substance to the stories that some of Finland's international companies have had to put on training for executives in 'how to show interest' and 'small talk'. If a Finn asks, "How are you?", he's not engaging in small talk; he genuinely wants to know how you are. Many a Brit has been astonished that a polite introductory conversation with a Finn has led into a detailed description of someone's ailments! So, if you are not truly interested in the well-being of your Finnish friend, don't ask how they are. The Finns are interested in you as an individual, but they don't need to show this by using small talk. As they say, at -20°C (-4°F), they just get straight to the point. It seems as though the Finns believe they will lose some of their integrity if they become more articulate. So, to some extent you have to be a mind reader. One Finnish friend says she tries to be deliberately controversial with her staff just to stimulate them into communicating with her about the business. As she puts it, "I can't expect to be a mind reader all the time!" It is important to remember this point in negotiations with Finnish businesspeople.

In the winter months, 'winter behaviour' sets in. Many people become depressed and even more silent; they have a tendency to stoicism and quietness, and become very introspective. Many suffer from SAD, seasonal affective disorder, and Finland has a high suicide rate. However, in the summer months they go crazy! As a friend of mine Janne says, "The Finns put their life on hold during the winter months, and then let up when the light comes".

Sue R: 'I was hiking through East Finland when I reached a tiny village. There were very few people about and I needed to know how long it would take me to reach the nearest camping place. I spotted an old man sitting on a bench and I approached him. I asked in good Finnish, "How long will it take to reach the camp site?" He didn't answer, so I repeated the question, but still nothing. I assumed he was deaf and I turned and walked away. After a few paces he called out, "15 minutes!" I asked why he hadn't said something sooner, to which he replied, "I didn't know how fast you walk."'

Once the average Finn has had a couple of alcoholic drinks, you may wonder whether I am talking about the same nation. Watch out when they have a party—it's hard to keep up with them. When the Finns get together for socialising, they can become extremely talkative and noisy. They especially like singing and need very little excuse to start singing some of their old traditional ballads. However, it should be said that it is the male of the Finnish species that is more silent than the female. Finnish women, wanting to be romanced or entertained, live in frustration at their silent partners.

## HUMOUR

It is said that the Finns rarely smile, and that they appear to be very dour. Many a newcomer to Finland will think Finns guarded and serious. Indeed, a Finn shys away from any demonstrative behaviour. However, I know lots of Finns, and under their very quiet, reserved exterior, they really are quite a bubbly and humorous people. The Finns love to laugh and most of all they tend to laugh at themselves. Their humour is devoid of cynicism and has a startling frankness about it. Their jokes are rarely cutting or bitchy, but more a laugh about their own national characteristics. They have a very natural intelligence concerning their behaviour. Rather than getting overconfident and bullish, they tend to self-doubt and use humour to put themselves down—or put themselves back in their place. Remember, bragging has no place in Finnish behaviour!

Most jokes reinforce Finnish stereotypes, an example are those told about people from Savo. People in Savo speak in a coded way, they cannot be direct, they are prone to cunning, and their reason is more developed than their emotions. They always want to be the chief, but they are lazy and they work hard at getting others to do the work. However, they have sharp business acumen and are resourceful when dealing with other people. They are commonly said to say things like, "Well, you can buy it if you like it" or "It might be this way or it might be that way." Cunning and deceitfulness are the two words most commonly assigned to these people and, to top it all, they have a very pronounced accent about which people like to make fun. The Finns especially tell jokes about the Swedes and they also add Russians to their list of people they pick on.

An American, a German and a Finn are looking at an elephant. The American wonders if the elephant would be good in a circus, the German wonders what price he would get if he sold it, and the Finn asks himself, 'I wonder what the elephant thinks of me?'

**Two Words Only**

Virtanen, wandering around Greece, came across a monastery and was allowed in for a meal. He told the Abbot he would like to stay there, as he was tired of the modern world.

"You are very welcome," replied the Abbot. "We need more inmates here to till the fields and maintain the buildings. But I must tell you that we have certain rules. There are only two meals a day—porridge in the morning and soup in the evening. You must work ten hours a day, and we observe at all times the rule of silence. You are not allowed to speak at all."

"No problem for a Finn," said Virtanen, "in fact it will make a nice change from Helsinki."

Virtanen worked at the monastery for five years without speaking. At the end of this time, he was summoned to the Abbot, who told him, "You have been an excellent worker. As a reward you are allowed to say two words."

"I'm hungry," replied Virtanen.

"Give Virtanen an extra bowl of soup this evening," said the Abbot to the cook.

Virtanen worked another five years in silence and once more was asked to see the Abbot. "Your fine work has continued," said the good man. "You are permitted to say two more words."

"I'm cold," said Virtanen.

"Give Virtanen an extra blanket from December to March," instructed the Abbot.

After a further five years, Virtanen was summoned again. "You have performed magnificently once more," said the Abbot. "Your reward is to speak two more words."

"I'm going," said Virtanen.

Quoted by: Richard D Lewis (*The Cultural Lone Wolf*, 2005)

The Finns often joke at their inability to express their feelings. There is the story told of old Seppo who was sitting at the breakfast table reading the paper, when his wife came down the stairs looking rather disgruntled. Eventually, the old wife says, "Seppo, do you love me?" He replies, "Pirkko, I remember the day 40 years ago when we got married. I told you then I loved you, if anything changes, I'll let you know."

## FLIRTING

Many who are used to the overt ways of flirting in the Mediterranean countries think that the Finns don't flirt. They do do it—it's just a very different style. As I have been told, if Finns are flirting very openly, it's usually because they are drunk. Flirting in Finnish is coded in the speech. It's in the look. It tends to be very direct, frank, short and simple. It would appear that men never go for a long seduction and never bother to use flattery. Many foreign women can interpret this as being a bit of a put-down, and certainly a put-off! One Finnish man promised to write me an 'interpretation guide for foreign women'. This has not yet been forthcoming, but so far has led to an understanding of the following:

If you're at a dance and a man says to a woman, "Shall we go, or shall we dance?" First, the interpretation should be that this is the equivalent of a man saying to a lady that she is the most beautiful creature that ever walked on God's earth. Secondly, this also allows you to cut out the first three or four dates and arrive at the same point in time! One Finnish lady said this was the Finnish men's concept of equality but that somehow it had lost its politeness and finesse.

However, in terms of manners at social occasions, the Finnish ladies do not realise how lucky they are! Without equivocation, I can say that etiquette is alive and well and living in Finland. Gentlemen still help ladies on with their coats, hold doors open and stand up when they enter the room. Okay, the younger generation may not be so keen, but there are a lot more men in Finland observing the social 'niceties' than there are in the UK.

A Finnish joke: Juha meets Johanna at a dance. They leave together and he says, "Your place or mine?" She replies, "Why are you talking so much?"

## HOW TO BE A GOOD GUEST

The Finns are conscientious workers—they work hard and they play hard! It is an honour to be invited into the home of a Finn, so the first thing to remember is never refuse the offer of a sauna or a cup of coffee! However, first things first. If you are invited to a Finnish home, take your shoes off—or at least offer to. Remember! The Finns have outdoor and indoor shoes. It is quite normal for people to bring other shoes with them to change into, especially in the winter.

Dinner parties are not the norm in Finland. If you are invited, turn up with either some flowers or a bottle of wine. This would be very acceptable. But the most important thing is to bring an open mind. The Finns assure me that being interested in tasting their food is what they really want. Finns really like to be good hosts and give of their best. The norm in Finland is that people usually come round for coffee, and this will be served with biscuits or cakes. Traditionally, one had to serve seven varieties of cookies or cakes, as this is what etiquette demanded.

**Coffee Lovers**

Coffee is to the Finns as petrol is to cars, or so they say. In fact, Finland has the highest consumption of coffee per capita of anywhere in the world. The majority of entertaining in Finnish homes is about popping in for a short time to have coffee.

## DANCING

The Finns love to dance. Even the men, honest! I was dumbfounded when I took my first group of Finns out in London. After a formal black-tie dinner, they wanted to go out dancing and we ended up in a discotheque. After arranging the first round of drinks (we were in England remember!), everyone was soon up on the dance floor—ballroom dancing! The native Brits stood down and let the visitors take over the floor space. They, too, were as astounded as I was. Some of the time, the dancers formed a circle and a man would choose a lady from the gathering to dance a few bars in the centre of the circle. Then the lady would chose a gentleman and so the dance would proceed. When the music was slow, they would dance a rumba; if they could make the rhythm fit, they would dance a tango; and when the music was quick, they danced their humppa. Foxtrots and waltzes were also on their menu. I had a great time. I haven't danced like that since my mum sent me to ballroom dancing lessons as a teenager!

## ALCOHOL AND SMOKING

It is said that the Finns like moderation in everything—except alcohol! There are Finns who are teetotallers. There are those who drink socially and in moderation. However, there are those who keep alive the Finns' reputation for heavy drinkers. These are people who drink to get drunk. It seems any occasion can be an excuse to have a good drinking session—especially the many festival days they have in the year.

Alcoholism was the scourge of Finland (and other Scandinavian states) and alcoholism is still a major socio-medical problem. I am told that you can see drunks overtly staggering around the streets and witness teenagers hopelessly intoxicated at weekends, though I have not noticed this. However, the Finns yearly consumption of alcohol is below the EU average, and today they attending to drink more wine and less vodka.

There is still a state monopoly in the distribution of alcohol, which is done through Alko shops. Alcohol is extremely expensive and taking a 'Booze Cruise' to Tallin or Stockholm is popular to stock up on your bottles. Production, importation and advertising are strictly controlled. Alcohol is sold exclusively through the Alko stores, but light beer can be purchased in supermarkets. Spirits can only be bought by people over the age of 20, while wine and beer can be bought by those aged over 18. Nowadays, beer and wine are far more popular than spirits. Alko stores are open till 8:00 pm on weekdays and 6:00 pm on Saturdays.

In a restaurant or bar, wine is readily sold by the glass in two sizes—small (12 cl) and medium (16 cl). There are no grapes in Finland although there are some locally produced wines made from berries, so wine is imported. Beer (*Olut*) is light-coloured and is sold by its strength. This lager-type beer is most popular in its medium strength (strength 3) called *keskari* or *kolmonen*. The strongest is IVA (strength 5), or *nelosolut*, with 5 per cent alcohol. The weakest (strength 1) is *mieto* or *pilsneri* with less than 2 per cent alcohol. The size of the drink is either small (*pieni tuoppi*), medium (*iso tuoppi* 0.3l) or large (*pitka* 0.5l).

Alcoholic specialities include vodka and flavoured vodkas, and liqueurs made from cloudberries, arctic berries and cranberries. The Finns love to joke about their 'Finnish white wine' called *koskenkorva* (a foreigner, you might be caught out on this one!). It may look harmless enough but it has a real kick—it isn't wine at all—it's vodka!

Remember—alcohol is expensive in Finland, so be warned!

To my very great surprise, the Finns smoke like chimneys! Or so it seemed to me when I first went to Finland. It appears that smoking is not limited to certain generations as can be witnessed in the UK. Therefore, it looked as though everyone smoked, whatever their age. However, this is an overgeneralisation.

Many Finns do not smoke at all, but those who do, smoke heavily. There are strict 'no smoking' laws restricting smoking in public places to a very small confined space, where the smoke cannot escape and contaminate the environment. It is important to note that you may not smoke in any public place unless you are in a specially designated area. Also, it is no good just stepping outside the door to have a quick 'drag'. You have to be at least five metres away from the building in case there are any open windows. There is talk of restricting smoking on people's private balconies, which is not popular as some smokers will not light up in their apartments but go out on to the balcony to smoke.

## WHAT TO DO AT A SAUNA PARTY?

Finland is the land of the sauna *par excellence.* If you do not want to join in with the sauna, nobody is going to mind. It's quite accepted that women can feel particularly uncomfortable having saunas and then having to do their hair

and makeup again. Some men feel that going from extremes of temperature, especially in the winter, is not for them. So if you are invited to a sauna party, just relax and enjoy the time spent with your Finnish hosts—and forget about the sauna. Whether you sauna or not does not matter. In fact, if you are invited, it will be quite an honour.

What tends to happen in a mixed crowd of adults is that the ladies will be asked to enjoy the sauna first, whilst the men socialise and have a few beers. When the women have finished, showered and started to change, the men will then take their turn in the sauna. During this time, the women will enjoy beer or wine and sit and talk. This all sounds very civilised. And it is. However, there have been a few startling incidents when I have been around with a group of foreigners. For instance, it is usual that on coming out of the sauna, people will stand around naked, or wrapped in a towel, to cool off. This might well be down on the balcony. I have heard many a scream from unsuspecting guests stumbling across a group of the opposite sex during their cooling off period!

Finnish proverb: First build the sauna, then the house. The sauna has its own name day—the second Saturday in June.

The Finns enjoy their saunas. One of the greatest compliments they can pay you is to invite you along to enjoy a sauna with them. Jumping in and out of the lake, smearing a paste over your skin, and slapping you with birch twigs, is all seen as beneficial and invigorating to your circulation and skin tone. This is not to be thought of as torture! The Finns enjoy it—really!

However, once the enjoyment of the sauna has passed, it is then time to get on with the eating and drinking. At a conventional sauna party, you will be offered a mixed salad and a mixed meat and rice dish to accompany it. All this will be prepared in advance so that the hosts can join in the fun along with their guests. As an aside, the Finns will shower completely naked along with others of the same sex, so this is no time to be prudish. Take a leaf out of their books and throw your inhibitions away! A family with children under the age of seven will probably sauna together. After that age, the sexes will take their sauna's separately. Usually a child will be introduced to the sauna in their first year, but definitely before their second birthday.

The typical and traditional sauna is a log cabin with windows overlooking the lake. The original type was a smoke sauna but then the heating form changed to a stove. If you have the opportunity to go out to the lakes and enjoy a sauna, the format of the event will be similar to the above. The difference will be that you are expected to be masochistic enough to have a short sauna, then jump into the cold waters of a lake, or through a hole cut in the ice (*avanto*) in the winter, before returning to the sauna again. This is a process which is repeated about three times! I am assured that the hot and cold dipping is quite invigorating! Be prepared to be whipped with birch twigs, which is said to do wonders for the skin. After showering and changing, food will be served. Often the food served will be sausages, grilled in the open air and washed down with beer. A wonderful way to spend a warm sunlit summer's evening.

Saunas are seen as a necessity, not a luxury. Originally a sauna was a place to wash and keep clean, and to warm up in the winter. It was also viewed as a hygienic place to give birth, to dry herbs for folk medicines, and to smoke fish and meat. There are 1.7 million sauna in Finland—one

From Paul Thomas: 'It was my first sauna and I was being taught all about the methods and etiquette of sauna. Being new in the country and a little naïve, I believed everything they were telling me, including that following a sauna somebody had to clean the sauna stones—I fell for it and even offered to do it!'

for every three people. They are in houses, apartments, companies, government offices, summer cottages and public swimming pools.

A good friend of mine had quite an eye-opening experience when she first visited Finland. Unaware of Finnish traditional habits, she was invited to a meal with a Scotsman and an Englishman at the abode of some Finnish people who lived in the forest. They played games like archery and shooting at first. Then, when they arrived back at the house, she was whisked away to have a sauna with the wife of the household, which included 'skinny-dipping' to cool off. Needless to say, as a Brit she was totally out of her comfort zone! However, when the wife started to whip her with birch leaves and smear her skin with a therapeutic paste, she

decided enough was enough. By that time, it was the turn of the other two foreigners. The Scotsman had a great time, but the Englishman declined the offer!

**Sauna Mats**

From C.K: I had been invited to my in-laws' summer cottage for the first time and I had greedily accepted their offer of going to the sauna first. I remembered my husband once telling me that you should sit on a sauna mat for hygiene, so I took one that was hanging up to dry in the bathroom. After I had finished, I asked my husband what I should do with it and he collapsed in a fit of giggles. It turns out that it was not a sauna mat, but a place mat for the table that his mother had been drying.

One morning at breakfast in a hotel, with surprise I met up with a colleague in some far-flung town in Finland. I explained that I was in town with two of our colleagues and we intended to go out for a meal in the evening, and asked whether he wanted to join us. He replied that his wife's family lived not far away and that he had been invited to spend the evening 'having a sauna with my mother-in-law'. To the English, this sounds quite heroic, but it is quite common place in Finland.

## REGIONAL DIFFERENCES

My understanding of regional differences has come from Roman Schatz, a German who has lived in Finland for over 30 years. He is a mini-*julkkis* (celebrity), having presented language and travel programmes on TV, and recently his own show—all in Finnish! He has a distinctly irreverent view of the Finns. In Finland, people never ask what you do for a living, as he commented: "This goes far beyond small talk!" This question can be considered offensive (though in the UK and other cultures, it's perfectly normal). The Finnish identity is based on places and ancestors rather than on work and career.

Somewhere in their not-too-distant past, they have been displaced in either their personal or collective history. Many lost homes during the war. Many have moved to the bright lights of the city for a more fulfilling future. But, for what ever reason, everybody is from somewhere else and nearly everyone, within one or two generations, can trace back to their rural backgrounds.

Regional stereotypes which the Finns love to humour:

- Häme: People from this region are serious by nature. They represent the true essence of Finnish-ness. They work hard, are robust and practical, but considered a bit slow. They like farming (so they must be slow!).
- Karelia: A Karelain is agile, talkative and active. Unfortunately, he doesn't have much stamina when it comes to work (as he doesn't like farming) and prefers to make a living through trade. They are traditionally very musical.
- Ostrobothnia (*Pohjanmaalaisert*): These people are a special breed—tough, brave and a robust temperament. They are good field workers and skilled craftsmen. They love to show-off and their celebrations are famous for overindulgence.
- Savolax: The Savo people are playful and enjoy communicating. As such, they make good salesmen. They are therefore considered untrustworthy and rather deceitful by the rest of the Finns (who hate talkative people).
- Swedish-speaking Finns: They have supposedly a happy disposition and are committed to purity. They especially like to preserve valuable old traditions—like drinking and singing!

> 'The Finns have a nasty little expression for something that doesn't have any value: "This isn't from anywhere!" (*Tämä ei ole mistään kotoisin*).'
>
> —Roman Schatz, *From Finland With Love*, 2006.

# SETTLING IN

CHAPTER 5

'With Finns it's sometimes hard to tell whether they hate you or love you...The secret is simple. The Finnish concept of politeness works differently than in most other countries. In most countries it's considered polite to communicate. In Finland it's polite to leave people alone.'
—Roman Schatz, *From Finland with Love*

## ADMINISTRATIVE PROCEDURES TO ENTER AND LIVE IN FINLAND

Foreigners must have a valid passport or other approved travel document to enter Finland. Nordic and EU citizens do not need a visa or residence permit. Finnish citizens who have lived abroad and retained their nationality do not require a visa either. However, a person arriving in the country may need a visa or residence permit depending on the country of origin. Different permits are needed for entering Finland and staying in the country. Details can be found at: http://www.suomi.fi/suomifi/english/subjects/migration/index.html.

**Useful Resources**

An organisation called Expat Finland provides information and networks for living in Finland. More information can be found on their website: http://expat-finland.com/index.html

The following link provides a list of the embassies operating in Finland: http://formin.finland.fi/public/default.aspx?nodeid=32311&contentlan=2&culture=en-US

## FINDING A HOME

Unlike most well-populated countries, in Finland even the largest cities are quite small and therefore the matter of 'what location in the town' is not at all relevant. There is a new 'rich' class in Finland, and as a consequence there are some very costly apartments these days in the Helsinki region and they are acquired as soon as they go on the market. But nowhere is very far from the city centre, so don't worry about where you are—and there are no down and out places.

Finding an apartment for yourself couldn't be easier—do it the Finnish way! Look up real estate agents on the Internet! People shopping around for apartments tend to do this on the Internet nowadays. Most real estate agents have their own web pages showing the apartments and houses that they have for sale or rent and the price levels. This gives you a good indication of price level and sizes of homes in the location that you want to live in. Information about privately owned rental apartments can be found from the local newspapers as well. Newer apartments are always very well equipped, including saunas. A two-bedroom will be between 50–80 sq m. Be mindful that newer apartments tend to be smaller than the older ones. Please note that in Finland, most of the rental accommodation is not furnished!

**Accommodation for Students**

Universities or other educational institutions usually help foreign students to find affordable accommodation. Many universities also have their own organisations for student housing: e.g. http://www.hoas.fi/webV2/ase_inetV2.nsf/Frameset?OpenForm&01

## Setting Up Your Home

What really counts for a Finn is his home—they all dream of their having their very own. Very characteristic in Finnish society is that young people first go and live in an apartment in the centre of the town. It is a common dream to own their own homes so they usually buy a plot of land and begin to build their own house. Planning permission is needed to build these houses, and you will be required to build in harmony with the district. In other words, you get permission and you follow the district guidelines. Loans to build houses can be taken out and these are repaid over ten years. About 70 per cent of people age 65 and over own their own homes.

Younger people rent them, and as they get older, at some stage they will make the decision to buy and build.

## INSIDE A FINNISH HOME

In the English language, we have a word to describe a certain style called 'Scandinavian'. This look will be very minimalist, modern, stylish and light in colour. Most things Scandinavian are aesthetically beautiful. Finnish homes can be described as being Scandinavian in style. The décor is usually white or cream painted walls with a few choice pictures and white painted in-built cupboards with either white or natural wood skirting boards and architrave. Light wood bookshelves, light coloured sofas and chairs, and perhaps a leather comfy chair are almost the only furniture. Side tables, coffee tables and all the 'clutter' of a British home is kept to a minimum. One theory for this white and minimal look is that style has been heavily influenced by Lutheranism. There is just one thing that strikes a British person as decidedly odd, and that is the doors all open outwards on to the passage ways (or most of the time, anyway)! So, beware as you walk down a corridor.

### Flooring

An apartment or house will be floored throughout with wood and will usually be of a very pale colour. The floors have a highly polished finish and can seem quite slippery, and there may be a few rugs thrown about, especially in corridors or walkways. The Finns do not like carpet. One Finnish client of mine asked, "How can you live in such dirty houses?!" She was referring to the British custom of having wall-to-wall carpeting. In her perception, the houses must be very dirty because we would be unable to clean the carpets thoroughly. To her way of thinking, the carpets must be full of germs and bacteria.

### Windows

One of the things that surprised me the most when I first visited was the windows. Windows tend to be non-openable. Coming from a family where everyone throws open the windows whatever the weather to let some fresh air in, I found this extremely irksome. Modern day windows are usually heavy wooden frames with triple glazing. There will be a double glazed sealed unit on the outside, and a single glazed pane on the inside, usually all within the same frame. Between the units of glass, there may well be a venetian blind. (What a great idea! Dust-free blinds). The opening mechanism only allows you to open the window by a few centimetres, just enough to cause a draught. However, the lounge or living room will usually have large windows and a French door leading on to a garden or the balcony. The curtains hanging at windows in a home tend to be very thin, although quite stylish in their design, but they are there more for decoration than for cutting out the light. The Finns like their privacy and do not like to think they may be seen from the outside, so blinds and curtains are important to them.

## The Sauna

There is thought to be about one million saunas in Finland, and no Finnish home is complete without one. Some apartments may have a shared sauna in the basement, but everyone has ready access. In a home, the sauna may only be the size of a large cupboard. It is fitted into the shower room. As with all Nordic saunas, it is completely lined with wood and is usually heated electrically by a small heater in a box, covered with stones onto which you will throw water to make you really sweat.

The heating stove, called a *kiuas*, heats up special stones. Normally, the sauna is warmed until it reaches 70–110°C. The best material for sauna benches is Aspen wood because it will not become too warm to sit on, even in a hot sauna.

### Hot Stones!

Some Finns like to show off with foreigners by continually throwing water on to the stoves. This, of course, will produce enough steam to cook everybody in there, but they do it just to see how long you can last.

The best way to enjoy a sauna is to shower first and then enter the sauna naked. Then just sit and relax and enjoy the steam. The steam makes you sweat and increases your blood circulation. If you want to give yourself a real treat, then get someone to beat you with birch twigs and smear you with some gooey paste! This process is supposed to be really revitalising and good for the circulation. The Finns are very vociferous about the benefits of taking saunas. There is an old Finnish proverb that says, 'First build the sauna and then the house'. The Finns take their saunas very seriously and it is actually part of their social life. Incidentally, the Finns get most upset when they hear English speaking people pronounce sauna in the same way as we would pronounce the name 'Lorna'. The pronunciation that they use for the 'sau' is more like the way we pronounce the word 'how'.

## Heating, Gas and Electricity

In urban areas, everybody's heating is generated by one central organisation that supplies heat to all the homes. Our translation would be city heating or distant heating (*Kaukolampo*), and this supplies hot water too. For cooking, only the old houses might have gas. These days, nearly everyone has electric cookers with ovens and built-in grills that are rarely used. Most cooking is down on the hob. The majority of houses are fully electrical, using 220 volts and the European two-pin plug. All weights and measures are in metric. There are still a few houses that use oil for heating, but these would mostly be in rural areas. Even though homes have city heating, many of them have open fires that they use to heat the home, with fire ovens built at the sides. This is from tradition and adds to the cosiness of the home. One of Finland's growing exports is fireplaces made of soap stone. These are now the 'in' thing to have and are favoured greatly by Hollywood superstars. These fireplaces can be immense but extremely stylish, and have the property of staying warm for a long, long time and heat the whole of the home.

## Television

Prime time television in Finland is from 7:00–10:00 pm. Programming reflects the Finns' interest in the news, the economy and sports. These subjects take up the majority of time on the television and many people take part in the national ritual at 8:30 pm—watching the evening news. Apart from the news, the Finns are hooked on two particular soaps. One is *The Bold and Beautiful*, which is an American series, and the other is a British series called *Emmerdale Farm*, both of which are on early in the evening. On Saturday and Sunday evenings, the programmes change. There is often a crime series imported from England, Germany or America, and is something like the Miss Marple series from England. Saturday evenings might well have some sort of light-hearted match-making series broadcasted. On Sunday evenings, an American movie is broadcast, preceded by some political comedy/satire.

### TV and English

If you've ever wondered why the Finns are so good at speaking English, you will find the reason out now. A good proportion of television programmes are imported from Britain and the USA. They are broadcast in the English language, with Finnish subtitles. This even includes some children's television. So youngsters from a very early age begin to pick up English. I was most impressed when I heard a little tot on a train journey once. She could have only been about three or four years old, and she was singing the lyrics to *Postman Pat*. Political figures on the news are always broadcast speaking in their own language!

As an aside, a Finnish lady friend of mine said that one Sunday she was driving in her car and there was nothing on the radio other than sports all day long. Having said that, most women in Finland are just as keen on sports as the men.

## GETTING A TELEPHONE AND INTERNET LINE

No worries here! Finland is the most Internet ready country in the world—telephone lines and the highest speed broadband are everywhere. Contact the landline company of your town and you'll soon be connected.

For mobile phones, you can easily open a pay-as-you-go (called 'pre-paid') connection at several providers. They are available in kiosks as well as in special mobile operators' stores. For a pay-monthly connection, you need to have a Finnish social security number, or some operators will provide this if you give a hefty deposit.

## DOMESTIC HELP

It is not common for the Finns to have someone to help with their household chores. This is actually not built into their culture or their traditions. One reason may be because the rate of pay for cleaners is extremely high. However, you can join a type of 'circle' at the employment office and they will supply someone to come to you one day per fortnight to clean and tidy your home. This becomes an affordable way to get help because these people are on the unemployment register and are claiming unemployment benefit. So in effect, this service is subsidised by the government. It is also possible to hire a company to come and clean for you, and you can put the cost of this against your earnings and claim tax relief on it. There is a certain amount of money you can claim in a year, which would equate to perhaps five visits from a cleaning company.

## THE EDUCATION SYSTEM

The Finns have a very healthy respect for education and have set themselves high targets in the educational field. Ninety-nine per cent of the country is literate and investment in education is just over 7 per cent of GDP (Gross Domestic Product). In 1990, a government commission recommended that one of the strategic aims of the country should be to make the Finns the best educated people in Europe by the year 2010. They added as a warning that this would call for considerable increases in financial resources. In 2007, they were formally acknowledged as being so.

**Finns and Their Books**

The number of newspapers and books printed per capita is one of the highest in the world, and the Finns borrow books from the library at the highest rate in the world at 9.7 books or recordings per person per year.

### Pre-school

At the age of six, children go to a pre-school establishment. For one year, they learn how to work in teams, to cooperate and be a little disciplined. It is mostly play with a little education. Although there is debate in Finland currently about getting children to start school earlier, the Finnish people believe in letting children be children. Almost as a whole, the nation believes that children at this age should learn to be themselves, have confidence and explore their own creativity. However, by the age of seven, most children can read and count.

## School

At the age of seven, children move into school. This consists of nine classes and takes them through to age 16. In school, they will do the usual variety of subjects which most Western societies cover. They have to learn Swedish as their first foreign/domestic language. Apart from that, through their school life, they will learn two or possibly three more foreign languages, and these will be English, German or Russian.

At the age of 16, young people will go on to one of two types of school: the high school or a technical/vocational school. Youngsters wishing to go on to university will go through the high school route. They will have up to four years to pass the high school examination, which is their minimum requirement to apply to university. At the vocational schools, youngsters will learn the skills required to prepare them for a job as a mechanic or a hairdresser, for example. Just recently, people in these schools have been allowed to study to take the high school examination. This does entail a lot of work for them. For those who, at the age of 16, have not been academically gifted, this gives them an extra chance to pass the examination and perhaps go onto university.

## University

Entrance to university is awarded on a points scale. Young people who have the highest pass in the high school examination will be awarded more points. However, this will not be enough to get them into university. The university themselves set an entrance exam, and this exam is more important than the grades achieved when leaving high school. University is totally funded by the state, and students get a generous grant, although some of them work to subsidise their incomes. One of the knock-on effects of such generous state subsidies is that students will sign up for university and stay there. The majority of young people sign up for Masters degrees and it is very unusual for people to get a degree just at Bachelors level. Currently, there are discussions about limiting the course duration to five years.

There are 21 universities and colleges of higher education in Finland, with about 80,000 students altogether. Every year 18,000 students start. These students obtain state grants. State guaranteed low interest loans, subsidised health care, meals and student hostels are available to most students. The majority of students stay an average of seven to eight years at university.

## Open University

In recent years, an open university system has been established for adult learners. This is especially targeted for professional people who have had no university background and wish to study for a degree. Prior learning and experience are taken into account, and the adult learner needs to study for various modules to complete a degree. The Finns I know that are doing courses under the open university scheme have said they are being welcomed with open arms.

## Language Teaching for Foreigners

The diversity of cultures can be seen in day nurseries, schools and the streets of the city. In primary and high schools, students with immigrant backgrounds are offered special services to support their studies and integration into Finnish society. The following section is only a guide to what happens in some regions in Finland.

Mother tongue teaching is arranged for students at the preschool, primary school and high school level in about 15 different languages. The biggest language groups are Russian, Dari and Kurdish. New language teaching groups are set up if there are at least four students attending the group who speak the same mother tongue. It doesn't cost the students anything to take part in the lessons in their own mother tongue. Students who don't speak Finnish as their mother tongue learn Finnish as a second language.

At a comprehensive school, the students are offered so-called preparatory teaching, which means that they learn the Finnish language intensively in addition to their regular subjects. The aim of this intensive teaching is to acquire sufficient knowledge of Finnish so that the students can participate in the ordinary Finnish language group. After that, students are offered a language assistant who speaks their own language. An interpreter is used in cooperation between home and school, whenever necessary. Preparatory teaching usually lasts one semester, but a student can attend the group as long a period of time as required.

High school students apply straight to the Finnish language high school that they have selected. Instead of preparatory teaching, the schools aim to organise effective Finnish language teaching, and arrange teachers who can

## Education System Summary

- School obligatory from the age of seven.
- Six years of primary and junior school are followed by three years at the secondary stage. After that, pupils can stay on for further three years to obtain their high school certificate.
- Half of all young people obtain high school certificates, of which 60 per cent are girls.
- The nine-year comprehensive school (*Perus-koulu*)—tuition, books, meals and commuting to and from school are free.
- The secondary school (*Lukio*) is three years in length—stepping stone to university.
- First university in Finland was in Turku, established in 1640, transferred to Helsinki in1828 and now with 26,000 students approximately.
- Swedish schools are provided under the state system in communes where the numbers justify it. Some universities still have split departments in which instruction is given in each language separately.

speak the students' own languages to help them succeed in school.

### Enrolment in Schools

The enrolment process varies between schools and cities. However, International schools are only in the largest cities, but there are some international classes integrated in Finnish schools.

## MEDICAL FACILITIES AND HEALTH INFORMATION

In Finland, medical facilities and their staff are as a rule excellent and are widely available for emergency services. English is commonly spoken by Finnish medical personnel. Helsinki is a frequent medical evacuation point for emergency cases from the countries of the former Soviet Union. The public hospital system and many private hospitals accept credit cards. Most pharmacies (*apteekki*) are open during normal shopping hours and major cities have at least one 24-hour service pharmacy.

If you are a tourist or temporary visitor to Finland requiring immediate emergency medical assistance, you may visit a local medical centre or clinic, called *ensiapuasema* (first-aid station) in Finnish. Usually, these stations are located at hospitals and provide a full range of services. The emergency telephone number 112 can be used throughout Finland to contact emergency medical services.

**Health Insurance**

Those resident in Finland are automatically part of the national health insurance scheme. Find out more information on the Social Insurance Institution of Finland website at http://www.kela.fi/in/internet/english.nsf. You can also apply for an additional private health insurance from Finnish insurance companies.

## PROVISION FOR RELIGIOUS GROUPS

There are two official religions in Finland: the Evangelical-Lutheran Church of Finland (about 85 per cent of the population) and the Orthodox Church (currently 1.1 per cent of the Finnish population). Other churches and religious communities operating actively in Finland are the Catholic Church, Anglo-American Christianity, Judaism and Islam. There are about 30 other registered religious communities in Finland besides those mentioned already. As in other European countries, numerous new religious movements are active in Finland.

A list of Buddhist groups in Finland can be found at http://www.buddha-dharma.info/ihmisia.htm and the website of The Islamic Society of Finland is at http://www.rabita.fi.

### Purchasing Special Foods

Various ethnic and religious minorities are able to purchase food products of their special requirements from small shops located mainly in the largest cities in Finland. More specific information can be found from the Internet about their specific town.

## TRANSPORTATION

### Taxis

The word for taxi in Finnish is spelt *taksi* and so is easily recognisable. You will usually find taxi stands at bus and train stations, or in Helsinki at other central points. It is not customary to hail a taxi in the street. Taxis can also be booked over the telephone. However, if you book them more than two hours in advance, they will put a modest surcharge on the cost of the ride—the equivalent of two pounds. Taxis are nearly as expensive in small towns as they are in the large towns. Unlike some countries, there is no shared taxi service available in Finland, the exception being airport taxis. If there is a group of you travelling a fair distance, you should negotiate for a good price for this journey before you start out.

### Buses

According to the tourist board, the bus service covers around 90 per cent of the roads in the country. The buses are generally comfortable and the service is efficient and on schedule. Apart from around the town where there are local services provided, there are two types of services: the inter-city service and the express bus. The inter-city features regular buses that stop frequently at small towns and villages on the way to the next. The express bus travels swiftly between cities—generally acknowledged as 100 km in less than two hours and 400 km in about six hours. Whichever type of bus you take, they all have the same ticketing system.

Each town has a bus terminal. This is called *Linja-Autoasema* and is generally within walking distance of the rail terminal. Most buses run Monday to Friday with restricted services on Saturday and on public holidays. Very few buses operate on a Sunday, and bus stations close at 6:00 pm Monday to Saturday, and 4:00 pm on Sunday. If you are travelling long distances, it is usually better and cheaper to travel by rail. However, from village to village, buses are the most expedient forms of transport.

For Information on long distance and express buses:

- OY Matkahuolto Ab
  Lauttasaarentie 8, 00200 Helsinki
  Tel (09) 682-701
  Website: http://www.expressbus.com.

## Railways

I was much impressed with the Finnish rail service when I first encountered it on a journey from Helsinki to Joensuu. I arrived at Helsinki station and encountered an old vaulted building which reminded me of something off a spy movie set in Moscow. I was about to travel on an inter-city train. The train was modern, very clean and tidy, and seemed very quiet and smooth as it travelled. The first class had Pullman seats, but the whole train seemed to be very roomy. The train left dead on time and kept to its schedule throughout the journey. A first class ticket on an inter-city train has food included in the price. The restaurant on the train was very cosy and, although it didn't serve the greatest of cuisine, the food was more than adequate. There was also a bar area rather like a pub. The whole journey was very pleasant and with little hassle. There is just one thing to take special note of: there is

The Joensuu railway station may be buried in snow during winter but usually remains open for business and, being Finnish, the trains will still run on time.

a huge step up from the platform onto the trains in Finland. If you have luggage with you, you will need a push up with it. This really is my worst nightmare when travelling in Finland and I always try to reduce the weight of my luggage when I know that I will be travelling on and off trains.

On the longer routes, there are sleeping cars available and special car carriers and all of these will have dining carriages, serving snacks and meals that are tasty and good value for money. Seating is either in first class with Pullman-type seats, or in second class which are open carriages with soft chairs. Seat reservations are mandatory on inter-city trains and the high speed Pendolino express trains. Tickets can be bought from the guard on the train at a small supplement. First class tickets are 1.5 times the cost of a second class. Trains are cheaper than buses. If you are aged over 55, there are rail passes available for travel throughout Scandinavia for nationals of any country.

Helsinki is the main rail terminus for the south of the country, and Rovaniemi is the main northern terminus. There is a fast and efficient service on North South routes, but this is not duplicated on the East, West routes. The trains are fewer in number. There are three main rail lines: the

Pohjanmaa line runs between Helsinki and Oulu in the north, and continues to Kemijasrvi in Lapland; the Karelian route runs from Helsinki to Nurmes via Joensuu; and the Savonian route runs from Kouvola in the south to Iisalmi in the north continuing to Kajaani.

## Cars and Bicycles

Be warned: petrol is expensive in Finland. There are petrol stations throughout the country, but in isolated regions—especially in Lapland—just remember to check your petrol gauge often as petrol stations are few and far between. It's very common for Finnish petrol stations to have cafes or restaurants where meals or snacks are served at reasonable rates until very late. True to the Finnish trait of everything modern, petrol pumps are automatic, which means you can insert your bank note or credit card straight into the pump. First you need to insert your method of payment, then press *setelikuittaus*, choose the right pump, choose the right petrol type and fill the tank up!

**Driving Licence**

You do not need an international driver's licence for Finland. You only need your own home country's licence. The Finnish National Motoring Organisation is called Autolitto (Tel: (09) 774-761, Hameentie 105A, 00550 Helsinki).

This may be a sweeping statement, but Finland seems completely empty of traffic. One of my French colleagues says it's the only place on earth where she sees pedestrians waiting at the sides of empty roads for red lights to change to green, so that they can cross. Although the roads may be empty and you may be tempted to take short cuts, traffic laws are strictly enforced. In fact, the government receives hundreds of millions of Euros annually as income from traffic tickets alone. The wearing of seat belts is compulsory for all passengers in a car, when driving outside urban areas and on rural roads. It is also compulsory to have your headlights turned on. Failure to comply with these simple rules means you will have to pay. Drink driving is an absolute taboo; the blood alcohol limit is 0.05 per cent. There is a great social stigma against those who risk drinking and driving.

As with most of the world, the Finns drive on the right hand side. Most Finnish roads are two lanes wide and the speed limit varies, depending whether it is summer or winter. Generally the speed limit is 50 km per hour in built-up areas; on motorways the summer limit is 120 km per hour; and in the winter it reduces to 80 km per hour. There are two classes of roads: first class (*valtatie*) and second class (*kantatie*). The motorways or stretches of bypass around large towns are called *moottoritie*. The highways between major cities bear the pre-fix 'E', then one or two digits. Trunk roads have numbers, but there are many smaller roads with no numbers at all!

As Finland is a bilingual country, many street signs are in both languages. Finnish comes first, followed by Swedish. If the local area is mostly Swedish speaking, the signs used for places, hotels, restaurants and things to see will be written in Swedish. The province of Åland is totally Swedish speaking and little Finnish is used.

Here are some things to take note of when driving in Finland. There are no stop signs to regulate the traffic flow. This tends to cause a lot of confusion for foreign drivers. The rule is that cars entering an intersection from the right always have the right of way, whether they are on a major or minor road. If you spot a reindeer, slow down! This is not a joke. Truly, moose and reindeer can make motoring very hazardous. These animals don't respond to car horns and, as I once read, they feel they deserve the right of way! Whatever direction the animal seems to be heading in, move slowly, as they might just come towards you. About 4,000 reindeer are killed each year by cars, and it is a legal requirement to notify the police about any incidents involving moose or reindeer. There may be legal implications if you do not. There are two seasons in the year which seem to be particularly bad for reindeer related accidents. These are November/December and July/August. It is hardly surprising that the vast majority of accidents happen near tourist centres.

Another thing to be aware of is that it is compulsory from the 1 November to the first Sunday after Easter to have winter tyres on your car. There are two types of winter tyres: the first is a standard snow tyre, and the second is a snow tyre which has tiny metal spikes stuck into the rubber. It is illegal to drive with tyre chains in Finland. It is the spiked tyres that allow Finnish drivers to motor along as though they are on some sort of rally, even in the middle of winter with very icy slippery roads. The Finns generally tend to be good drivers, but your first impression is that they drive like the Italians. Distances between destinations are shorter during the winter months—no I'm not kidding. Being extremely efficient, the Finns mark out official roads across the frozen lakes for traffic. Hence, instead of having to spend a large proportion of your journey time driving around lakes, as happens in the summer, you just make a bee-line for the far shore. This is not as dangerous as you may think. The ice is very thick, thick enough to take trucks. Roadways are clearly marked and are regularly checked for safety.

Cycling is extremely popular in Finland. There is very little traffic on the roads and the country is fairly flat, making Finland a haven for cyclists. Bicycles are allowed on all public roads, except motorways. There is a very good network of cycle paths in and around most major cities. Due to the distances in Finland being so vast, buses and trains are very bike friendly, so you are allowed to take your bike on either mode of transport. And many people frequently do.

Apart from when there is a red light at a crossing, it seems to me that pedestrians and cycles have the right of way. Although this may not be entirely true, it is certainly in the culture of the nation that if a pedestrian or a cyclist is knocked over by a car, it has to be the car driver's fault.

## TRAFFIC SAFETY AND ROAD CONDITIONS

Finland has an extensive network of highways throughout the country, as well as excellent public transportation services. A valid EU or US driver's licence may be used while visiting Finland, but drivers must be at least 18 years of age. Driving in Finland is on the right. Traffic approaching from the right usually has priority, even if entering a primary roadway from a secondary one. Road signs use standard international symbols and Finnish text. Many urban streets have traffic lanes reserved for public transportation only. Unless otherwise noted on traffic signs, the speed limit is 50 km/h in urban areas, 80 km/h on open roads, and 120 km/h on motorways during summer (reduced to 100 km/h during winter). Vehicles must use headlights at all times. Use of seatbelts is mandatory for drivers and all passengers. Minor children must be seated in approved child or booster seats. The emergency telephone number for police/fire/ambulance in Finland is 112.

Drink-Driving: Be aware—drunk-driving laws are strict, and acceptable blood alcohol levels are much lower in Finland than elsewhere. Police strictly enforce all traffic laws and institute random roadside Breathalyzer tests. Drivers who register a 0.05 or above alcohol content are subject to immediate arrest.

Driving in Finland during the winter months can be hazardous. Daylight hours are very short and one should be comfortable with driving in darkness. Icy road conditions are common. If driving in Finland, the vehicle must be winterized with studded snow tyres (mandatory), and engine heaters are strongly recommended. When driving at night, drivers must be alert to elks wandering onto major roadways. There have been incidents of elks being struck by vehicles, causing severe damage to the vehicle and injury, sometimes fatal, to the occupants. For real-time updates on road conditions throughout Finland, see the Finnish Road Administration's travel and traffic information website at http://www.tiehallinto.fi/eindex.htm. Visit the website of the country's national tourist office and national authority responsible for road safety at http://www.mek.fi.

## WHAT YOU CAN IMPORT

### Importing Food into Finland

Finland is very strict on its food safety standards. The importation of food products containing meat or milk products for personal consumption is prohibited unless accompanied by the necessary documentation from the official veterinary services of the country of origin. Infant milk, food and special foods required for medical reasons can be imported under the condition that these products do not require refrigeration before opening, that they are packaged proprietary brand products for direct sale to the final consumer, and that the packaging is unbroken. For details of what you can and can't bring into the country, contact the Customs of Finland and/or Finnish Food Safety Authority. More information: http://www.tulli.fi and http://www.evira.fi/portal/en/

## Importing Animals From EU Countries and Norway

The requirements applied to the import of dogs, cats and ferrets are designed to prevent the spreading of animal diseases. Import regulations vary therefore depending on the animal disease situation in the country of origin. Compliance with the regulations is necessary to prevent the spreading of diseases, eg rabies. These requirements concern only pets which accompany their owner or person responsible for them on behalf of the owner and which are not intended to be sold or transferred to another owner.

- The animal must be identified by a microchip.
- The animal must be vaccinated against rabies.
- Dogs and cats must be given echinococcus treatment at least 30 days before arriving in Finland.
- The animal must have a pet passport.

Further details can be found at http://www.evira.fi/portal/fi/evira/julkaisut/ or Tel: (020) 772-5104

## Finland Import Prohibitions

The following commodities are prohibited:

- Atlantic red tuna fish (Thunnus Thynnus) originating from Belize, Panama and Honduras
- Toys and games containing copper sulfate
- All forms of asbestos fibers
- L-Trytophane and any items having L-trytophane as an ingredient
- Certain US beef hormones

- Rubber erasers that are similar in appearance to food products that are easily ingested
- Medical thermometers containing mercury intended for human consumption
- Items having a flexible metal blade entirely contained in a plastic, paper or fabric sheath
- Illicit narcotics and drugs
- Whale meat
- PCB and PCT chemicals used in transformers and condensers causing problem wastes

## SHOPPING

Finland is not a cheap place to shop. Generally, it is cheaper than the other Scandinavian countries. However, goods are very good value for money because they only sell high-quality items—you cannot buy inferior, low-priced 'value' products. Finns prefer high quality to cut price goods. That's not to say Finns don't like a bargain. Many take a day trip from Helsinki to Tallin, in Estonia, to pick up some real bargains. Here you can buy the same type of goods as in Finland but for far less money.

**Shopping in and around Helsinki**

There are numerous shopping centres in and around Helsinki. The best known are Stockmann, Sokos and Forum in central Helsinki. Around Helsinki, you find some malls like Itäkeskus (easily accessible by metro), Jumbo (by bus), Iso Omena (by bus) and others. Moreover, big foreign companies have errected huge, massive shopping areas here and there, for instance IKEA, Gigantti and ON/OFF (electronics), Stadium (sports gear) and Bauhaus (building tools).

Finland is famous for its glassware, pottery, woollens, furniture and other wood products, all of which are exquisitely designed. One well-known piece of glassware that is typically Finnish is the Aalto Vase designed by Alvar Aalto and this can be bought in shops and departments stores all over Finland. From Lapland come intricate jewellery and handicrafts made from wood, reindeer hide, wool and metal. Lappish hand-knitted sweaters, woollen mittens and woven wall-hangings can be purchased throughout Finland. Genuine articles made in the true Lapp traditions are authenticated by a *duodji* token.

Department stores have a good range of products, very similar to those found elsewhere in Europe. However, they do seem to have a different and varied range of clothing. You will be able to find well-known expensive off-the-peg brands, but there is a full range of Finnish designed and made clothes. The quality of these is good and the price sensible. You will not find very cheap clothing or shoes in Finland. The Finns would not put up with the poor quality.

**Shopping Tips**

From Elina ,a Romanian in Finland: Finland is quite an expensive country to do shopping, especially if compared to Eastern or Southern Europe countries. However, if you avoid the most expensive boutiques and shops, you won't lose all your money. Here are some examples of affordable, inexpensive and expensive shops.

- Stockmann—Definitely has all you need, at least more than any other department store. You get good, even personal service, but the prices are the highest. (Same product may be twice as expensive as in another shop). Stockmann department stores are in Helsinki (in city centre and in Itäkeskus), Turku, Tampere and Oulu. Stockmann is also abroad, in Latvia, Estonia and Russia.
- Anttila—Becoming more and more expensive, yet the service and quality of products remain the same. Has mostly basic products but also some quality ones. Has an affordable music department.
- Sokos—I would say it is between Stockmann and Anttila. Quality is better than in Anttila, and the prices are a bit lower than Stockmann's.

I enjoy looking around the kitchen and home furnishing departments. Finnish design is very evident in even the

The Finns value the aesthetic. Whether creating furniture, clothes, jewellery or buildings, design is the core ingredient of their products. Shopping is a delight as there is such a variety of unique items of suberb quality.

simplest utensils. Amazing bottle openers, innovative egg-timers, slender glasses, must-have saucepans, intricate candles and delicate paper napkins are just some of the goods which make shopping such a delightful experience.

The Finns have a wonderful range of materials on the reel for home furnishings and dressmaking. I am always so pleased to see their traditional haberdashers shops, spilling over with knitting wools, buttons and hobby kits. The UK saw the demise of these types of shops about 20 years ago and they are only now beginning to surface again.

There are some spectacular pieces of jewellery for sale reflecting the traditional designs of Finland. These are both unique in appearance and very striking. Some of course are costly, but those made from copper or bronze are good value for money and unique.

# FOOD AND ENTERTAINMENT

CHAPTER 6

'Nutritional experts have distressed Finns by claiming that the most lethal killer isn't the green mamba but sausage. Ingest just one kilo of this additive-infested and widely sole poison and face dire consequences: if you survive it, at the very least you'll end up in early retirement. But Finns have been impervious to these warnings. They consider sausage a proper summer snack to be eaten all year round.'
Hese Hyvärinen, Marja Nurmelin & Timo Mäkelä, *A Survival Guide to Finnish Cuisine for Business People*

FINNISH FOOD HIT THE HEADLINES in July 2005 when France's President Jacques Chirac pronounced Finnish food as almost inedible. Earlier comments by Italian Prime Minister Silvio Berlusconi compared Italian and Finnish food culture and found the latter vastly inferior. However, Finns have a mixed reaction to this criticism. Public commentators, restaurant owners and food critics think it is nonsense to deride all Finnish dishes, even though there are some traditional specialties which are a bit of an acquired taste. For instance, a very popular dish especially in eastern Finland is the *kalakukko*, a loaf of dark bread filled with herring and very fatty bacon. Some commentators have, however, admitted that sometimes Finnish food can be a bit bland. This is partly a question of tradition and spices available. Spices used to be very expensive. But it is also a question of healthiness. During the past two decades, the Finns have been brainwashed to avoid butter, salt and other ingredients that are bad for your heart. And herein may lie the problem for Mr Chirac, as any French cook knows that for a delicious dish, you need only three ingredients: cream, cream and cream.

Finnish food suffers from a poor reputation because in

> 'Chirac and Berlusconi are wrong! Finnish cuisine is much more international than I expected. I have eaten very good food in wonderful restaurants, visited market places and enjoyed in good cafeterias. Cheese is very good in Finland. I also love Finnish cloudberry and smoked fish.'
>
> —Ute Junker, *Australian Financial Review Magazine*, Sydney, Australia

Liliane Delwasse, Le Figaro, Paris, France: 'Food in Finnish restaurants is extremely good. I especially love Finnish salmon, mushroom soup and desserts. There are very good Finnish wines. The worldwide reputation of Finnish cuisine isn't very good—but it should be!'

the olden times, the country's harsh climate meant that fresh fruit and vegetables were largely unavailable for nine months of the year, causing a heavy reliance on staple tubers (initially turnip, later potato), dark rye bread and fermented dairy products, occasionally enlivened with preserved fish and meat. Traditionally, very few spices other than salt were available, and fresh herbs like dill were limited to the summer months. Many Finnish traditional dishes are prepared by stewing them for a long time in an oven, which produces hearty but bland fare. Famines caused by crop failures in the 19th century caused Finns to improvise by eating, for example, bread made from pine bark (*pettuleipä*), which was nutritious but rock-hard and anything but tasty. However, joining the EU in 1995, with the consequent elimination of trade barriers, prices of some products like grains, meat and milk dropped by up to 50 per cent and more varieties of food became available and affordable. Now Finnish supermarkets and restaurants serve up a wide variety of food from all over the world. The simplicity of traditional Finnish food has also been turned into an advantage by placing an emphasis on freshness. Finnish restaurateurs now blend high-quality Finnish produce with continental cooking techniques.

**Enjoying Finnish Food**

Visit http://www.finfood.fi for everything you want to know about Finnish food culture, cuisine and recipes. It also has a list of restaurants from around Finland that bear their 'Taste of Finland' symbol.

## THE CUISINE

Finnish cuisine is traditionally a mélange of East and West; of European, Scandinavian and Russian cuisine, with modern day food liberally laced with an international flavour. Also, it is very seasonal. Finnish cuisine since the 1970s has been

constantly changing, but would always be influenced by age-old traditions such as smoking meats. It is said that the traditional foods are still those favoured by their Bronze and Iron Age ancestors, namely salmon, reindeer, rye bread, dill, highly aromatic berries and beer. According to the *Kalevala*, the Finnish national epic, the Iron Age Finns enjoyed frosty, foaming beer. (Finland has the oldest breweries in Scandinavia). And for those Finns living abroad, rye bread and salted herring are the two things that they miss the most.

A friend of mine related the story about her time working with the Finnish Trade Delegation. She explained that whenever they were entertaining foreign visitors, the menu would always be *gravalux* (a delicacy of cured salmon), followed by reindeer as a main course with ice cream and cloudberries as a dessert. Occasionally the menu would change to smoked reindeer as a starter, followed by poached salmon as a main course. She lamented that this type of food was served more often than the Finns would actually eat it, for their real favourite is meatballs. At home in Finland, the number one dinner is meatballs and mashed potatoes, with the sauce in the pan made into thick gravy by adding butter, flour and cream.

The Finns use cream a lot in their cooking and this is most notable in the soups they prepare. 'Cream of ......' takes on a new meaning here. Cream of mushroom soup is so thick you can stand a spoon in it; salmon soup, too, is very rich. Rich but exceedingly delicious! You either love it or hate it, and the Finns love it. Many dishes are served with a rich creamy sauce, so it is common to have steak, pork fillet or chicken breast covered with a sauce that is slightly spicy. Just to ring the changes, you will often encounter a bright red or yellow sauce served with your meat. The sauce will be made from berries and I have developed a real taste for this. I have noticed that whenever liver, bacon and mashed potatoes are served, this dish comes with both a creamy sauce and a berry sauce. The best of both worlds! Dill is a favourite herb in Finnish cuisine and is often used when preparing fish dishes.

Strawberries, cranberries, gooseberries, blueberries and raspberries are also popular and provide a good flavour for many local types of liquor. Cloudberries are bright yellow in colour and are only found in the Arctic Circle. It is also popular to drink a shot of vodka with a couple of berries in the glass.

So, what are the other dishes that are eaten daily by the Finns? *Makkara* (sausage) has to be the next on the list. The Finns eat *makkara* and drink beer with a passion. This sausage is more similar to a frankfurter than a British-type sausage and is very tasty. Often cooked on bonfires in the open air, the *makkara* is the favourite food for a summer night at the summer cottage. *Lenkkimakkara* (ring sausage) and *grillimakkara* (grilled sausage) are so popular that the joke is they are 'Finnish vegetables'.

At home, sausages are eaten frequently and, as a change, cheese is placed in the middle of them and then they are warmed slowly in the oven. Mashed potato is part of the Finns' staple diet, but nowadays everyone tries to include vegetables and/or salads in their meal. Bread is also a staple commodity in the Finnish diet. It seems wrong to call Finnish bread a commodity as that seems to demean it. There are many delicious types of bread and it is said that nearly

Working up an appetite in the spring usually involves sitting round a bonfire cooking sausages (*makkara*)!

every village has its own recipes. Like the Italians, the Finns love mushrooms and there is a real appreciation for all the different varieties that can be picked wild in the forests. A usual week's shopping trolley will have lots of milk products such as yoghurt, milk, *viili* (Finnish yoghurt), cheese, cold cuts of meat and sausage. The Finns are fond of casseroles and stews. *Pirro* stew is made with reindeer and potatoes, while Karelian hot pot, *lapskoussi*, is made with veal, pork, mutton and vegetables. *Sekali* is a heavy stew made of pork, beans and sauerkraut.

**Sausages Delight**

The first time I ate Finnish sausage was after an afternoon snow-mobiling in the spring. A group of us snow-mobiled over the frozen lake near Kuopio, around the little islands off-shore and alighted on an island that was completely out of sight of civilisation. The sun was just beginning a gradual descent and the sky had turned a magnificent colour of golds and reds. Awaiting us was a roaring fire, a crate of beer and a stack of *makkara* ready for cooking. After the exhilaration of snow-mobiling and all the fresh air, we were ready to eat. How good those sausages tasted!

Lunch may be a smorgasbord. The Finns mostly prefer the fish and the seafood courses, leaving very little

'Everything is sugar-free, fat-free, politically correct, well-balanced, anti-allergic and enriched with live-enhancing bacteria... they [the Finns] stood up against the Russians and they'd do it again any time, but they're s**t scared of cholesterol.' —Roman Schatz (*From Finland With Love*, 2006)

room for the rest of the food. The best restaurants have an incredible variety of foods to choose from. The Finnish way to eat a smorgasbord is first to help yourself to the fish dishes, then take a clean plate and help yourself to the cold meats. After that you can continue with the warm food and follow on with the dessert.

## LAPPISH FOOD

Winter in Finland is often associated with Lapland and that's when Lappi food comes into its own. The most popular dishes are fried sirloin of reindeer, grilled fillet of elk, glow-fried breast of snow grouse, and fried arctic char. Also, there is smoked and dried reindeer, arctic char, smoked ciscoes, forest mushroom salad, vendace and a collection of Lapland's cheeses with cloudberries and lingonberries.

Reindeer and moose are the real delicacies. They are slightly more expensive than other meats. Served as a steak with potatoes, salad or in a stew, apparently they are becoming the 'it' menu item of the moment. Reindeer meat has a distinctive taste of game and is fine-textured and tender. It is also very low in fat and rich in vitamins and minerals. It is like beef but more tender and really rich in flavour. Reindeer meat does not need that much sauce, so it is light and the taste is just so powerful. You can also find the meat served as chops, on sandwiches, as soups, as meatballs, as burgers, sautéed, roasted, cold smoked and every which way you can think of. Moose meet is similar and is also used a lot in the winter time.

Reindeer and moose meat come from Lapland where the cattle roam freely. Herding is an integral part of the Lapp heritage and provides a livelihood from about 2,000 Lappish families. The export of reindeer meat has become big business in recent years, and is said to be one of the fastest growing parts of the Finnish food industry.

**Recipe: Sautéed Reindeer**

- 400 g meat for sautéed reindeer (reindeer shoulder and/ or fore loin cut into thin shaves)
- 50 g butter or oil
- 50 ml water or beer
- Salt
- Black pepper
- (Crushed garlic)

Melt the butter in a pan and add the frozen meat. Let the meat melt in the pan under a lid and fold it carefully from time to time. When the liquid is vapourised, add the crushed garlic, salt and pepper. Fry the meat for a while, folding carefully. Add the stock and let it simmer under the lid for about 30 minutes. Check the taste. Serve hot from the pan, with mashed potatoes, cranberries or lingonberry sauce.

## TYPICAL FINNISH DISHES

Just some of the many traditional dishes you will encounter on a journey through Finland are:

- **Bread**
  There are dozens of varieties: rye, wheat, oat, potato and mixed grain; heavy, light, crisp and unleavened; sour-sweet and malted. These are made into the best-ever sandwiches you will come across.
- **Kaurapuuro**
  This is the Finnish equivalent of porridge. Made from oatmeal, this is the way to begin the morning.
- **Karjalanpiirakka** (Karelian pie)
  This is a small pie whose crust is made from rye. It is shaped like a moccasin as it has a 'ruffled' edge along the top. Filled with a rice mixture, it is delicious served in the traditional Joensuu manner spread with butter and chopped egg. They are served for breakfast, lunch or dinner.
- **Kalakukko**
  This is a well-known delicacy from the Kuopio region and is a 'fish pie'. It is a loaf-shaped pasty filled with fish

and fatty pork. A rye pastry is filled with vendace, perch, rainbow trout and pork, wrapped in foil and baked in the oven

- **Poronkäristys**
  Sautéed reindeer, a special treat in Finland, except in Lapland where it is an everyday meal.
- **Mustamakkra** (Black Pudding)
  This is a speciality from Tampere and is served with lingonberry sauce.
- **Hernekeitto**
  Pea soup, extremely thick, traditionally served on Thursdays. In February, on Shrove Tuesday, it's followed by pancakes, berry sauce and thick cream!
- **Baltic Herring**
  Baltic Herring is served in a variety of fashions. Sweet pickle, sour pickled, cold in a spicy, curry sauce, marinated, salted, smoked, charred or cooked hot. Don't miss the Helsinki Baltic Herring Market every October.
- **Loimusiika**
  A dish not to be missed; Flamed whitefish. Whitefish filets are nailed to a board and slowly smoked over an open flame.
- **Caviar**
  Finland has its own caviar which comes from whitefish, burbot and vendace. Three different coloured caviars are served with sour cream, onions and tasty bread, usually as a starter or light-bite.
- **Smoked meats and fish**
  Smoking is an age old method of preparing food. Particular favourites are smoked reindeer, lamb and ham. Salmon, of course, is one fish that is often smoked, along with trout.
- **Korvasienimuhennos**
  Creamed morel mushroom stew.
- **Berries**
  Artic berries that are popular in Finnish cuisine are the cloudberry (which looks like a golden raspberry but tastes of honey), the Artic Bramble, the Sea Buckthorn, cranberry and the lingonberry. There are cultivated berries, currants, raspberries, strawberries and gooseberries which are

A wide variety of food is available in a smorgasboard: smoked, pickled or steamed fish; all manner of salads and raw vegetables; meats, pâtés and poultry; and different types of bread.

especially suited to the colder climate and have a distinct flavour compared with those grown in sunnier climes. These berries are made into jams, sauces, are frozen or turned into Finnish liqueurs or wines. Lingonberry jam is served with meat, especially with game and reindeer. It is common to have ice cream served with golden cloudberry sauce. Vodkas are flavoured with these berries and Finnish sparkling white wine is mainly made from the white currant. White currants are also used to make fresh, fruity white wines.

- **Ohukainen**

  Pancake. Ok there are pancakes as 'usual' pancakes (or crepes), which in Finnish are called *ohukainen* or more unofficially but more commonly *lätty*. A better version is the ones made outside with a big frying pan—known as *muurinpohjalätty*. Also, there is what in Finnish is called *pannukakku*, which is a direct translation from the word 'pancake'. It is much thicker and baked in the oven, and tastes a bit different too. Pancakes are usually consumed with some jam—most preferably with homemade jam made from Finnish strawberries, cloudberries (*lakka* or *hilla*).

- **Cheese**
  Finnish-made Emmental cheese is a favourite and is found all over Finland, and is often exported.

**Recipe: Roast Fillet of Reindeer with Cranberry Sauce**

- 600 g fillet of reindeer
- Butter for frying
- Salt and freshly ground black pepper

Cranberry sauce:

- 1 tbsp butter
- 50 g of vegetables:
- Celeriac, parsnip, carrot, shallot, leek
- 100 ml cranberry juice
- 400 ml game or beef stock
- 2 tsp sugar
- 2 tbsp corn flour
- A dash of red wine
- Freshly ground black pepper
- Freshly ground white pepper
- Sea salt
- A total of 400 g raw vegetables (e.g. turnip, celeriac, parsnip, potato, carrot) cut into decorative pieces

To garnish:

- Cranberries
- Fresh sprigs of herbs

First prepare the sauce. Sauté the finely chopped vegetables in butter, in a saucepan. Add the cranberry juice, stock and sugar. Simmer for about 20 minutes. Strain the sauce and thicken with corn flour dissolved in red wine. Simmer for 5 minutes. Cut the fillet of reindeer into 4 pieces and fry in a pan until medium. Season the meat with salt and pepper. Cut the pieces diagonally into slices. Boil the vegetables until *al dente*. Place them onto a plate and arrange the meat onto the bed of vegetables. Surround with the sauce and cranberries. Garnish with a fresh sprig of herbs.

## SPECIAL OCCASIONS

There are two particularly grand occasions for eating in Finland. First, of course, is Christmas and the highlight is the meal served on Christmas Eve. Mulled wine is served with oven-baked ham, mashed swede and potato, lingonberry sauce, blackcurrant jelly and apple sauce. Traditional Christmas sweets often have prunes in them and Finnish Christmas pastries are filled with prune jam. And Christmas would not be Christmas in Finland without large, spicy gingerbreads. The Christmas 'cake' is a beautifully created gingerbread house which sits in the middle of the table for decoration until the time to eat it up! During December, restaurants serve a Christmas buffet which includes herring, salmon, smoked reindeer, duck, ham, sausage, cod served with a thick milk-based sauce, melted butter and potatoes.

The second grand occasion is at 12:00 pm on 21 July. This is the gastronomic peak of the summer and is the official beginning of the crayfish season, which will last until the end of August when crayfish parties will be the vogue. The essential ingredients for a really good party are paper lanterns, a warm August evening, great friends and family, toasted bread and butter, *koskenkorva* vodka and crayfish. The crayfish are boiled in salted water, with sugar and lots and lots of dill.

Thursday is traditionally pea soup day. Runeberg's day on 5 February is when bakeries sell a special cake named after the national poet. At Easter, the children look forward to *Mignon*, real egg shells filled with delicious Finnish chocolate. 1 May is a time to drink *sima* mead, sparkling Finnish white wine and eat sweet pastries.

From Maria M, a Finn: 'With Americans and food, the problem is usually waste. In Finland, you only take what you want to take but then you are expected to finish what's on your plate. Some Russian friends of ours nearly starved when they visited Finland, because we would only put food on the table and ask them to take some. They thought it was impolite to take food themselves and so would say that they were not hungry. If we had been Russians, we would have insisted that they eat, but as Finns we said "fine, if you are not hungry". Serving is not commonly done unless a dish is really difficult to move around, and even then you are always asked how much you'd like. Anything that can be passed around is passed around for everyone to take what they want themselves.

**Recipe: Pea Soup**

- 500 g dried peas
- 1.25 litre water
- 1/2 tsp salt
- 1 onion
- 300 g smoked knuckle, slightly salted pork shoulder or side
- 1 tsp marjoram

For soaking the peas:

- 2 litre water and 2 tsp salt

Soak the peas in salted water for 6–12 hours. Pour the water away. Place the peas, water and salt into a pot. Bring to the boil; skim off the residue and excess pea cases with a skimmer. Peel and chop the onion. Add the onion and the whole amount of meat into the soup. Simmer for about one hour. Take the meat away from the soup and let it cool. Slice into small cubes. Let the soup simmer until the peas are done. Add the meat cubes and season with marjoram.

## EATING OUT

Most Finns eat their main meal at lunchtime (12:30–2:30 pm), when restaurants (*ravintola*) offer special meals from about € 7. In the evening, most Finns will eat in their family homes from 6:00–8:00 pm, although if dining out, most will eat between 8:00–10:00 pm. For more informal dining, *baari* and *kahvila* serve less expensive options. Service charge and VAT are always included in the advertised price of food, so there is no extra charge to your final bill. Payment can be made by credit/debit card, however small the bill. Tipping is not customary. Most restaurants have menus in English. In Helsinki, the main eating districts are all centrally located around or on the streets off the Esplanadi, Bulevardi and Mannerheimintie.

In the summer, many restaurants are full of fresh, locally grown produce including the Helsinki speciality, crayfish. In the autumn, mushrooms, berries and game are on offer. Firm staples throughout the year include meat, potatoes, fish, milk, butter and rye. Salmon is one of the most popular mainstays, grilled, fried, or made in the Helsinki version of sushi (wrapped around new potatoes) and it is used for making soup. Roasts, diced meat, pork chops, mince and speciality sausages are also firm favourites.

When you've had a few too many drinks and it's the early hours of the morning ... *Lihapiirakka kahdella nakilla ja kaikilla mausteilla* will steady the legs and set you up for your journey home. Bought at fast-food kiosks, this is a popular late-night snack consisting of a meat pie with two hot dogs and all the condiments!

The Finns have developed a taste for international cuisine, especially Italian food. There can hardly be a village in Finland that hasn't at least two pizzerias and there must only be a handful of restaurants that do not offer both pizza and lasagne on the menu! Helsinki is extremely cosmopolitan in its choice of good restaurants, which ranges from Japanese to Mexican, from trendy bistros to traditional farmhouse. The variety is plentiful and, added to this, a multitude of cafés, tearooms and bars can be found serving light snacks and delicious pastries. In the major cities in Finland, the choice of restaurants is not so varied. However, there always seems to be a good Russian restaurant around, along with Greek and Italian food. Chinese food is becoming popular with the Finns, though Chinese restaurants tend to be few and far between. Nowadays, there is a good range of vegetarian restaurants and health food cafes and, whatever your preference, all menus are minutely detailed with symbols demonstrating the ingredients of each dish—even in trucker's cafés.

I suppose it goes without saying that McDonald's has a heavy presence all over the country. My daughter has taken great delight in telling all her friends that she has eaten a Big Mac in the most northerly McDonald's in the world—and has the hat to prove it! But, not to be outdone, the Finns have their answer to the American chain. They have Hesburger—their own home-grown burger chain and these are usually located within a stone's throw from a McDonald's. Needles to say, Hesburger is the more popular. Apart from hamburgers, another popular fast-food is the hot-dog and hot-dog kiosks abound.

**Pineapple Craze**

From a foreigner in Finland, Penelope: 'Finns and their tinned pineapple chunks! I would bet money on Finland being one of the highest per capita consumers of tinned pineapple in the world. It is, as you all know, a must on pizzas up here (peaches as well!) and there's usually a few bits lurking around in the side salad!!! Anyway a butcher I know, who is also a hunter, says there are chemical reasons why marinating elk meat in pineapple juice tenderises the meat.'

## DINING OUT WITH A FINN

If friends want to see each other for longer than just a coffee, they will probably arrange to go to a restaurant for lunch or dinner. In this case, each person will be required to pay their own bill. The Finns are very particular about this. They won't split the bill equally 'down the middle' or by the number of people attending (customary in the UK). They like to pay precisely for what they have had. They like to pay their own way. As the Finns would say, "I don't like to travel on your wing". In other words, they don't like to be beholden to anybody else. People who don't pay, or are looking for other people to pay for them, are called 'wingers' (*siipeilisa*—our equivalent is 'sponger'). This very precise and careful way of splitting bills is the Finnish concept of fair play. As a foreigner, you may well be asked out to dine. In this case, you probably will be invited as a guest and not expected to pay, but do remember that alcohol is extremely expensive. The next time you meet, be prepared to pay for your portion of the bill.

When drinking out, Finns never drink in rounds. Everyone always pays for their own beer, and buys it when they want, even when drinking with friends. As a foreigner, you often feel obliged to buy a round, but I have heard said that no one feels the compulsion to return the compliment!

From a Finnish reader, Jarmo H: 'Offering rounds in the pub in Britain is really so unpleasant that I try to avoid those situations. It forces me to drink more than I want to, stay awake longer than I would want to and spend more money than I would want to and leave me in debt, at least morally. I think I am not the only Finn who feels this way.'

My French friend Christine cannot get over how little importance the Finns seem to

give to enjoying their meals. Of course, the French like to sit over their meal, sipping wine and debating till all hours of the morning! The Finns, on the other hand, seem to eat as quickly as they can and get up from the table as soon as they are finished. Obviously they all have something more important to do! Of course, hardly a meal will go by without half the diners making or receiving a phone call. If you are eating in a group, once four people are served at the table, you can start eating; you need not wait for everyone to be served.

## THE COFFEE CULTURE

A surprising fact about Finland is that they drink more coffee per capita than anywhere else in the word. I'm not convinced they have acquired this accolade because they drink more cups of coffee in a day but because the coffee they drink is so strong that you could hang wallpaper with it! However, the Finns have a very long established coffee tradition which started at the beginning of the 18th century when it first arrived in Scandinavia. It had become so popular by 1767 that the government tried to make this 'unhealthy luxury drink' illegal. But those with money were able to

### Savoury or Sweet?

From Maria M., a Finn: 'One of the most difficult things to explain to foreigners is the difference between savoury foods (eaten first) and sweet foods (eaten usually with coffee, after savoury foods). We've had some American friends who have thought of *pulla* as bread, put butter on it, and tried to eat it with the main course. This is utterly wrong; *pulla* is sweet and therefore should be eaten with coffee.'

buy it on the black market and eventually the government of the day gave up.

By the 19th century, the coffee habit had spread throughout the countryside. The wealthiest amongst the population drank it daily but villages would use it just for their public celebrations and holidays. Ordinary families soon wanted to have coffee for themselves and so began the Sunday ritual of having coffee after church. Unfortunately, coffee was so expensive that other ingredients like rye, barley, beans, peas, dandelion roots, acorns and chicory were mixed with it to lessen the price. But when times were hard and the harvests had been bad, coffee was the luxury that was given up.

By the 20th century, coffee was being consumed three times a day and was established as the national drink. All kinds of coffee cultures arose and people began to drink it with sugar and cream. Then they began to buy coffee beans raw and roast them at home in a special pan called a *rannali*. This way, each family produced its own distinct blend of coffee depending on what other ingredients they had mixed with the beans. Coffee was in such short supply during World War II that when the container ship *The Herakles* arrived from Brazil with the first consignment of 35 tons of coffee in 1946, the day almost became a national flag day. There is a sweet bread called *pulla* that is traditionally eaten with coffee. It contains lots of cinnamon and cardoman. In the old days, the *pulla* was baked as a large circular bun with a scooped hole in the middle. When the *pulla* was served, the centre would be filled with all sorts of cookies and biscuits (traditionally seven varieties).

## CAFÉS

The Finns' enormous appetite for coffee means that a café culture is alive and thriving in most towns, but especially in Helsinki. When visiting, treat yourself to a visit to some of the following. Opened in 1861, one of the most reputed cafes is also its oldest, Café Ekberg, Boulevardi 9. Its pastries are the most revered in town. Try *korvapuusti*, the traditional Helsinki sweet roll loaded with sugar and cinnamon, at Café Success, Korkeavuorenkatu 2. Choose from over 100 coffees at Robert's Coffee Garden, Kanavakatu 5, which is a 'gourmet roastery' which freshly roasts and grinds coffee beans on the spot. To step back in time to a more refined atmosphere, the Tamminiementie Kahvila, Tamminiementie 8, is set in an old manor house. Here the coffee pot is bottomless. Alternatively, sipping coffee by the seaside at Café Ursula, Ehrenstromintie 3, is a great place to simply watch the world go by.

**Getting it Wrong**

From a foreigner in Finland, Dino Desfiges: 'My girlfriend and I were in a bookstore looking for a Vietnamese cookbook. While she was reading one particular book, I was looking around and noticed that almost every book had 'Keittokirja' on the cover. I knew *kirja* (book), so I just asked her what *keitto* meant. She replied 'soup'. Surprised and confused, I blurted out a bit too loudly, "All these books are about soup?!" (*Keittokirja* means Cookbook.)'

## RESTAURANTS

This guide is extracted from *Helsinki Happens*, a free English-language magazine for visitors to Helsinki (http://www.helsinkihappens.com). You may want to try some Russain restaurants as those in Helsinki are rated to be the best outside St. Petersburg.

Lappi Restaurant is a piece of Lapland tucked away in Helsinki, on the corner of Annankatu and Kalevankatu. Its long-standing popularity is based on serving traditional Lappish cuisine, originating from Muonio. The variety of dishes served in Lappi are indeed delicious and exotic. The restaurant is richly decorated with images of the aurora borealis, drawings and sketches by northern artists, and pictures of reindeers and elks. The interior is covered with genuine wood brought from Lappish, the tables and

The Finns enjoy a sunny afternoon chatting with friends at a cafe near the harbour in Helsinki.

A converted warehouse by a lake in Kuopio is an enjoyable venue for an outdoor summer drink or meal.

chairs are made of wooden logs, comfortably carved to follow the suite. The friendly staff are dressed in traditional Lapland costumes.

## Fine Dining

- Chez Dominque
  Tel: 612-7393
  A highly imaginative French-Scandinavian gourmet restaurant with attention to season and detail.
- G.W. Sundman's
  Tel: 622-6410
  The former sea captain's house has an experimental spirit of Scandinavian flavours.
- George
  Tel: 647-662
  A comfy classical restaurant with international gourmet dishes exploiting the best of fresh Finnish produce.
- Kaarlen Kruunu
  Tel: 622-4133
  A gastronomic delight, serving from an open-plan kitchen.
- Kanavaranta
  Tel: 622-2633

Located in an old red-brick warehouse, this restaurant offers historic atmosphere with quality taste and good service.

- Kamp Restaurant
  Pricey yet excellent international flavours and broad selection of wines in a glorious, thoroughly restored interior.
- Savoy
  Tel: 176-571
  Has the reputation of having the best price-quality ration of all the finer restaurants in the city. The marvellous dining room is one of Alvar Aalto's most celebrated designs.
- Sipuli
  Tel: 179-9000
  Exceptional quality international cooking, broad selection of fine wines.

## Ethnic Eateries

- Antiokia Atabar
  Tel: 694-0367
  Tasty Turkish flavours and belly dancing on weekend nights.
- Namaskaar
  Tel: 477-1960
  One of the first truly ethnic restaurants in Finland, still has the reputation for serving the best Indian cuisine in town. Pricey yet delicious.
- Saslik
  Tel: 742-555
  The romantic atmosphere of Czarist Russia offering many Russian specialities and delicacies. Russian troubadours nightly.
- Maithai
  Tel: 685-6850
  Traditional Thai food in the Far Eastern venue has plenty of vegetarian dishes. Reservations recommended at weekends.
- Mexicana
  Tel: 666-797
  A small cosy restaurant with full-flavoured spicy dishes and Latin American ethos. Good lunches.

- Lotus
  Tel: 605-167
  Oriental atmosphere with tasty Chinese dishes at reasonable prices.
- La Petite Maison
  Tel: 260-9680
  Cosy, modest interior serving classic French cuisine with appropriate wine.

## BUYING FOOD

Finnish towns have a daily fresh food market that is held outside during the summer and has a permanent indoor home during the winter. The choice of food will be somewhat limited but is not restricted to only Finnish-produce goods. However, you can find all kinds of food in Finnish supermarkets from meats and fish to cheeses, pizzas and milk. Finnish supermarkets are very modern and pleasant and much more on a par with British stores than those of their Scandinavian neighbours. They also offer a far wider choice of chilled and frozen foods then those countries. In recent years, the offering has become far more international, especially with the coming of foreign competitors such as Lidl who now have 10 per cent of the market. Large department stores such as Sokos and Stockman have their own food halls, while large supermarkets such as Prisma and CityMarket also stock clothes, shoes, CDs and DVDs, electrical goods, magazines, sports equipment and much more.

From an American in Finland: Once you're in the store and ready to check out, don't get in the first cashier line you see. Finns have this strange ailment that whenever they see a line, they feel they must be in it. Every week at my local supermarket, I think there are huge lines at the checkout, then I'll stroll 20 registers down and there's a bunch of girls sitting there without any customers.

Finland produces 85 per cent of its own food needs. Much of this is traditional, including bear, mouse and reindeer meat and berries with 400 times the vitamin C content of oranges. The Finns have a highly developed system of ensuring food safety. Their milk and egg safety is considered by many to be the best in Europe.

Medicine is purchased in chemists called APTEEKKI. There is usually more than one chemist in town, with one of them staying open very late or even all night. Villages and larger ski resorts also often have a chemist, or another point such as a village shop or a post office, where non-prescription medicine is sold over the counter.

### Doing It Yourself

From Annabel Battersby, an Australian in Finland: 'The first time I went to a Finnish supermarket, about a week into my first visit to Finland, I made an accidental blunder. I picked up fruit and vegetables with my shopping and went straight to the counter to buy it all. To my surprise, the girl at the checkout told me I had to weight and label the fruit and vegetables myself before coming to the counter. So I obediently went back and did this—trying hard to figure out which label was for which fruit or vegetable with my non-existent Finnish, and remembering the numbers. In Australia, the check-out assistant does this for you, and everywhere else I've lived come to think of it. Going to the supermarket in Finland has meant making an effort to remember to weigh and label all the fruits and vegetables myself. After the first couple of months, I still occasionally forgot to weigh one thing or another, and I feel it's a real achievement to remember to weigh everything. It's such a conscious effort. But even better, I've picked up some Finnish more quickly!'

From an American in Finland: 'At all Finnish supermarkets, you need to have a coin to get a shopping cart, the coin is then given back to you when you return the cart. And not just any coin, often only 50 cent or € 1 pieces. I never have coins in my pocket and forget about this fact each and every week as I enter the store! And grocery bags cost money, like 20 cents a bag, but they're much more durable than the free ones in the States.'

Please note that you will not be able to buy alcohol, apart from mild beer and cider, in Finnish supermarkets. Wine, strong beer and spirits are only sold in off-licenses called ALKO to those over the age of 20. Some shopping centres include a separate ALKO shop, while you can also find one in some of the larger ski resorts and most towns. ALKO shops are closed on public holidays and Sundays.

# ENJOYING THE CULTURE

CHAPTER 7

'I am often tired of myself and have a notion that by travel I can add to my personality and so change myself a little. I do not bring back from a journey quite the same self that I took.'

—Somerset Maugham, *The Gentleman in the Parlour*

ONE OF THE BEST WAYS TO UNDERSTAND a nation is to learn something about who they respect and worship. Who are their heroes? Who are seen as role models for the nation's children? Who are the people who hand down tradition or guidance, values and direction? Then find out what they do. How do they spend their leisure time? What is the most popular leisure activity or hobby? What do they become fanatical about? How musical are they? What art do they appreciate? Finally, you could travel around the country and see the sites and understand how a nation's geography has shaped their culture. This chapter highlights all of the above to help you get a flavour of the Finnish culture.

## FINNISH HEROS AND CHAMPIONS

As previously mentioned, Finland is not as celebrity conscious as many other 'Western' cultures. So, let's take a look at who are their national heroes.

### Alvar Aalto

An architect and designer, he is sometimes called the 'Father of Modernism'. He was the most influential of Finnish architects, developing a style that became known as Nordic Classicism. Aalto's wide field of activity ranged from furniture and glassware designs to architecture and painting. His vase designs are world-famous. He invented a new form of laminated bent-plywood furniture in 1932.

Aalto furniture is manufactured by Artek, a company Aalto co-founded. Aalto glassware (Aino as well as Alvar) is manufactured by Iittala. Aalto's career spanned the changes in style from pre-modernism (Nordic Classicism) to purist International Style Modernism to a more synthetic and idiosyncratic approach.

## Jean Sibelius

A Finnish composer of classical music and one of the most notable composers of the late 19th and early 20th centuries. His music played an important role in the formation of the Finnish national identity. Sibelius' best-known compositions include *Finlandia*, *Valse Triste*, the *Violin Concerto*, the *Karelia Suite* and *The Swan of Tuonela* (one of the four movements of the *Lemminkäinen Suite*).

## Carl Gustav Mannerheim

A career officer in the Russian imperial army (1889–1917), he commanded the anti-Bolshevik forces (1918) in the Finnish Civil War and expelled the Soviet forces. He served as regent of Finland (1918–1919) until the new republic was declared. As chairman of the national defense council (1931–1939), he oversaw construction of the Mannerheim line of fortifications across the Karelian Isthmus. As commander in chief of Finnish forces (1939–1940, 1941–1944), he won initial successes against greatly superior Soviet forces in the Russo-Finnish War (1939–1940). Named president of the Finnish republic in 1944, he negotiated a peace agreement with the Soviets.

## Urho Kekkonen

Served as prime minister of Finland (1950–1953, 1954–1956) and later as president of Finland (1956–1981). Kekkonen continued the 'active neutrality' policy of President Juho Kusti Paasikivi, which came to be known as the Paasikivi-Kekkonen Line. This policy allowed Finland to retain independence and trade with both the nations of the North Atlantic Treaty Organisation and the Warsaw Pact. Kekkonen was the longest-serving president of Finland. He also became the

Finnish high jump champion in 1924. He has a park and a musuem named after him, and until recently was one of the faces featured of Finnish currency.

## Jorma Ollila

Prior to joining Nokia in 1985, Jorma Ollila worked eight years in corporate banking at Citibank's London and Helsinki offices. When he joined Nokia, his tasks involved international investment deals. A year later in 1986, Ollila found himself as head of finance during Nokia's renewal under then CEO Kari Kairamo. His career at Nokia continued as he was appointed as chief of the mobile phones section in 1990, and CEO two years later in 1992. When Ollila first came into power, the company had suffered from internal disputes and had run into a financial crisis over a number of years. As CEO of Nokia, he has been the leader of the strategy that restructured the former industrial conglomerate into one of the major companies in the mobile phone and telecommunications infrastructure markets.

And then comes a long list of sports people...

## Hannes Kolehmainen

Credited with 'running Finland onto the world map' when he won the 5,000 m, 10,000 m and the marathon races in 1912 at the Stockholm Olympics—three gold medals. He is considered to be the first of a generation of great Finnish long distance runners. At the time, Finland was still a part of Russia and, although there was a separate Finnish team at the Olympics, the Russian flag was raised for Kolehmainen's victories, making him say that he 'almost wished he hadn't won'.

## Paavo Nurmi

Called the 'Flying Finn' because of his distinction in running events between 1920–1928, winning nine gold and three silver Olympic medals in the 12 events he competed in. To this very day, Nurmi is the single athlete in track and field who has won the most Olympic medals, 12 in total. Due to this fact, he is often considered as the greatest athlete in track and field of all time.

### Jari Litmanen

A Finnish footballer, widely considered the country's greatest ever. He was chosen as the best Finnish player of the last 50 years by the Football Association of Finland in the UEFA Jubilee Awards in November 2003. Litmanen also finished 42nd in the 100 Greatest Finns voting in 2004. He went off to play for Barcelona.

### Mika Häkkinen

World-famous Formula 1 racing driver and twice the winning champion. He is considered to have been Michael Schumacher's greatest rival and is said by the German to be the rival he most respects. However, Häkkinen follows a long line of well-known and loved rally and racing drivers.

### Teemu Selänne

A professional Finnish ice hockey right winger currently playing for the Anaheim Ducks. He holds the NHL record for the most goals by a rookie with 76; his rookie season point total of 132. The 'rookie' record is officially held by Selänne.

### Marja-Lisa Kirvesniemi

A former Finnish cross country skier. She was the big figure at the 1984 Olympics in Sarajevo, winning all three individual cross country skiing events (5, 10 and 20 km) and a bronze medal for Finland in the relay. She is an all-time legend in Nordic skiing events, competing long after others of her age had given up.

### Mikko Ilonen:

An amateur golfer who was said to be 'putting frozen Finland into the golfing world's consciousness'. He was the first Finnish golfer ever to take part in one of the four Major tournaments in 2000, and had a spectacular and unexpected win in the British Amateur Championship the same year. He turned pro in 2001 and was the first Finn to win a European Tour event and to feature in the top 100 of the Official World Golf Rankings.

Then, some 'others'...

### Aki Kaurismäki

Film director, producer and screenwriter. In terms of awards, Kaurismäki's most successful movie, for the time being, has been *The Man Without a Past*. It won the Grand Prix at the Cannes Film Festival in 2002 and was nominated for an Academy Award in the Best Foreign Language Film category in 2003. However, Kaurismäki refused to attend the gala, noting that he didn't particularly feel like partying in a nation that is currently in a state of war. Kaurismäki's next film *Lights in the Dusk* was also chosen to be Finland's nominee in the category for best foreign film. Kaurismäki again decided to boycott the Awards and refused the nomination as a protest against US President George W. Bush's foreign policy

### Armi Kuusela

A Finnish beauty queen. On 24 May 1952, she won the national beauty contest Suomen Neito and was presented with a trip to the United States to participate in the first-ever Miss Universe contest. She was the first winner of this beauty pageant

### Unto Mononen

The most successful tango composer of the 1960s was Unto Mononen, a semi-professional bandleader. Mononen made his living by playing in rural dance halls. In the 1950s, he had published a number of songs, including *Satumaa*, which had been recorded in 1955 with moderate success. In 1962, Reijo Taipale recorded Satumaa again, and by the beginning of 1963, it was the best selling record in Finland. After 1965, the Beatles overtook him in popularity.

And now some foreigners...

### Richard D Lewis:

A Brit who works in the field of intercultural communication. Although relatively unknown to the average Finn, he is well respected in the business, political and diplomatic circles for helping to promote their country. His recent book: *Finland, Cultural Lone Wolf* (see Further Reading) has been well-received. Mr Lewis was knighted by President Ahtisaari of Finland in March 1997 for his services to Finland.

### Roman Schatz

A German-born Finnish TV show host and writer. Born in Western Germany, he has been living in Helsinki since 1986. He has appeared on TV in various programmes, including his own show *Toisten-TV* and just recently in *Dancing with the Stars*. He has an absolutely irreverent sense of humour and says some 'outrageous' things about the Finns—and they love him for it! His book *From Finland with Love* (see Further Reading) is full of humourous insights.

## THEY CALL THIS SPORT

Just so you would know how wonderfully way out and wacky the Finns are, I thought I would list for you some of the eccentric things they get up to in the year. As mentioned previously, the Finns are obsessed with sport. Anything and everything they will turn into a sport. The Finnish word for sport is closely related to bravery and heroism—it's all about fighting and winning against all odds—and, above all, not giving up. As a foreign observer, it appears that the most important thing is not the method or how well you play/do it, but that you take it deadly seriously! But how do you take the following seriously?

- The World Mosquito Killing Championship
- The Anthill Competition—the person who can sit naked in an anthill the longest is the winner!
- Flirting, National Championship
- Chatting up contest for singles
- The International Ice Swimming Contest which takes place in a different location each year. A hole 25 m long and five lanes wide is cut out of the ice on a frozen lake. The

winner is the person who can swim the fastest!

- Bowling with logs
- Swamp football
- Kissing festival
- Arguing competition
- Finger Pulling
- The World Wife Carrying Competition takes place each summer in Sonkajarvi. The team consists of a married couple and conventional means of carrying have long since fallen into disuse. This is a game of tactics where the ham-fisted do not stand a chance. Just to complicate matters, there is a water obstacle to overcome.
- Running around a forest
- Swarming around a field
- The Kick-Sledge Championship held in Piesamaki has the holders of the record kicking a sledge for 24 hours and covering a distance of 500 km (311 miles).
- Throwing rubber (Wellington) boots
- Dragon Boat Racing is an annual event in Kuopio.
- The Ice Fishing Contest in Joensuu—but no one ever catches very much!
- The enduring Finnish puzzle—For a nation of shower lovers, why are there so many baths out in the countryside and where did they all come from? Apparently when the 'well-to-do' changed their plumbing from baths to showers in the dim and distant past, they threw out their old baths which were then seized by the farmers and used as troughs for their cattle! Thank you, Mike, for this fascinating puzzle.

There are many other smaller events going on in communities all over Finland. For further information, look on the website of the Finnish Tourist Boards (http://www.mek.fi).

## HOLIDAYS

The Finns traditionally get about five weeks paid holiday a year, plus bank holidays. Usually, the time they take off during the summer will be spent at their summer cottage or enjoying the long daylight hours of mid-summer in Finland.

A winter skiing holiday and a trip to sunnier climes will be built around the other weeks. One warning to foreigners who may be tempted to come to Finland to join in some holiday festivities is that the Finns themselves tend to leave the cities in their droves and everything is closed—hotels, restaurants, museums etc. Not Helsinki, of course. You may well be able to find a small family hotel which will be open, but unless you have Finnish friends to spend time with, there will be nothing for you to do. Alternatively, you could stay in one of the increasingly popular holiday villages which have built-in entertainment.

Easter and Christmas are the most important holidays in Finland. Easter is the most important religious celebration in Finland. People flock to religious concerts, passion plays and religious services. Whenever Easter falls, the days are getting longer and the Finns like to make the most of this holiday. Easter is almost a Finnish version of Hallowe'en, with children dressing-up as witches or trolls and with trick or treat style traditions. The doorbell rings and when you open the door, you see three girl-hags clad in shawls and clutching pussy-willow twigs adorned with pink and yellow feathers. "Give us coins or candy," they shriek. The Easter chicken delivers Easter eggs during the night when children are asleep (just like Santa Claus with his presents at Christmas time) and the children experience the same wondrous excitement. People paint Easter Eggs and eat *pasha* and *mammi*. *Mammi* is an exclusively Finnish seasonal cake made of rye and malt that goes well with cream and a sprinkling of sugar. Lamb is the traditional meat for this festival.

Christmas Eve and Christmas Day (Joulu) are mainly family celebrations. This is not the time to get drunk to enjoy yourself. Almost everything is closed and if you are on your own, this is not a good time to be in Finland. The main Christmas meal is served on Christmas Eve, probably about 6:00 in the evening, after the afternoon visit to the graveyard. This is a very special occasion when the Finns will take candles and light them and put them on the graves of their lost loved ones. The cemetery will be full of light; the light from these flickering candles is enhanced by the

A December treat not to be missed in Rovaniemi is the traditional Lappish Christmas market. The market traders are dolled up in traditional costumes and the stalls stocked with handmade arts and crafts.

whiteness of the snow. They may also attend mass. The exchanging of gifts and feasting will be saved for Christmas Eve night. The whole family will probably enjoy decorating the trees, a Christmas sauna together before partaking of more food, including mulled wine, prune-filled, star-shaped pastries and gingerbread cookies.

The May Day holiday (Vappu) is always the first day of May, whatever the day on which it falls. So on the evening of 30 April, there are a lot of festivities. It is, of course, International Labour Day, but in Finnish tradition this festival is about celebrating springtime. A tradition at this time of year is for people to put on their white student caps—the caps that they wore for (school) graduation day. It is quite common for decorations to be put up a day beforehand, even in offices. It's said that Finland suffers the hangover of the year on May Day, as this is a time to 'let your hair down' and have a great deal of fun. This holiday is spent eating and drinking and is definitely a time for partying with friends.

Mid-summer (Juhannus) is of special importance to them. This holiday celebrates the longest day of the year. For those who live in areas of the world where the length of the day differs only slightly during the year, I must emphasise that having 'white nights' is so uplifting for the soul. Even in the southernmost part of Finland, the wee small hours of the morning will be just 90 minutes of twilight. The festivities always take place on the Friday night and Saturday between 20 and 26 June. The Finns leave the towns en masse to spend mid-summer in the countryside. There is usually a mid-summer festival full of music, dancing and food; and a gigantic traditional bonfire is lit.

Independence Day is another bank holiday which falls on 6 December. This is always a sombre and serious day to mark Finland's independence from Russia in 1917. Independence Day is a time when Finns like to eat a festive lunch in a restaurant with relatives and friends. Bakeries will make special blue/white pastries and shops will have blue/white displays. People light candles and put them in their windows, and then they visit cemeteries and light candles there. In the evening of Independence Day, the president of Finland always holds a huge formal party for all the VIPs in Finland. This party is televised and becomes the highlight of the holiday.

New Year (Uudenvuodenaatto) is celebrated like elsewhere in the world. Speeches, fireworks, partying and making New Year resolutions! However, there is a tradition of melting tin in a dipper and pouring it into a bucket of cold water. The resulting form is then interpreted to predict the future.

**Public Holidays in Finland**

- 1 January: New Year
- 6 January: Epiphany
- March/April: Easter including Easter Monday
- 30 April evening: May Day Festivities
- 1 May: May Day
- May: Ascension Day
- May/June: Whit Sunday
- 3rd weekend of June: Midsummer Holidays
- 1 November: All Saints Day
- 6 December: Independence Day
- 24–26 December: Christmas

From Annabel Battersby, an Australian in Finland: 'Since living here for a longer time, I realise that the year is punctuated with traditions and customs, some involving flag raising, eating special foods and decorating your home in various ways. It's very different to Australia where there are no such well-enforced traditions, and I am beginning to really like it. But I will never forget the Finnish silence that greeted my first giggle about the graduation cap....'

Take a look at her wonderful photos and read about her life in Finland: http://annabel-jaakko.blogspot.com/

Flag Raising Days are very common in this northern country. Hardly a month passes without the blue and white flag of Finland being raised to celebrate some Finnish tradition or person. There is an official calendar with the flag days in it and Finnish janitors have clear instructions as to when to hoist the flags and take them down. Finland has 16 flag raising days—six of them official and ten unofficial. On official flag days, government institutions are obliged to fly the flag. Spring is known as the high season for flag-raising which begins with Agricola's Day (the father of the Finnish language, 9 April). Only two of the flag-raising days are public holidays; May Day and Independence Day.

**The Flag-Raising Days (Liputusäivät)**

- 5 February : Runeberg's Day (was a famous poet and writer)
- 28 February: Kalevala's Day (national epic of Finland)
- 9 April: Mikael Agricola's Day (father of the Finnish language)
- 27 April: Veteran's Day
- 1 May: May Day
- 12 May: Snellman's Day (father of the Finnish currency)
- May: Mother's Day
- 20 May: Remembrance Day
- 4 June: Finnish defence forces/military Day
- 23 June: Finnish flag's Day
- 6 July: Eino Leino's Day (a famous Finnish poet and writer)
- 10 October: Aleksis Kivi's Day (was a famous Finnish writer)
- 24 October: United Nation's Day
- 6 November: Swedish Day
- November: Father's Day
- 6 December: Independence Day

Further information regarding Finnish festivities can be found on http://www.festivals.fi or Finland Festivals (09-621 4224) info@mail.festivals.fi.

## SEEING SANTA CLAUS

No book on Finland would be complete without mentioning Santa Claus because Finland is the home of Father Christmas.

The Finnish version of Father Christmas is rather different from the modern day equivalent that we have in the UK and the USA. We tend to depict him as a kind, rounded, jovial, old man (this image was originally designed by a Finn for the Coca-Cola company!) However, in Finland he is depicted as a mischievous elf and is rather peculiar looking. He's certainly dressed in red, but it's more like a Lappish costume than the red and white outfit that we see on Western Christmas cards and in Hollywood movies.

Santa Claus lives in Lapland. I know because I've been to his house. Santa's village is located just outside Rovaniemi, and it is built right on the beginnings of the Arctic Circle. In fact, strung across the village is an electric cable filled with red lights marking the boundary of the Arctic Circle. You can,

A visit to Santa Claus's village is a must. Whilst at the village, you can go on a reindeer safari and snow-mobiling.

therefore, straddle the Arctic Circle with one foot in and one foot out, just as you can straddle the time line in England, at Greenwich.

Santa's village is commercialised in a Finnish sense, which means it is modestly promoted and modestly commercialised in our terms. For those of us who are used to theme parks in America or in well-populated parts of Europe, you will find visiting Santa's village a very gentle and pleasant experience. The gifts in the shops are often handmade goods crafted by the Laps themselves. Their craftwork is quite unique. The designs are colourful and intricate and really something that you will not buy anywhere else on this earth. Whilst in the village, do remember to go to Santa's post office and send all your young relatives and friends an official card from Santa's village. Rovaniemi is the town in Lapland to which Concorde used to fly on its one-day trips to visit Santa. And what a glorious site it was—looking like a huge silver bird hovering a pale-blue wintry sky!

There is some discrepancy as to where Santa Claus actually lives. He has a rival who says he is the real Santa Claus and lives in a town called Korvatunturi, also in Finnish Lapland. Here, too, you will meet Father Christmas, his wife and all of

Santa's helpers. And you should remember to use the post office here as well.

It is probably worthwhile mentioning, while we are on the subject of Santa Claus, that during the months of November and December, while you are flying on Finnair flights, you will get the opportunity to be able to commission Santa Claus to send letters from Santa's village. A couple of years ago, I sent all my step-grandchildren some letters and they were highly delighted, because they did come from abroad and they truly did seem to come from Santa Claus himself.

Now, Santa Claus is quite remarkable. He has an incredible knowledge of foreign languages. Whilst we were queuing up to see Santa Claus, I personally heard him speaking Japanese to some young Japanese visitors, he also spoke French and, of course, English to my own daughter. We had the official Santa photograph taken whilst we were there. Digitally mastered and prepared within seconds, it is of course one of those treasures to keep!

In Finland, you can hire an 'official' Santa Claus or official 'Santa Claus Helper' to come and visit the children on Christmas Eve. These men are called *Tonttu*. They are officially registered and licensed to act as Father Christmas, and there is a set fee for their services. I was surprised to learn that Father Christmas' services are not only required at Christmas time.

My friend, Tonttu Hannu Rosberg, is an official Santa Claus helper. Many families employ the services of *Tonttus* around Christmas-time to visit their homes and deliver presents to their children.

### A Modern-Day Santa Claus Helper

I remember quite well one day early in February. I was flying out from Helsinki airport, north bound, when I saw a gentleman turn up to check in for the plane. He was dressed in a most peculiar outfit. Later on, both he and I shared the same airport taxi. Although his English was not too good, I gathered that he was an official Tonttu. The photograph in this chapter is one that he gave me when I told him I was writing a book and would dearly love to mention him in it. His name is Hannu and he even has his own website! These *Tonttu* are not as quaint and old fashioned as you might believe. Perception is the name of the game. His costume was definitely old fashioned and traditional. The shoes he had on were handmade from reindeer skin and he carried a sort of wooden box tied with string to keep his belongings in. I was quite surprised when I was in the taxi to see the string untied, the box opened and a mobile phone appear. My illusions were shattered. I laughed and it made a very good starting point for beginning our conversation. We both laughed in the end; he because he couldn't believe that I thought he didn't live in an electronic age, and I at my own naivety.

Outside Rovaniemi, there is Santa Park. This is the underground theme world of Santa Claus. When we visited , it had only just been opened a few months. Do not go with the impression that you might be visiting another Disney World. It certainly is not like that. In fact, my impression was that it

The main entrance to Santa Claus's village is also where you can catch the snow-train to Santa Park. When in the village, don't forget to send some letters to your friends and family and have them arrive franked with Santa's official postmark.

was aimed really for young children. At the time, there was not very much to amuse older children or adults. However, it is certainly a very interesting place to visit and it gives you an idea of how the Finns think of Father Christmas. For me, it lacked a certain magic or sparkle. In hindsight, that was probably because I had too great an expectation (a cultural one) and was a little disappointed for my daughter, aged 11. However, we were all decidedly glad we had made the effort to go. I suppose I am used to some sort of 'Hollywood gloss'. The Finns, as I mentioned before, regard Father Christmas as being a mischievous elf and, indeed, Santa Park was very much built on that perception.

Both my husband and I had to smile about the organisation, therein. They are obviously not expecting to be overwhelmed by thousands of visitors at any one time. Indeed, getting on and off the bus at Santa Park was at the same bus stop. The food hall had no clear indication of a queuing system. Retrieving hats and coats at the end of your visit is quite a free-for-all. For the amount of people attending when we visited, the whole thing worked well and was civilised. With larger numbers and more foreign visitors, it could have been

The gift shops in Santa Claus's village were filled with many traditional Lappish goods and handicrafts. There were many unusual gift items. One of my favourite buys is the Lappish doll in traditional costume, which can be bought in varying sizes. Look out for Mother and Father Christmas dolls, as their costumes are a delight, though their faces are very mischievous.

chaos. I really think this reflects the calm, quiet, non-pushy nature of the Finns. They are obviously assuming their visitors will all behave as they do—stick to the rules!

**Contacting Santa**

If you would like to write to him, the address is:
Joulupukki, 96930 Napapiiri, Finland; or go to his website at http://www.santaclaus.posti.fi.

## THINGS TO DO

### Music

Finland has a well-established music culture and has had many gifted classical composers. From an international prospective, Sibelius is synonymous with the musical identity of Finland and dominates this culture. Much of his work was written to glorify his own people and culture, and one of his most famous compositions, *Finlandia*, became a strong expression of Finnish patriotism and pride. Sibelius wrote his music during the time that Finland was a Grand Duchy of Russia and his music was seen as the rallying call to defy the giant oppressor. Today there is a Sibelius Academy in Helsinki, which has an international reputation for turning out many fine young composers, conductors and musicians. There is also a Sibelius Museum and a Sibelius Park.

The true richness of the musical life and traditions of Finland is witnessed through the 13 professional orchestras, 18 semi-professional orchestras and the many ensembles in the country. Helsinki has two Finnish radio symphony orchestras and the Helsinki Philharmonic Orchestra. There are also opera and ballet companies and solo performers, many with international reputations. For a country with such a small population, there is a remarkable number of world-class conductors, composers and performers covering a great range of artistic skills.

Good classical concerts can be heard in many towns during the summer. These are held in churches or in outdoor venues; most are free and are extremely popular. Helsinki has a lively all year round jazz scene. In the rest of the country, the jazz and rock scene takes off during the summer. There are numerous open-air concerts in parks featuring, as they say, 'the best and worst' of Finnish music. The summer festivals attract acts from all over the world. The most famous jazz festivals are held in Pori, Tampere and Espoo in June. Just north of Helsinki in Jarvenpaa, the Puisto Blues Festival is held. The best of the rock festivals can be experienced at Kuusrock in Oulu and Saapasjalkarock in Pihtipudas. Some festivals attract about 25,000 visitors. The Provinssirock Festival in Seinajoki in June has three stages and has attracted such stars as Bob Dylan, Billy Idol and R.E.M. There is little or no drugs problem.

One of the most internationally acclaimed festivals in Finland is the annual dance and music festival held in Kuopio which attracts performers from all over the world. One of the great opera attractions of the year is the Savonlinna opera festival. This is held in a courtyard of a medieval castle, and with world class performers, it is an experience never to be forgotten. Finland also has a wealth of modern operas that have been successfully performed all over the world.

Traditional Finnish folk music blends elements of both Eastern and Western culture. In fact, Karelian-type folk music is a popular alternative to pop and rock. Traditional music features a combination of violin, clarinets, accordions and the Finnish national instrument called a *kantele*.

Music is in the heart and the core of the Finnish people, demonstrated by the diversity of its musicians. There are melancholy tango singers, *jenkka* crooners, swing-time singers, jazz groups, big bands, rock-and-roll and Finnish pop including Jari Sillanpää, Eino Grön and Arja Koriseva. In 2006, Finland won the Eurovision song contest with the group Lordi (looking like a lot of monsters) performing the winning song 'Hard Rock Hallelujah'.

**Jari Sillanpää's Music**

Early spring, I was holding a seminar at a hotel on the outskirts of Helsinki that was about to open for the summer. Whilst there, Jari Sillanpää came to rehearse for a concert, away from the madding crowd. My colleague Timo and I sneaked in to listen and watch. As someone who loves crooners and romantic music, I could listen to Jari gleefully. Of course, at the airport on my way home, I bought his best hits CD. A couple of years later, I was being interviewed on BBC radio about Finland and was asked to bring a record with me. Yes, you've guessed, I took Jari's CD and had it played on British radio during a popular lunch time chat show. Anyone reading this who knows Jari, please tell him that he had a few minutes claim to fame in Britain!

## Dancing

The Finns love to dance, many of them ballroom dance superbly. Every city and town has its dance restaurants where patrons do the waltz, tango, *humppa*, *jenkka* and the foxtrot. These restaurants engage small orchestras that play evergreen tunes. Local hotels have their dance evening too, the most popular evenings for this being Wednesday, Fridays and Saturdays. The mid-week dance is usually advertised as *Naistentanssit*. This is the 'ladies excuse me' dance evening. If a woman asks a man to dance, he should accept her offer graciously. Similarly in a dance restaurant, men should feel free to ask a lady to dance. It is considered good manners to accept the invitation, and you normally have two dances, and then the gentleman will accompany the lady back to her chair.

One of the things not to miss out on during the summer months is a visit to an outdoor stage dance called *Lavatanssit*. This is where local singers and their bands play popular music and people dance. The noisy dance stages seem always to be situated in the middle of nowhere. *Humppa* is extremely popular on these occasions. *Humppa* always looks to be great fun and appears to be a cross between very rowdy ballroom dancing and the hoe-downs held in the mid-west of the USA. The instruments that usually accompany this sort of music are the accordion or violin.

### Tango in Finland

Believe it or not, the tango has been wholeheartedly adopted by the Finnish nation. Every year the tango festival is staged in Seinajoki. It attracts thousands of people to the venue and is televised live to thousands of viewers.

## Sports

You cannot mention the Finns without using the word 'sport' in the same breath. The Finns are fanatical about sports and hero worship their athletes, sports people and fitness. Outdoor activities are still an enjoyable part of the Finnish way of life. As it is so much a part of their lifestyle, this may help to explain why the Finns, for such a small nation, perform particularly well in international athletics and sporting events. The pre-eminence of Finland in motor sports, whether it be formula one, rallying or cross–country motor-racing, is well known and of course their golden boy, Mika Hakkinen, is a world champion.

The Finns as a whole nation walk extremely quickly. In fact, they have a very different gait from anyone else I have seen. They walk as though their upper torso is completely rigid, with just arms and legs swinging at great speed. Nearly everyone walks in this manner. In 1998, the latest craze was something called stick walking which has now caught on in many other countries and is known as 'Nordic pole walking'. This is something akin to cross-country skiing without the skis and without the snow! People go out walking with ski poles that they dig rhythmically into the ground at great

The author (back) and her French colleague (front) on their first terrifying but enjoyable snow-mobiling lesson. The author expected to ride it like a motorbike but was in for a surprise. As a novice, she found it too heavy to steer and her arms ached for days afterwards, but she found it truly thrilling!

speed. This type of walking takes place during the snowless months and is particularly good for your health. It's said to use twice the calories that normal walking uses.

Trekking is a popular pastime in Finland, and there are many wilderness huts and long trails established for visitors. The lake lands are an idyllic area to cruise on old ferry steamers, whilst canoes and kayaks can be rented to explore the river ways. Cycling is also a major pastime in Finland, along with sailing on the lakes or around the large coastal areas of the country. The Finns are never far away from a fishing rod, both in summer and winter. However, if you want to go fishing, you must do so with a permit. There are several different types of permits and these can be acquired from post offices or banks. However, a local permit can be bought from a fishing location by the hour or day.

The Finns are potty about ice hockey—it's their national sport. They are just as keen on this as other nations are on football. The big matches are televised and it seems the whole of the country comes to a standstill when these take place. The high spot of Finland's sporting year is the World

Championships in Ice Hockey, and this is just as much a part of the Finnish Spring as the May Day celebrations. You can tell how involved the Finns are with this sport—they have created small talk around the subject! Football, during the summer months, is a very popular pastime with most towns having their own club playing in the leagues. The success of some Finnish players abroad, Jari Litmanen at Ajax and Barcelona, Jonatan Johansson at Glasgow Rangers and Charlton, and Sami Hyypia at Liverpool, for example, has created an enthusiasm for the game. You will often find some very famous international teams playing friendly matches in many parts of the country, and Finland's first purpose-built football stadium has just been built in Helsinki.

Golf is a sport which is attracting more and more attention. Although the golfing season may appear to be short in terms of other countries, it has to be said that you can play golf 24 hours a day. The Finns are now promoting their country as a golfers' paradise, encouraging people to play golf at midnight. For the fanatics, there is winter golf—played on the frozen lakes with red balls.

During the winter, some of the activities which take place are ice fishing, dog sledding, reindeer safaris, snow mobiling and snow shoeing. Finland offers 35 centres for cross-country skiing and ski-trekking, and there are a few areas in the north of the country—in Lapland—for downhill skiing. Whether it is cross-country or downhill skiing which takes your fancy, most of the trails will be illuminated for the winter duration. Kuopio and Lahti are famous for ski jumping and these areas are where their Olympic participants train.

Sport in Finland is a time-honoured tradition and is ingrained in every child. The Finns are well aware that modern means of transport could easily suppress the instinct for physical exercise and make them lazy. Therefore, they encourage Finnish schools to have a rigorous sport's programme, and every individual takes a personal responsibility to keep themselves fit.

### Cinema

Cinemas can be found in every city and town, all showing the latest releases from an international market. Over 80 per cent of the films showing will be imported from abroad, and these will probably be screened in their original language with Finnish subtitles. The most up-to-date releases are quickly rolling out in even the most out-of-the-way towns. I have managed to see some of the latest blockbusters in Finland before they have arrived in the UK. Films classified with an S are for general audiences, whilst those with a K rating are restricted to those over the age of 16 or 18. The majority of foreign films come from America, then France, followed by Britain and Sweden.

## TRAVEL

Most people travelling to Finland will arrive by plane, arriving at Helsinki International Airport. The first thing that will strike the visitor is that they have arrived at what seems to be a very well-ordered and civilised society. The number one thing on my list of what is great in Finland is the trolleys they have at the airport. These are miniature versions of the shopping trolleys you would find in a supermarket. They are just big enough to take a heavy coat and some hand luggage—excellent! (You will find them just as you exit the aeroplane right next to the gate).

Other passengers to Finland might arrive by boat either from Estonia or Sweden, on mini cruise liners which sail straight into Helsinki harbour located virtually in the middle of the town. Others might arrive by train from St Petersburg or other parts of Russia, and they will find themselves coming into Helsinki station, again in the centre of the town.

## Mosquitoes

From a Finnish reader, Taavi Suorsa: 'I would like to correct one assumption that seems like all the Dutch people have of Finland: The mosquito situation is not nearly as bad as people over here think. People seem to think that at the moment they step out of the plane in Finland, the cloud of mosquitoes is attacking them. This is not true, as we know.'

However you arrive, you will find ready and easily accessible transportation to your next destination. Whether you are able bodied or not, you will find Finland an easy country to get around. Disabled visitors should not feel at all anxious about visiting Finland. In fact, outside of the USA, this is the best country I have ever visited for facilities for disabled people.

Frozen lakes begin to thaw during May and lake systems become a hub of activity. Mini ferries and working boats are the most popular means of transport during the summer months.

There is a superb selection of city and regional maps that are free of charge and obtainable from local tourist offices. There are also maps for waterways and lakes, trekking areas and national parks, and 19 different road maps.

## Visas and Documents

If you are a citizen of the Nordic countries of Denmark, Iceland, Sweden or Norway, you do not need a passport to enter Finland. Citizens of the EU countries need either their national identity card or a passport to enter (except Greece). Other foreign visitors will need a valid passport. You will need a residents' permit for any stay longer than three months except for citizens of the Nordic countries mentioned above. For stays of less than three months duration, most western nationals will not need a visa. It is always best to apply for a resident's permit before you leave home. Work permits are required for all foreigners other than those coming from the EU and EEA. Employment must be secured before applying for a permit. For more information, apply to the Finnish Directorate of Immigration (Tel: (09) 4765-5857, Siltasaarenkatu 12a, 00530 Helsinki; http://www.uvi.fi).

## International and Domestic Flights

Helsinki Airport has once again won the International Airport of the Year. There is a good choice of merchandise for sale in the various shops, including a wonderful selection of Finnish jewellery and Scandinavian glassware. Make sure to get some bear or reindeer meat before going home, what a souvenir! If you are buying gifts for children or want a really unusual present, you can buy Lappish dolls in their traditional dress with their reindeer skin coats and bright coloured hats, or you can buy wonderfully detailed Father Christmas and Mother Christmas. I have to mention to those who are interested; my favourite shoe shop is here at the airport! There are plenty of restaurants and cafes selling good quality food at fairly inexpensive prices compared with other European airports. In the International terminal, there are various lounges for frequent flyers or business class passengers. Everything is close to each other, so you don't waste time walking endlessly around.

**More about Helsinki Airport**

Helsinki Airport is located in Vantaa, about 20 km to the city centre. If you are taking a domestic flight, you are using Terminal 1. International flights leave from Terminal 2. Terminal 2 is actually also called Terminal 3 and 4, depending on which check-in area you enter. But don't worry about going to the wrong place, the airport isn't that big so you will not need many minutes walk to get to the right place.

You can get to the city centre by Finnair airport buses, local buses (No. 615 and 617) or taxis of different companies. A taxi will cost you around € 30.

The Finnair Shuttle Bus runs from 5:00 am to midnight, every 20 minutes during most of the day and every 30 minutes very early in the morning and late at night. It costs only € 4.90 and it'll take you only 25 minutes to get to Helsinki.

The buses depart from right outside the terminal, so there isn't a long walk with your luggage. They stop at the Inter-Continental Hotel and the central rail station where you will find the Finnair City Air Terminal. The buses sometimes make stops along the route to drop off passengers on request.

Bus No. 615 and 615T both leave frequently from platform 10 of the bus station on Rautatientori, right by the central train station. Tickets cost € 3.40 and are purchased from the driver as you enter the bus. Upon arriving at the bus station, you will see clear signs indicating where the buses to the airport leave from. There are even pictures of aeroplanes on the bus stops at the relevant departure points. Buses generally leave every 20 minutes or so during the day and the journey takes 35–40 minutes.

There is no free parking at the airport—10 minutes = € 1.

There is no business class service on domestic flights within Finland, and therefore there is no business class lounge in the domestic terminal. However, there is a lounge for the members of the Finnair frequent flyers club. Unfortunately, many a business class passenger, arriving in

Helsinki and travelling on, has found their way to this lounge and been turned away.

Finland can offer some of the cheapest domestic flights within Europe. The principle domestic carrier is Finnair, and now Blue1, a low-cost airline, has started business. Golden Air will fly internally to a few smaller destinations. They fly to all the big centres in Finland but all flights are routed through Helsinki. This means that it is almost impossible to fly east to west across Finland. You have to go south to Helsinki and then fly on. The smallest aircraft in the fleets are used on routes that have few passengers or for late night journeys with only a handful of customers. Unfortunately, these internal journies will take longer on the small aircrafts rather than the normal jets. However, I do have to say that the Finnair pilots have to be the best in the world at landings! No others like them—so smooth!

Having arrived at your destination airport, there is NEVER a problem travelling on from there to your hotel or place of stay. At the very small airports, you will be asked whether you want a taxi whilst you are on board the aeroplane and a taxi will be booked for you. At larger airports, taxis will be waiting outside; alternatively you can catch either the airport taxi or the Finnair bus. At Helsinki airport, the airport taxi will take you to your destination. When leaving, you can order the airport taxi to come and pick you up. Likewise, at other large airports around the country, airport taxis will be waiting to transport you onwards. Airport taxis differ from normal taxis because they will take up to ten passengers. However in reality there is never normally more than five. The Finnair bus is great value for money and very reliable. You will recognise the coach by the blue and white Finnair logos on the side. The drop-off points are usually the main railway station, the main bus station, the centre of town and probably a few of the hotels. The Finnair bus operates like a regular bus service so you can catch this bus on your return to the airport. It will make the same stops and will collect you probably one hour 15 minutes before the flight takes off.

The airports around the country are small, so there is no need to check in hours before your flight. Generally speaking, half an hour before the flight takes off is usually long enough even if you are catching an international connection. When travelling abroad via Helsinki, you can check your baggage right through to final destination and still check in just a short time before take off.

In all the time I have travelled with Finnair, I haven't suffered much of a problem with lost luggage. Once my luggage didn't turn up in Finland, but arrived a few hours later on the next flight. On another occasion, my luggage was lost three times. Spectacularly it was on the same trip, and my case eventually caught up with me in Dublin 24 hours later. However, I have met two people whose luggage are constantly lost. One person had lost her luggage so many times in one year that she was featured on the BBC's *Watchdog* programme.

If your luggage doesn't turn up on the conveyer belt at your destination airport, this is what you need to do. First of all, go along to the Finnair desk which is usually the check-in desk for outgoing passengers. You will need to report how many pieces of luggage you are missing, and you will be asked to identify a generic type of case from various photographs. If you arrive in the middle of the day, you will probably find that your suitcase will follow you on the next plane. Therefore, within about three hours, you will have it. However, if you arrive last thing at night, you should ask them to give you an overnight bag. This bag contains all the essentials: ladies' and gentlemen's toiletries, and some clean underwear. If your luggage hasn't turned up by the next day, you can claim compensation by writing to Finnair.

* Customer care! Be warned. None of this information will be given to you. You need to know that you can have the overnight bag, and that it is your right to claim compensation for a bag that has been lost for more than a few hours.

If your luggage is broken during transit, report this at the Finnair desk on your arrival. There will be some paperwork for the airline to fill in. However, you will be given a letter or a voucher to go to a local luggage shop to pick yourself a new case. All you need do is choose a new case and they will swap it over without any fuss whatsoever.

## HOTELS AND LODGINGS

It is difficult to make comparisons of Finnish hotels with international star ratings. Star ratings have to be taken into context and what is one country's 4-star may be another country's 3-star. Therefore, the comments that are made in the next few lines are very subjective and are my opinion, and not necessarily the 'official line' printed elsewhere. My observations are biased towards comparing star ratings within the UK and travelling within Europe.

There are luxury hotels, but they are few. In Helsinki, the most luxurious is probably Hotel Kamp, opened originally in 1887 to bring a taste of great European cities to Helsinki; it has recently had a faithful restoration. Most hotels are geared towards catering for business people and belong to a few national chains of hotels: Scandic, Sokos and Cumulus. I would tend to put these into a lower 4-star bracket. Generally speaking, these will have a swimming pool and saunas, restaurants and nightclubs (which may well be the most popular in the vicinity). Do be warned that Finnish hotel swimming pools are freezing! Don't do as I did on my first visit and plunge into the pool expecting to have a nice leisurely swim. The swimming pools are there for people to plunge into straight from the sauna to cool themselves down. Of course, the other reason for their existence is to amuse the Finns when foreigners like me jump in and scream from the shock!

There is a group of independently owned hotels called the Finlandia Group. In reality, these are equivalent to 2/3-star accommodation elsewhere. Sometimes, first impressions may not be too good, but do not under any circumstances let this put you off. In my experience, the bedrooms are always more than adequate, and of course being Finnish, everything is immaculately clean. These hotels are modestly priced, and whilst they may not have many public facilities, they will have a restaurant. My friend Leena owns The Amado Hotel in Pori, a member of this Finlandia group, and she stakes the reputation of her hotel on the food she serves. Her restaurant has been voted the best restaurant in town three years running and the National Sales Representatives Association

Towards the end of the summer, hotels rates are reduced quite heavily. This also applies to the weekends, Friday night through to Sunday.

has just awarded the hotel 'The Best Value for Money in Finland' accolade.

Breakfast in Finland is always a buffet consisting of cheese, ham, boiled eggs, pickled fish, fresh salad vegetables, dried fruit and nuts, cereal, oats and porridge. Quite often, there is a hot choice which will be a Finnish version of scrambled egg and either meatballs or tiny cocktail-sized frankfurters. Finnish bread is tasty and of multiple variety and the butter is delicious. Being Finland, there is always a large dish of natural yoghurt around and hot porridge.

**A Word about Curtains...**

Because Finnish buildings are triple glazed, there is no need to have thick curtains at the windows to stop heat loss such as in the UK. Also, because Finland hasn't been used to having many foreigners, there has been no custom of having thick curtains to shut out the light during the summer (the Finns are used to this). It is still extremely common to go into a hotel bedroom and find very thin cotton curtains hanging at the window. Nowadays, Helsinki hotels and the better hotels have recognised the need to provide more sumptuous and plush soft-furnishings. These hotels hang heavy curtains and behind them they have metallic drapes or blinds, such as they have in Spain, to create total darkness.

When checking into a hotel, you will always be asked whether you want a smoking or non-smoking room. The Finns are very fastidious about this. If you want a bath in your hotel room, you will have to request it. All rooms have showers, but very few have baths. A carpet in a hotel bedroom is a real rarity, so it is advisable to take slippers with you to wear. From experience, I would say that the temperature in Finnish hotel bedrooms is not as high as you might imagine and it is easy to get cold just sitting around. The secret of being warm in Finland is not to allow yourself to get cold. The quilts on the bed are extremely lightweight and at first do not seem at all cosy or warm. However, once you and the bed have warmed up, you'll be as warm as toast. I always take a hot water bottle with me.

Although I have first-hand experience of all sorts of hotels throughout Finland, I have no experience of either the hostels or guesthouses. However, perhaps the following information will provide guidelines for anyone wishing to stay at these establishments. The Finnish youth hostel associations own the majority of hostels. You will be required to bring your own sheets and pillowcases, but there are occasions to rent them if you haven't got any. Quite often, there are special family size rooms that can be rented. Breakfast will not be included in the price of the room. Guesthouses should always be inspected before you decide to stay. These tend to be found in town centres and near train stations. If you are in one of Finland's old villages, you might find that the guesthouse is an old wooden house.

If you are visiting Finland during the summer, consider renting a Finnish summer cottage. This will be the true way to experience Finland. A summer cottage will normally be located near a lake and comes supplied with the compulsory rowing boat and a sauna. Apart from that, many rental cottages come fully equipped with cooking utensils, a fridge, television and telephone. You will have to check carefully because not all of them will have electricity and running

Traditional Lappish dwellings are either log cabins or tents made from reindeer skins. They are sturdy and heated by a central open fire.

water. If you fancy experiencing the tranquillity of the countryside, these summer cottages can be booked through regional tourist offices.

Other possibilities are to stay at farmhouses, rented accommodation or even in wilderness huts while out trekking. Further information about these can be obtained from regional tourist offices.

## THE REGIONS

### Lapland

Lapland is the ancestral home of the Sami people. This is the land of the midnight sun. The area covers about one-third of the total land mass of Finland and almost all of it lies within the Arctic Circle. There are large expanses of tundra, rounded hills, silent lakes, flowing rivers and some isolated birch trees. Summers are short and from October to May, snow covers the ground. Reindeer are semi-domesticated and roam freely across the land. Reindeer farming has been the traditional livelihood of the Sami. However, other Sami are now involved within the tourist or forestry industry. I am told that one of the typical delicacies/traditions of the region is buying a coffee at a bar, along with a couple of hard boiled eggs.

Reindeer farming is still a means to make a living for many Sami (Lapps). Semi-domesticated animals, the reindeer are allowed to roam freely over vast acres of tundra.

Finland is rich in natural beauty, as seen in this picture of Lapland on a calm May day.

## Karelia

Northern Karelia shares a border with Russia. As a consequence of World War II, the southern part of Karelia was ceded to the Soviets. Thus, Karelia is regarded as a symbol for national patriotism. The Orthodox Monastery of Valamo, which was founded 800 years ago on an island in Lake Ladoga, was transferred to within the Finnish territory of Karelia where it now stands. If Lapland is the land of the midnight sun, then Karelia is the land of song. The musical instrument *kantele* derives from this region. The capital of the region is Joensuu. Nearby, in the Kuusamo area is the beautiful National Park of Oulanka with Koli Hill as its highest peak.

## The Lake District

The main features of the central part of Finland are the thick, verdant forests and the thousands of lakes which make this part of the world unique. There are a variety and an abundance of waterways, rapids and streams, where one can go canoeing, rafting, rapid-shooting and sailing. Some of the most stunning national parks are located in this region.

Savonlinna has the beautiful Castle of Olavinlinna dating from 1475 where one of the most famous of Finland's summer events is held—the Savonlinna Opera Festival. Kuopio is an important commercial town in this area and is located in some spectacular wooded lakeland scenery. This can be enjoyed best on an evening cruise on a restaurant boat. The best view of the town can be seen from the top of the revolving tower on Puijo Hill, which is open as a restaurant during the summer months (read more below under Kuopio).

## Southern Finland

This is the most populated area of the country. There are many historical reminders of this area's past and its rich cultural diversity. Here you will find castles, fortresses, churches and historical cities, including Turku, the original capital of Finland (read more below under Turku). The cathedral in Turku is the country's only medieval cathedral. It

The restaurant at the top of the revolving tower on Puijo Hill in Kuopio offers fantastic views of the surrounding countryside, even at 11:00 pm.

is a national shrine which has been rebuilt many times after fires and enemy attacks, and has had great significance in the formation of a Finnish identity. Rauma, a 500-year-old village near Pori, is a world heritage site. The countryside is very gentle in this part of the country.

## THE TOWNS

### Helsinki

The capital of Finland is Helsinki and it is sometimes referred to as the White Capital of the Baltic and the Daughter of the Baltic Sea. It is surrounded by sea and green forests and is set on a rocky promontory. It is not a great sprawling city as other capitals of the world. There are around one million inhabitants. Along with Espoo and Vantaa, Helsinki makes up the Greater Helsinki Area.

In 1812, Helsinki succeeded Turku as the capital of Finland, when Tsar Alexander decided to move the capital nearer to St. Petersburg and thus further from Sweden. The city burnt down in 1808 and destroyed virtually all the important public buildings. Immediate reconstruction took place, the results of which are the buildings you see today in the centre of the town. There are many new and modern buildings which add to Helsinki's rich variety of interesting architecture.

The cathedral dominates the quayside in Helsinki. Sailing boats are a common sight here, and one has even been converted into a restaurant serving delicious Finnish food.

There are plenty of museums to visit, most notably the Museum of Modern Art (Kiasma). There are some magnificent churches including one carved from rock (Temppeliaukion) and the beautiful Lutheran Cathedral. Parks abound. There is the Helsinki Zoo and the Suomenlinna Sea Fortress to visit just off the coast of Helsinki. The Opera House, the National Theatre and Finlandia Hall all draw many visitors to their performances.

The first day of May is a great time to visit Helsinki. The May Day celebrations will be in full swing. May Day is actually a two-day event. The partying starts the night before at 6:00 pm when students ceremonially place a white student cap on the Havis Amanda statue on the edge of the Market Square. The rest of the evening is then spent wandering the town and joining in with the festivities. The next morning, May Day, it is essential

From a Finnish reader, Hannu Sivonen: 'When my wife and I talk to foreigners from faraway countries who plan to come to Finland in the summer, we suggest that they take a plane to Stockholm, see around them there, take a boat for Helsinki and watch the marvellous Stockholm Archipelago from the top of the ship. Then we also recommend to them, as extended sights of Helsinki, to visit Tallinn and St. Petersburg. So all these cities, Stockholm, Tallinn and St. Petersburg can be viewed as sights of Helsinki.'

The author recommends that you take the ferry from Helsinki to the Island of Suomenlinna. Declared a UNESCO World Heritage Site since 1991, Suomenlinna is an artisan's refuge and houses more than five museums.

to be at the mass picnic in Kaivopuisto Park. Arrive by 10:00 am at the latest. Here you will be greeted by the most extraordinary sight. The park will be filled to the brim with happy, partying picnickers wearing white student caps. May Day has gradually evolved from a working class celebration into a spring festival for all people. Whatever the weather, the Finns will be outside in the park enjoying themselves—for this is their first day of Spring.

In January and February, a huge church made completely of snow will stand on Senate Square. Built every year, this is a major attraction.

## Turku

Turku has a cultural identity as Finland's historical centre as it was the largest city in the country for a very long time. In 2011, it will be the European Capital of Culture.

- Turku Castle is an impressive grey stone castle dating back to 1280s. It is the largest surviving medieval building in Finland, and one of the largest surviving medieval castles in Scandinavia. The castle was the centre of the historical province of Finland Proper, and the administrative centre of all of Finland. Its strong walls and dungeons also served as the state prison for centuries. The castle's heyday was in the mid-16th century during the reign of Duke John of Finland and Katarina Jagellonica. The castle is Finland's most visited museum.

- Luostarinmäki Handicrafts Musueum is an outdoor museum with over 30 pre-industrialsied workshops offering information and demonstrations of craft skills from 200 years ago. During the summer season, the museum's workshops have craftspeople working there every day. The museum's shops, postal office and cafeteria serve customers round the year. The highlights of the year are the 'Handicrafts Days' in August. It is the only part of Turku that survived the Great Fire of 1827.
- The Christmas City: In 1996, the Turku City Board made the decision to declare Turku the Christmas City of Finland. It is a string of events taking place over a six-week period. It begins on the first day of Advent and lasts until the day of St. Knut on 13 January. Over 100 event producers participate in planning and executing a total of approximately 400 Christmas City events.
- Moomin World is the theme park dedicated to the children's Moomin characters created by Tove Jansson. Located in nearby Naantali, on the island of Kailo, the blueberry-coloured Moomin House is the main attraction. Tourists are allowed to visit freely all the five storeys. Hemulen's yellow house is situated next door to the Moomin House. It is also possible to see Moominmama's Doughnut Factory, Fire Station, Pancake Factory, Snufkin's Camp, Moominpappa's boat etc. in Moomin World. Visitors may also meet Moomin characters there or the Witch in her cottage.
- The Sibelius Museum contains exhibits relating to the great composer, Jean Sibelius, and houses hundreds of musical instruments from all over the world. Live concerts are a regular feature of this museum of music.
- 'Ett Hem' Museum. In their will, Alfred and Hélène Jacobsson donated their home as a museum. They owned a two-storey house that was designed by Carl Ludwig Engel. It is a fine example of upper class life in Turku at the turn of the 19th century.

## Tampere

Compact and lively, Tampere sits between two lakes joined by rapids and is renowned for its fresh, innovative cuisine, quirky museums and some of Europe's most interesting conversions of industrial buildings.

- Tampere's Cathedral: The grey granite exterior was completed in 1907 and is one of the best examples of Romantic architecture in Finland. The frescoes of the Resurrection and the Garland of Life (depicting 12 naked boys), once considered controversial, are now regarded as masterpieces.
- Pispala is a very colourful and unique housing district with small wooden houses built very close to each other. It was founded in the late 19th century as a neighbourhood on a hillside. The area is now protected so that its unique character will be preserved for future generations. Pispala is no longer a workers' district but more famous for its artists, authors and musicians. The plots are understandably very expensive here because of the magnificent views over lakes Nasijarvi and Pyhajarvi.
- Särkänniemi Adventure Park has seven superb sites, the only one of its kind in Finland. This family destination offers the following attractions: Rides, Aquarium, Children´s Zoo, Dolphinarium, Planetarium, Näsinneula Observation Tower (tallest in Finland) and Sara Hilden´s art museum. It is open all year round—Rides and Children's Zoo are open only in summer.
- Vapriiki Musuem Centre is housed in what used to be the engineering works of Tampella Ltd, the old factory area. It exhibits 350,000 items from modern art and technology to handicrafts and nature.
- The Spy Museum: The history of spying and present-day spying as well as famous spies and spying equipment—don't miss its collection of lethal umbrellas!
- The Excursion: A three-hour boat trip with Finnish Silverline passes tree-lined shores and pretty lakeside homes before reaching Lempäälä Lock, 12 miles north. A short walk from here is Villa Hakkari Manor Restaurant, a 200-year-old wooden house in which the young but

skilled chef prepares excellent local dishes. In the grounds are half a dozen museums, including one dedicated to hairdressing, which features one of Wella's first perming devices. From Lempäälä, catch bus 71 back to Tampere.

- Tampere Film Festival takes place in the middle of March each year and outdoor concerts abound in the summer months.
- Viikinsaari is a summer recreation island for the whole family, only 20-minute boat trip away from the city centre. Boats leave on the hour at the Laukontori quay. The western part of the island is a charming nature reserve, and various activities and events take place throughout the summer in the eastern part. Find playgrounds, swimming shores, gaming fields, summer theatre, dance pavilion, small boats harbour and public campfire sites amongst many other fascinating objects of interest. You can borrow petanque, croquet, badminton, dart, football and volleyball.

## Kuopio

Kuopio is located in the province of Eastern Finland and is surrounded by beautiful lakes and forests. A charming and lively place, there is lots to see and do. It's a well-known venue for winter sports enthusiasts.

- Puijo Hill and Tower: A vast panorama of an endless mosaic of blue lakes and green islands that can be seen from the Puijo Tower. It is a spectacle not to be missed by anybody visiting Kuopio. The tower, situated about 1.5 km from the city centre, has a revolving panoramic restaurant that serves local specialities. The tower and the hostel at the foot of it are surrounded by a unique primeval forest.
- Puijo Sports Centre: Especially well-known as a venue for winter sports events, including cross-country skiing, ski jumping and downhill skiing. Top international ski jumpers train and compete at Puijo, and top-class cross-country ski events also take place at Puijo each year. The centre has two downhill slopes, one for experienced and one for beginner skiers. The services in the area include equipment hire, a ski school and a café.

The daily outdoor market in the Kuopio town square is a riot of colours in summer. The stalls sell summer-flowering plants which, once planted, grow quickly.

- The Orthodox Church Museum: Most of the exhibits, which feature gold and silver objects, lavishly embroidered church cloths and other valuable icons, are from the monasteries and congregations of Karelia—a region in south-east Finland that was partially ceded to the Soviet Union in connection with World War II.
- The Old Kuopio Museum: Consists of 11 old wooden houses which form an enclosed block. The oldest buildings date back to the 18th century and the most recent to the end of the 19th century. The interiors show homes and workshops of different kinds of families from 19th century to the 1930s. There is a pharmacy museum in the block and a café for refreshments. There is also a display of photos of old Kuopio.
- Kuopio Dance Festival: The oldest and longest-running dance festival in Finland. As well as several première performances, the festival hosts 30–40 dance courses and seminars for dance professionals, enthusiasts and beginners, as well as a variety of events on the Market Square, a Festival Club and many other fringe events. First-rate performances. Lots of participation from the audiences.

- Nature/Bird Watching and Hiking: The Kuopio area is ideal for walking, hiking, moderate climbing, boating and generally being out in the peace and quiet of the surrounding countryside. Take a picnic. An ornithologist's dream, there are many rare species to be spotted.

# THE LANGUAGE AND THE LITERATURE

CHAPTER 8

'Every country has its way of saying things.
The importance is that which lies behind people's words.'
—Freya Stark, *The Journey's Echo*

ANOTHER ONE OF THE FASCINATING CONTRADICTIONS you encounter in Finland concerns its language. As previously mentioned, Finland has two official languages: Swedish, which is spoken by about 6 per cent of the population and whose presence came about through Swedish supremacy over 700 years, and Finnish. Yet, Finnish is both old and new. As a spoken language, Finnish has existed for years and was thought of as the language of the common people. It was only in the Middle Ages that Finnish was written down, when Mikael Agricola (1510–1557) created the first Finnish written alphabet. Hundreds of years passed before Finnish was elevated to the status of a true, written, cultural and official language. This was in 1863. Until then, Finnish folklore was an oral tradition and early literature was written in Swedish, with more scholarly work written in Latin. In modern times, the Finns have found knowing foreign languages essential to their economic well-being. Thus, the vast majority of Finns use and understand English in their business transactions (the author's experience claims 98 per cent of her contacts) and many speak German and Russian.

## THE LANGUAGE

The early inhabitants of Finland were thought to come from the Ural mountains in Russia and they brought with them a language which belongs to the Finno-Ugarian group of languages, part of the Uralian family of languages. Other related languages in this family are Estonian, Hungarian, Lapp and several lesser Russian languages spoken by minority groups. These languages have been around for thousands of years. Finnish was established in the geographical region of Finland around 3,000 BC. While Hungarian and Finnish are thought to be related, they have developed separately over the last 6,000 years, and are now quite dissimilar.

**Rugs and Worms**

A foreigner in Finland, Mato: 'When pronouncing Finnish, I have trouble differentiating between a single letter and a double, such as *matto* (rug) and *mato* (worm). The worst moment was at a party with some friends and somebody asked me what I enjoyed about Finland, to which I replied, in Finnish, "I love to watch people beat their worm!" The whole room fell about with laughter and *mato* has now become my nickname.'

Today Finnish has numerous word loans borrowed from its many neighbours which demonstrates millennia of contact and interaction between its peoples. An Indo-European influence has been gained through Baltic, Germanic and Slavic languages. More Finno-Ugarian influence was borrowed through Estonian and the other Baltic-Finnic languages of Karelian, Lude, Vepsian, Vote and Livonian. However, modern day influence has come especially from Swedish, with Germanic and Scandinavian languages making a contribution.

Although Finnish may have many word loans borrowed from other languages, its ability to absorb these into the language in a unique Finnish way makes them almost unrecognisable as 'foreign' words. Coffee, for example, has become *kahvi* and bacon is *pekoni*. The language is still being consciously developed and due to a flexibility within the language that allows you to 'glue' words together (Finnish

I was amazed when I first heard Finnish spoken all around me. The image I conjured up was of Italian. The language sounded so melodic, so soft and so pretty. Others have said it sounds like Welsh or Polynesian. It seemed as though every word ended in 'i' or a vowel, which gave the impression of people singing. In fact, within the grammatical structure of the language, there is a rule concerning vowel harmony, thus distortion does not appear. Some say its sounds like a symphony. The most common sound in Finnish is the vowel 'a' and the least common is the 'o'.

Spelling tests are unknown for Finnish schoolchildren. As every letter in a word is pronounced, they know exactly how a word is spelt from how it is said.

is an agglutinative language), international words are kept to a minimum. Whilst television is *televisio* in Finnish, computer is *tietokone* (knowledge machine) and telephone is *puhelin* (to do with speech).

The language is phonetic, where every letter in a word is pronounced. Any adopted words from a different language will be adapted to fit into the Finnish phonetic system. Vowel harmony can also affect some grammatical structures. So that pronunciation is clear, Finnish uses double letters as a distinctive feature. Thus, all eight Finnish vowels *a*, *e*, *i*, *o*, *u*, *ä*, *ö*, *y* and many consonants may appear in writing with two letters to denote a long sound and one letter for a short sound. An example of this is *kukka*, meaning flower, and *kuka*, meaning who.

Finnish has a fearsome reputation for being impossible to learn as an adult foreigner. However, I am informed that Finnish is very logical. It is not difficult, just different. Personally, I don't agree with this statement! I struggled with German and its four cases, others find Latin difficult with its six cases, so Finnish with 15 cases has to be as near

impossible as you can get! To demonstrate, Finnish has a rich system of word flexion which adds suffixes, pre-positions and post-positions to the root of the word. Thus, just learning and recognising basic vocabulary becomes exceedingly difficult as so many additions are made to the original form. These additions are used to show grammatical relationships and can express time, place, ownership, object, manner, etc. Finnish is, therefore, thought of as a synthetic language because it can use suffixes to express grammatical relationships and derive new words.

One word in Finnish, *talossanikin*, is translated in English by 'in my house, too'.

| | |
|---|---|
| *-ssa* | corresponds to the English preposition 'in' or 'on' |
| *-ni* | here means 'my' |
| *-kin* | corresponds to the English word 'too' |
| *-lla* | on or at |
| *-lle* | to |
| *asema* | station |
| *asemalla* | at the station |
| *kaupa* | shop |
| *kaupalle* | to the shop |

The length of Finnish words can be unbelievably long and usually needs a good few English words to translate: *kirjoitettuasi* when translated means after you had written. Because each noun or verb has so many additions showing its grammatical relationship, word order in Finnish is far less important than in English: Peter hates John means something different from John hates Peter. However in Finnish, *Pekka vihaa Jussia* (Pekka hates Jussi) can also be written *Jussia Pekka vihaa* because the direct object is apparent and it is quite clear that Jussi is the object of the hatred.

**He or She?**

Mark Reedman: I first moved to Finland back in 1998 and knew nothing about Finnish names. Finns don't have the concept of 'he or she' and often they mix these up when speaking English. I attended my first ever meeting and I was told "Jukka would meet me after the meeting. She will help me with orientation". I waited for a girl called Jukka to come and join me when this guy walks in and starts talking to me for over an hour! It also took me a while to know which were girls' and which were boys' names.

There are many features in the language that still show its Uralian origin, for example the absence of gender. The same Finnish pronoun *han* means both he and she. Often you will find that Finns get muddled, using those pronouns interchangeably when speaking English, so you have to listen carefully for a name to work out whether they are speaking about a man or a woman! Also, Finnish does not have the definite and indefinite articles, 'the' and 'a' in English. There is no equivalent of the verb 'to have' and no direct counterpart of the passive verb forms of Indo-European languages. The passive form exists and is used commonly, but it is formed using endings on words. Additionally, in order to express negation, the Finns use a word which corresponds to the English word 'not,' but this has to behave as a verb and changes according to the person. Questions can be posed by adding the suffix *-ko* after a verb.

From a Finnish reader, Hannu Sivonen: 'The passive form in Finnish is made using word endings as any other grammatical forms, but it definitely has the same meaning as in any Indo-European language. The passive form is even used more than in other languages, because Finns don't want to stand out from a group. So they prefer to say or write: "so and so was done..." instead of "I did so and so..". I find this funny sometimes.'

Finnish is said to be a very conservative language because it is slow to change and many borrowed words still have their original root. For example, the Finnish word *kuningas* meaning 'king' still has the same word as its root. It was borrowed from the Germanic languages and in other languages has changed its form quite radically through the years; king in English, *kung* in Swedish, *könig* in German.

## LEARNING THE LANGUAGE

Finnish is a language that you do not just 'pick up'! It seemed to take me forever to remember even everyday words such as *kiitos* (thank you), *kylla* (yes) and *hyvää huomenta* (good morning). As foreigners, our problem is that we have no hook on which to hang even simple information—nothing relative or similar to combine new knowledge with old. My experience of learning languages has been confined to European languages, but there is nothing in them to help me master even a modicum of Finnish. I've had two short bursts at learning Finnish and I can say that it is both challenging and fascinating. A dedicated linguist will be entranced. So, for anyone wanting to learn the language—best of luck!

Roman Schatz describes Finnish as beautiful and practical, like Lego bricks, 1,000 pieces all fitting together. Every word and piece means so much. It expresses very subtle differences that other languages can't.

However, a consistent and disciplined effort will let you achieve huge results, but dipping in and out of learning it will leave you none the wiser. The logic and the process of the language structure have been likened to mathematics, and studying Finnish can be seen as a similar challenge. I would like to thank my colleague Timo for his clear and uncomplicated explanations of his language, though after three years, I think he is almost giving up on me. A more in depth overview of the language can be found on http://www.virtual.finland.fi and http://www.hut.fi, whom I must thank for giving me the overall framework and the examples written above. Below is a summary of Richard Lewis' excellent chapter 'The Unique Finnish Language' from his book *Finland, Cultural Lone Wolf* (2005, pp 43–52):

The rules/structures of Finnish are as follow:

- No gender: nouns are not she/he/it as in Indo-European languages. There is one word for he and she—*hän*.
- No definite or indefinite article: *talo* means 'house', 'a house' and 'the house'.
- Stress on the first syllable of all words: Hélsinki, Róvaniemi.
- Large number of vowels (8): - *a, e, i, o, u, ä, ö, y*

- Few consonants: 13 of them in a 21-letter alphabet. *B*, *c*, *f*, *q*, *w* and *z* do not appear unless in foreign loaned words.
- No verb 'to have': use 'be' instead. The possessor is expressed by a dative or locative case e.g:

| | |
|---|---|
| *isä* | father |
| *on* | is |
| *talo* | house |
| *isällä on talo* | father has a house (literally 'to father is a house') |

- No prepositions: modern Finnish has developed some prepositions (e.g. *ilman* : without) but these are mostly due to a Germanic influence on the language. There is a declension system which negates the need for prepositions:

| | |
|---|---|
| *talo* | house |
| *talotta* | without a house |
| *talossa* | in the house |
| *talon* | to the house |
| *talosta* | from the house |

- Compound nouns: You can join two, three or more words together in modern Finnish; for example:

| | |
|---|---|
| *talo* | house |
| *ryhmä* | group |
| *taloryhmä* | group of houses |

| | |
|---|---|
| *sanoma* | word |
| *lehti* | leaf (page) |
| *toimisto* | place of activity |
| *sanomalehtitoimist* | press office |

- Conjugation: Finnish conjugates in a manner similar to Latin-based languages:

| | |
|---|---|
| *ostan* | I buy |
| *ostat* | you (familiar) buy |
| *hän ostaa* | s/he buys |
| *ostamme* | we buy |
| *ostatte* | you (formal) buy |
| *he ostavat* | they buy |

- Changeable negative markers: the Finnish equivalent of saying 'not' is much more complex than in English. The negative marker, derives from 'ei' meaning 'no', but changes and takes the person ending:

| | |
|---|---|
| *puhun* | I speak |
| *en puhu* | I don't speak |
| *puhut* | you speak |
| *et puhu* | you don't speak |
| *hän puhuu* | he speaks |
| *hän ei puhu* | he doesn't speak |
| *puhumme* | we speak |
| *emme puhu* | we don't speak |
| *puhutte* | you speak |
| *ette puhu* | you don't speak |
| *he puhuvat* | they speak |
| *he eivät puhu* | they don't speak |

- Interrogatives: questions are easily formed by adding ko and kö to words:

| | |
|---|---|
| *Tulet* | You are coming |
| *Tuletko?* | Are you coming? |

| | |
|---|---|
| *Menen* | I am going |
| *Menenkö?* | Am I going? |
| *Menet keskustaan* | You go to the city centre |
| *Menetkö keskustaan* | Do you go to the city centre? |

## THE LITERATURE

Until the 16th century, Finnish was a language rich in a folklore of songs and poetry handed down through oral tradition from generation to generation. It had no written form until Mikael Agricola began to construct a Finnish alphabet. As Bishop of Turku, he researched the old Finnish gods as a means to further the cause of Lutheranism and so began the research of documenting the folklore in a Finnish written form. The Bishop of Porvoo, Daniel Juslenius (1676–1752), is known as the first of many 18th century scholars to research Finnish culture, people and language. This was at a time when Sweden was a great power and dominated the political structure in Finland. His work was always in praise of the Finnish people. The language, cultural traditions and the feeling of a distinct national identity owed much to the survival of their oral traditions which had been passed on for centuries by a people with no written language, telling tales of the supernatural and legendary characters. Juslenius used folk song texts as proof of an ancient Finnish civilisation and his work drew patriotic appreciation from many scholars who followed in his footsteps.

> 'The Finns are a nation of tough guys and gals… It's only logical that they also like strong language. In most cultures swearing is considered something you shouldn't do. In Finland it is an essential part of effective communication. If you really want to verbally interact successfully with Finns, you have to learn to enhance your lingo with those special little words that add emotion, depth, and meaning to your message.'
>
> —Roman Schatz (*From Finland With Love*, 2006)

The first detailed account of Finnish poetry, *De Poesi Fennica*, was written in 1778 by Porthan. His approach was to compare and look for variants of the same song. This work was to lay the foundations of Finland's most significant literary masterpiece, *The Kalevala*, by Lonnrot (1835). Although Porthan was interested in history and folklore, he did not write about Finland as a 'nation'. However, nationalistic ideas were beginning to spread through scholarly circles in Finland and these were given voice through a literary association set up by Porthan, known as the Aurora Society. Promotion of the Finnish language and culture gave expression to their patriotic ideals. Sixty years after his death, Porthan was recognised as a national hero and a statue of him was erected in Turku.

In 1809, Finland was ceded to Russia after 700 years of Swedish domination, and Alexander I granted Finland the status of an autonomous Grand Duchy of Russia. It was during this period that the awakening of the Finnish Nationalist Movement came about. Research into the rich and authentic folk culture which was distinctly Finnish gave inspiration for the movement of national independence. Folklore was to play a significant role in the development of a national identity. The period from early to mid-1800s is known as the age of Turku Romanticism. Many scholars from the university collected and published folklore material, but it was one scholar in particular, Elais Lonnrot, who was to set the Finnish world on fire. With a grant of 100 rubles from the newly formed *Suomalaisen Kirjallisuuden Seura* (Finnish Literary Society), Lonnrot travelled to Russian Karelia to collect folk poetry. He made several field trips around the Finnish-Russian border and in a letter written in 1834 wrote that: 'a desire to organise and unify them [folk poems] awoke in me, to extract from Finnish mythology something corresponding to the Icelandic Edda.'

During his fifth field trip, Lonnrot met up with a renowned singer who was then aged 65. The singer had learned his songs as a child from his father and had an extensive repertoire. In two days, the singer sang over 4,000 lines of poetry to Lonnrot, which he captured as the vehicle to narrate his future *Kalevala*.

**More on the Kalevala**

The *Kalevala* has been translated into 40 languages. Kalevala Day is on 28 February. The national epic of Finland starts with the whole world being created. The main character is the god of the seas with a mighty voice called Väinämöinen, who sets out on a journey and has several mishaps. These include having his horse shot from under him by the wicked shaman, a young chap called Joukahainen. He challenges the older man to a singing contest and Väinämöinen literally gets sung into a swamp. As he is about to drown, young Joukahainen thinks up an idea to save his life. Thus, he promises his sweet sister Aino to Väinämöinen, who accepts the offer. However, Aino drowns herself rather than having to be with the old man. Väinämöinen also gets swept out to sea by a tempest, is rescued by an eagle, and eventually reaches land where he is shown hospitality by its rulers, Louhi, the Mistress of Pohjola.

In the evolution of the Finnish National Movement, the most important literary event was the publication of Elais Lonnrot's *Kalevala* in 1835. This was a compilation of the Finnish folk poetry he had researched and which he transformed into a national epic. With its publication, the status of the Finnish language and of Finnish literature heightened. The positive response to the *Kalevala* enabled Lonnrot to expand his work through collections made available to him by other scholars, and in 1849, a new edition known as the 'new' *Kalevala* was published.

'I am driven by my longing,
And my understanding urges
That I should commence my singing,
And begin my recitation.
I will sing the people's legends,
And the ballads of the nation.
To my mouth the words are flowing,
And the words are gently falling,
Quickly as my tongue can shape them,
And between my teeth emerging.'
(Kalevala Poem 1, opening lines 1–10, translation Kirby)

Towards the end of the 1800s, the study of Finnish folklore and Finnish culture assumed great importance. It gave the Finns a self-awareness which eventually made it possible to build a political movement and was instrumental in the process of nation-building.

In terms of modern day literature, Aleksis Kivi is seen to be the founder. He penned a book called *The Seven Brothers* about seven brothers who try to escape education and civilisation in favour of the forest. *The Egyptian*, published in 1945, is a world-class bestseller from the author Mika Waltari. His book depicts the ancient Egypt of the Pharaohs and contains so much detail that, to this day, it is still regarded as a masterpiece. (He never visited Egypt in his life!)

The most widely translated Finnish author is Arto Paasilinna. He writes picaresque novels which are especially popular in France. The titles of his books include *The Year of the Rabbit*, *The Howling Miller*, *The Forest of the Hanged Foxes*, *Charming Mass Suicide* and *The Sweet Old Lady who Cooks Poison*. The author Tove Jansson is known all over the world for her books about the Moomin Family. The popularity of the Moomin characters has resulted in them appearing in over 120 magazines and newspapers in 40 countries, in children's books and comic strips, and then in a 78-part Japanese television series.

## FINNISH FOLKLORE

In Finnish folklore, the gods were natural phenomena. The gods were seen as Nature herself, respected by the people who in return received respect from the gods. Tapio was the god of forests, Ahti ruled the lakes and waterways, and the oldest of them all was Ilmarinen the blacksmith who is said to be older than the skies. He was born at night and by early morning, he was already a fully-skilled blacksmith. As the world was completely empty, he made a forge out of his shirt, used his forearms as hammers, transformed his trousers into the chimneys of the furnace and let his knees be an anvil. From this, Ilmarinen forged the skies and the stars, created the northern lights to add wonder to the long wintry nights and welded red into the dawn and the sunset. Väinämöinen is a god even older than Ilmarinen and is the ancient sage and hero of the *Kalevala*. He is the god of the seas. At the end of the epic, Väinämöinen leaves Finland declaring that his services will be in great need some day.

Apart from the gods, there was a plentiful assortment of goblins, elves, gnomes and ghouls who would help people, especially if left a treat. It was common to leave these mythological characters grain, milk or even money to enlist their help. In Mediaeval times, the Finns were noted for their witchcraft. It was said that any sizable forest within Europe had a Finnish witch and people would travel miles to take their advice or listen to their soothsaying. They were especially well noted for their love charms!

## FINNISH SAYINGS

- Finnish is rich with sayings and wisdom. These proverbs have been passed from one generation to the next by oral tradition in time-honoured fashion. Here are a selection:
- The visitor has two choices, to come or to leave.
- Enjoy coffee when hot, a maiden when young.
- Age does not give you sense, it just makes you go slowly.
- Rather a summer without a cow than Christmas without a wife.
- Love makes you blind; marriage opens your eyes wide.
- Even horses kick you when they love you.
- The truth won't burn in fire.
- A fool boasts of his horse, a madman of his wife, the unable of his children.
- Each household lives by its own customs.
- Behave in the sauna as you would in a church.
- Closeness without conflict only exists in the cemetery.
- Tears from long joy, a fart from long laughter.
- Once uttered, the word won't return to the mouth.
- Money will buy your way into society, but a horse will take you there.
- The brave eat the soup; the timid die of hunger.
- A man comes back from beyond the sea, but not from under the sod.
- Envy will kill the fish in the sea.

- Remember what the fleas say in the sauna: you're just a man like any other.
- A cat's delight is a mouse's plight.
- Don't jump before you reach the ditch.
- He who wants to climb a tree must begin at the bottom and fly when at the top.
- The shoemaker's children never wear shoes.

# WORKING IN FINLAND

CHAPTER 9

'If we listen to words merely, and give them our own habitual values, we are bound to go astray.'
—Freya Stark, *The Journey's Echo*

BE WARNED, THE FINNS TAKE BUSINESS very, very seriously! They have been travelling and trading for centuries. Even Henry VIII (the English king with six wives in the early 1500s) was buying tar from the Finns to make his new fleet, and Finland still has a profitable and successful shipbuilding industry.

Anyone naïve enough to think that they have struck a win-win deal with a Finn will sooner or later realise that the Finn has really got the better end of the deal. This happens not because a Finn is trying to get the better of you, but because they are very shrewd. They have had to live by their wits for generations. Finns can be formidable and they achieve whatever it is they set out to do. Because they are modest, they make you out to be cleverer than they are, bestowing on you attributes that they lack—but be warned! You are about to lose the spotlight. Finns are perfectionists and managers are highly-qualified technicians or engineers. They have state-of-the-art working environments and training centres with the most up-to-date technology. They have sports facilities, saunas, creative thinking spaces, subsidised canteens and anything else to enhance productivity.

This fact really should not be ignored when considering the forces that shape the future of global economics. In 1998, I wrote, 'The Finns have all the attributes to become phenomenally successful in a global, commercial future'. And now they are placed top or within the top ten countries of the world in so many leagues. Their limited resources, both natural and financial, and their distance from large consumer markets meant that Finland has had to find a different way to compete in the commercial world. When Europe and the USA were competing in a mass production market of consumer goods, Finland recognised it could not hope to compete and concentrated on high-value, upmarket selling. They sell quality, not quantity. They sell applied knowledge, and it's good, very good. So what are these attributes that make them phenomenally successful?

- Meticulous attention to the quality of their goods
- Obsessive about cleanliness, hygiene and purity
- An obsession for high technology and anything modern
- Respect for nature and its forces at a spiritual level
- Hard-working and full of stamina
- Conscientious and reliable
- Straightforward, steady and using common sense
- Skilled workmanship
- Respectful of good education and its appliance
- Safety for all
- Deep-rooted entrepreneurial and trading skills
- In-built honesty and ethical behaviour
- Hatred of debt
- Innovation and 'out-of-the-box' thinking
- Impressive language skills
- Quick decision makers
- Flexibility in meeting customer demands
- Respect for all whatever their position in life
- Tolerant of others
- Create, adapt and improve—everything!
- Pioneering spirit of trying to build up their country, such as existed in the USA in the 1800s

Above all, Finland has a high-technology environment. She is commonly reputed to be the world's leading information society with an advanced communications infrastructure and with the highest penetration of mobile phones and Internet connections in the world. The Finns are also considered 'tech-savvy' and respond well to technological innovations, welcoming the benefits that they can bring to their working and domestic lives. It has been the rapid adoption of these new technologies by many industries, and especially financial institutions that has made them world leaders in several sectors. It seems hardly surprising then, that Finns always adapt to 'e-services' so quickly, such as online buying, medical and bank services.

My motto for Finish business: 'Solutions come from closing your ears to everyone who says it cannot be done.' This demonstrates their *sisu* (persistence in the face of adversity).

However, there are a few traits that let them down and which stops them from realising world domination. First of all, they are very poor at marketing themselves. They won't push themselves forward. They need to get over their shyness, their reserve and the attitude that anyone being 'pushy' is bragging. They have to come to terms with the fact that they can remain 'Honest Joe', not lose their integrity and still communicate better to the outside world. Remember, that Finns are suspicious of those who boast and are talkative—perceived as distrustful.

Secondly, they are uncomfortable with the idea of partnerships. There still seems to be an inbuilt suspicion of sharing. Things are changing, but I believe it will take another ten years before global partnershipping becomes the norm, rather than the exception. Thirdly, the Finns are only just beginning to understand the concept that all customers may have different needs. The Finns value the quality of products before all else and think that you will either want to buy them, or you won't. Because of the customs and traditions in Finland, the Finns are not used to being sold to. (Remember this is invading privacy.) This has a detrimental affect when they try to sell to or compete with other more 'pushy' nations of the world.

Fourthly, they are poor at small talk and striking up relationships. As one manager said to me, "I'm there to do business. Not to find out how his wife is!" As 90 per cent of the world's population buy on emotion and justify with fact, the Finns have a lot to learn in this respect.

As Russell Snyder writes, 'Although Finns are not the world's greatest experts in small talk, they are attentive and good listeners. You will find them eager to entertain you with sightseeing, a visit to the sauna, a meal in a good restaurant, an evening of drinking and dancing at a night-club.' They have a good sense of humour, especially at their own expense, and they love telling jokes and exchanging business cards. They are very disappointed that the world as a whole knows very little about them, especially when they are so well educated in geography, economy and current affairs! They will be much impressed if you can name a few of their famous athletes or racing drivers or any other facts you know about their country. Ask as many questions as you like about Finland, because the Finns enjoy talking about their country. This is the only time you will see a Finn passionate—in public, at least!

**Cultural Differences**

I heard of one Finnish single lady who had gone out to Hong Kong on a business trip. The trip was almost a disaster in her eyes because her contacts had spent the entire trip talking about her family, her home and her hobbies. They thought she was very stand off-ish and uncaring because all she would do was talk about business and never once asked them about their families! The contacts in Hong Kong were clearly trying to develop that all-important relationship before proceeding with any business, whilst the Finn was just trying to get down to business. One party was trying to build trust and rapport whilst the other party was trying to do the deal with typical 'Western' efficiency—a potentially dangerous situation.

## THE FINNISH HANDSHAKE

One of the most important things to remember whilst doing business with a Finn is a good handshake. You will need to shake hands with your Finnish business colleague every time you meet and every time you say goodbye, or until a time comes when you know each other so well that you drop the formalities. However, the important thing to note is that the Finns require you to be shaking hands as you say your name when introducing yourself. If, like me, you are a foreigner who is unused to these Finnish names, you may find that your handshake lasts forever. In Britain, our custom is to say our names to each other, then extend our hand for a handshake, and shake our hand whilst saying "How do you do". In Finland, however, you first extend your hand for

From a foreigner in Finland, Wayne Deer: 'Currently I am unemployed and regularly sending job applications to Finnish companies, which requires my CV to be in Finnish. I was recently updating my work history by adding a few recent part-time jobs. I thought I had written '*Minä olin pakkaaja*' (I was a packer), but accidentally wrote '*Minä olin pakastin*' (I was a freezer).'

a handshake, and then say your names. Unfortunately, by the time you have said, "Pardon", and the person you are meeting has repeated his name, and possibly repeated it for a third time, you have been hanging on to their hand for a long time! This really is not off-putting as long as you know the custom. However, ladies be warned, many Finnish men have a gripping handshake, so it might be advisable to take any big rings off first! Women, on the other hand, tend to have a very weak handshake.

## GETTING DOWN TO BUSINESS

You will really impress a Finn by getting straight down to business after shaking hands. The Finns are very frank, to the point and will tell you all that they think you ought to know to make a decision. On the other hand, they expect you to be the same with them. You will have your chance to say what you need to say and give them all the information they need to make a decision. They will rarely ask questions, believing that any information, if it were important enough, you would have already told them.

I still remember vividly giving my first presentation to a group of Finnish business people. It is still my worst nightmare! My brief was to give a half an hour presentation and allow time for questions and answers afterwards. I gave what I thought was a good and interesting presentation. I ended with a few words of Finnish, which I also had written in my PowerPoint presentation so that everyone would understand what I was endeavouring to say. The mere fact that I had tried to speak Finnish was obviously well liked and appreciated. However, when it came to the question and answer time, I thought I had died. No one spoke. There was a deadly hush. The faces of my audience were very sombre. There was no spark of emotion and there didn't seem to be any interest whatsoever in asking any questions. At that moment, I felt totally lost; I didn't know what to do. It was the first time that I had ever experienced anything like this. The Finnish boss duly caught my eye, gave me a reassuring little smile and a nod. Someone eventually asked a question, which I answered, and so the meeting ended. I was completely away from my field of experience. I had no way of perceiving whether I had done well or badly. As it turned out, I had done well and I was asked to give some more presentations.

On my third presentation to some Finnish people, I paused and asked whether anybody had any questions. After a long pause, huge grins appeared on the faces of the audience. Someone laughed and said, "Debby, hasn't anyone told you we're Finnish?" In surprise, I asked what being Finnish had to do with asking questions. Back came the reply and the enlightenment. The gentleman replied, "Oh, in Finland we don't ask questions. We give you one chance to say everything you need to say, and if it is important you will say it. Then, we will evaluate what you have said, but we don't ask questions. If we don't like what we hear, we will then go and listen to somebody else". So my initiation into doing business in Finland really did seem like a baptism of fire. However, this illustrates a point—the Finns are thinking about what you have said and, most importantly, they don't think and talk at the same time.

The Finns like to be viewed as specialists and experts and, believe me, the majority of them really are well qualified and well experienced in whatever it is they are doing. They are experts. They hate to look silly, and do not like to be shown up in front of others. One writer likens them to those in the Far East who cannot abide losing 'face'. They will expect you to be very well prepared, will take you at face value, but assume that you are an expert in your field. They will respect you, just as you should respect them. Remember that the Finns aren't used to being sold to. In practical terms, this means that if you begin to push your product and tell them how wonderful it is, especially if you are going through the process of an 'American sell', you will be seen to be bragging. They don't like this at all. A typical Finnish expert will be slow, calm and soft voiced. He will know his 'stuff', and the quality of the products will sell the goods for themselves. However, this said, the Finns are pretty tolerant of odd people and funny habits. There is no real formality about them and they are, therefore, generally very easy to do business with. They will accept you for what you are.

## MEETINGS AND APPOINTMENTS

It is important to note that you should arrive at any business meeting on time. That doesn't mean to say that the Finn will always be there and ready to see you, but s/he is more often than not. However, punctuality is seen as a virtue, though a few minutes either way is not seen as detrimental. Office hours are generally 8:00 am to 4:00 pm, Monday to Friday, and business meetings might well take place from 8:30 or 9:00 in the morning. Good manners would dictate that afternoon meetings should be arranged to finish by about 3:30 in the afternoon, so that people have the opportunity to make last minute phone calls before the end of the working day. People like to clear their desks and leave a little early on a Friday afternoon, so you need to finish promptly if you see anyone then. It shows respect for their work-life balance. The Finns do work hard; they work conscientiously and many work beyond 4:00 pm. It is not uncommon to find people still at their desks at 5:00 or 5:30 in the evening.

**Opening Hours**

- Banks are open from 9:00 am to 4:15 pm, Monday to Friday.
- Post offices are open from 9:00 am to 5:00 pm, Mondays to Fridays.
- Both are closed Saturdays.
- Office hours are from 8:00 am to 4:00 pm, Monday to Friday.
- The majority of shops are open from 9:00 am to 6:00 pm, Monday to Friday, and 9:00 am to 3:00 pm on Saturdays.
- Larger shops such as department stores are open until 8:00 pm, Monday to Friday, and 4:00 pm on Saturdays.
- As alcohol can only be bought in the state-owned Alko shops. It might be worth noting their opening hours: 9:00 am to 8:00 pm, Monday to Friday, and Saturdays from 9:00 am to 6:00 pm.

You will be served coffee, tea and pastries at whatever time of day you visit. There will be a very small amount of 'small talk' because you are a foreigner. You can then get straight down to business with a no nonsense approach. If there is an agenda, it will be followed efficiently. You may be invited to stay to lunch which will be in the company restaurant-cum-canteen. No alcohol is served. Most people drink water or milk, possibly fruit juice. Lunch, even though it may be three courses, will be light as Finns do not like to over-indulge. In true egalitarian fashion, everyone clears away their dirty plates and leaves the table clean and tidy for the next users.

## NEGOTIATIONS

If you want to sell something, you have to be very knowledgeable about the technical side of your product. You are better off sending your technicians to Finland rather than your sales people, as the culture is engineer-dominated. You need to be able to supply relevant facts and figures and know the specification details well. There are no long, hard bargaining sessions. Get straight to the point—you can even lay your cards on the table and you will NOT be taken advantage of. The Finns respect that you need to make a profit not only for your sake but their good as well. They are not deceitful, so take them at their word. They keep their promises and a friendly handshake seals the deal. Written contracts will normally be short and straightforward, outlining everyone's obligations and deadlines. However with the EU experience, they are learning to use carefully written agreements. Remember: Finns are shrewd, disarmingly honest and usually get the better deal.

**Finnish Business Values**

'Jorma Ollilla, Nokia's dynamic CEO … was asked in 2002 about the reasons for his and his company's great success. He answered that Nokia has gained its strength from its firm underpinning of uncomplicated, sincere, durable tenants taken straight from Finnish rural society.' —Richard Lewis (*Cultural Lone Wolf*, 2005)

## DECISIONS AND ACTIONS

The Finns come to decisions quickly, although there may well be more than one person involved in the decision-making process. Unlike the rest of Scandinavia, they certainly do not make decisions through committees. They have flat organisations, which means that anyone can approach the boss and voice their opinion. The boss will glean thoughts from everyone, even hold brainstorming sessions, but the Finnish boss is the final decision-maker. Once s/he has all the facts, a decision is made quickly and then any actions needed are taken immediately.

In my experience, the Finns become quite intolerant of the way the rest of Europe make decisions and get to action. They cannot understand why it takes us so long; they are far more spontaneous than we are. If you are doing business with the Finns, it is important to note that you should be ready to implement any promises or any deals as soon as they are made. This will be their measure of your integrity as a businessperson.

Finns are self-disciplined, industrious individualists who like teamwork and team spirit. However, they often demonstrate inventiveness and individual lateral thinking. They like to be given responsibility and held accountable and work well under organisation structures such as profit centres. Their responsibility and authority should be clearly defined, because they like to be left alone to get on with their job. They intensely dislike close supervision. They openly share their knowledge and expertise; its part of their culture. Therefore, organisational learning is a key feature of Finnish business—no wonder they have created such a high-tech environment. For Finns, good business consists of right action more than right words. They do things because they are the right things to do and have faith that this will deliver the best outcomes. They have an innate belief that 'cooking with good ingredients' will always make a good dinner. This is not just another business philosophy, but part of their deep, inner-feelings—part of their psyche.

An example of right action: In Finland, animal health control schemes have been established for cattle herds, pig herds and poultry flocks and are being planned for sheep flocks, goat herds and reindeer. The purpose of the schemes is to improve and monitor measures relating to food safety, animal health and animal welfare at the farm level and improve the economic efficiency of domestic animal production. A nation-wide computerised database collects data on how the scheme is being operated in the field and allows vets and farmers to input data directly. Finland adopted a zero-tolerance approach to infectious animal diseases and has totally managed to eradicate many such as salmonella in chickens and pork, and swine fever in pigs. They are the only country in the world to have done so and are currently described in a recent survey as having a 'disease-free status'. Other EU countries adopted a risk-containment strategy.

## CONSENSUS

Argumentative discussions are not looked on favourably. People take both criticisms and arguments very personally, and you may have a major disagreement on your hands if you adopt a conflict approach. It's always preferable to try a consensus-based approach and get people working together to solve a problem. Remember, the Finns are very much like the Asians in respect of 'face' saving. They are deep thinkers and don't show much emotion, so you could easily upset them and not know it.

One Swedish businessman I know who has worked all over the world refers to 'Finnish efficiency' as being one of this nation's strong points. This is their ability to make decisions quickly and get on with implementation effectively. A Finnish manager is more production orientated than people orientated, especially compared with his Swedish counterpart. There is always an informal relationship between the boss and the workers, and senior managers/bosses are approachable in a way that would be impossible in southern Europe. Because the Finns are

One Finnish managing director with a subsidiary in Sweden shocked his Swedish employees by telling them they had to 'pull their socks up' and become more productive. The employees could not believe they were being spoken to in such a fashion. They were not used to it. That is not the way to do things in Sweden, but it is the Finnish way!

straight talking, they can be very frank when they need to tell people when things are going wrong.

Finnish managers are well liked abroad. They never try to 'impose' their will on anyone. They listen first—to everyone—at all levels of the organisation and willingly believe that others might know best. When it comes to working abroad they have a very pragmatic approach; adopt, adapt, improve. It seems to suit everyone well.

## PRESENTATIONS

When giving a company presentation, there is a vast difference between the American/Anglo-Saxon and Finnish styles. (Apologies to those of other cultures—I make the comparison with the US/A-S style as this is generally accepted in business circles as the norm, a world full of spin-doctors and hype.). This section on presentations may be of value to note: the Finns are very much into structure and facts. They like to tell you exactly where they are located in Finland, even showing you a picture of their factory on a map; show you an organisation chart (probably with lots of names on it); give you a lot of financial details and tell you how they have grown year-on-year in figures not percentages; and generally put in their PowerPoint a lot of information and numbers. They will inform you of the quality of their goods, tell you about the good design and you will learn that everything incorporates the latest technology. You will also learn that everyone in their business works 35 hours a week and has six weeks holiday a year—implying that not only is the product of quality but their work practices too! The purpose of their presentations is to give you information and educate you. All this will be delivered in a calm and quiet fashion by an expert. You will be given sufficient information to draw the conclusion for yourself that the product/service is 'the best thing since sliced bread' and you can then make your decision whether to buy. You will rarely hear any stories, and no one promotes the benefits of using their product or service. The delivery is very 'black and white' and unemotional.

Therefore, many Finns tend to find US/A-S style presentations lacking in substance because we tend to heavily feature the benefits of buying from our company, illustrate with stories, wring emotions and bounce energetically around the room—very unlike a quiet Finnish expert. All this is confusing for the Finn and makes us foreigners seem very untrustworthy. Unfortunately, the non-plussed, silent response we receive from a Finnish audience is usually misinterpreted by the presenter as lack of interest, and the greater will be the effort to stir up emotion (or even a response). Wrong move! The Finns are uncomfortable with any emotional outbursts and are just waiting for you to give them some straight facts with which to make a decision!

## LETTER AND EMAILS

These can be a source of confusion, irritation and misinterpretation. Because the Finns speak such good English in a one-on-one situation, we tend to attribute them with having a good understanding of the way 'we' do business. 'We' in this instance means anyone who isn't Finnish. Unfortunately, written communications from them are often interpreted as commands and demands by other nations. Again, Finnish efficiency means they do not bother to use more words than they have to and there is no 'soft' language used. They are so concerned that the relevant information is understood correctly that they do not 'dress up' any correspondence. This abruptness can lead to them appearing very arrogant and unjustifiably demanding. Other nationalities can easily be offended. However, there is rarely any intention to offend.

Finnish business is mostly conducted over the telephone or with face-to-face meetings. Emails are for clarification and letters usually get sent as a final round-up or summary of agreements reached.

Just an interesting thing to note, where we in Britain are used to ticking boxes to indicate that something is correct, the Finns cross boxes (crosses do not mean that things are wrong). Another thing not to overlook is that the Finns use the continental numbering system with decimal commas, not decimal points. For instance, one may talk about 2,5 million Euros, whereas for the English speakers we would use 2.5

million Euros. This may seem just a small detail but I have witnessed some potentially disastrous misinterpretations!

**Please and Thank You**

In giving seminars to other cultures, I tell the story of my experience working with a Finnish company (whilst still living in England). I used to dread going to my fax machine or opening up my emails on a Monday morning. As Finland is two hours ahead of us, my instructions for the week would be waiting for me to read as I started work. An example of the instructions: 'Dear Debby, do abc, do def, do this, then do that. Speak to Mr xyz, tell him 123. When finished call the office. Please. Thank you. Hely.' In English, that note would have been full of words such as: could you, would you kindly, find the time, etc. and the instructions would have been shaped to be asking, not demanding. But along the way, someone has told the Finns that the English are excessively polite, so they must use 'please' and 'thank you'. Incidentally, there is no word for 'please' in Finnish.

## CUSTOMER CARE

Once again I bring up the subject which, for this purpose, I have called 'Customer Care'. Who is to say what is right and what is wrong in customer care? Who can say that one country's service is better than another's? However, what I can say is that many foreigners' impressions of the Finns are based on their interpretation of the service they receive; especially if they do not have the opportunity to meet some Finns on a one-to-one basis. To many, the Finns seem abrupt, rude, grumpy and uncaring. This greatly saddens me because I know they are not.

Remember, the Finns will only give minimal information to any question you ask. Therefore, it is important to get the question right in the first place. For example, last week I was at Helsinki airport being served at the Finnair desk on the international side, when two Japanese ladies came up and asked, "Is there a bank?" Without looking at the two questioners, the Finnish receptionist said, "No. Not on this side". The abruptness of the answer caused the Japanese ladies to stop in their tracks. They clearly expected an additional response. When that was not forthcoming, they eventually moved away. When I had been served, I sought out the two ladies and asked whether they were looking for somewhere to change money or an actual bank. Of course, they were looking for a Bureau de Change and I explained where it was. There are two points to consider here. First, the Finn answered the question and no more. It is not in their culture to expand upon the obvious. There is no thought as to what the 'customer' really wants, no ability to look beyond the question to see what the problem is or the question should be, and there is no responsibility to find a solution. It appears that the Finns are quite unable to use their initiative in this respect. This is really not the case, but 'going beyond the call of duty' is just not expected of them in their environment. The second point to consider is the lack of eye contact.

Eye contact, especially with strangers, is kept to a minimum. One Australian I happened to meet on his first visit to Finland was almost pulling his hair out at the treatment he was getting from a girl behind the airline desk. She was clearly telling him that he could not board the plane but kept averting her eyes from his. Whatever he said, she just repeated the same message like a stuck gramophone record, and continued the same averting of eyes. He was becoming very agitated and in desperation exclaimed so the whole room could hear him, "It's almost as though I weren't here. Why won't you look at me?" It was obvious the girl behind the airline desk was getting distressed. After all, she would be used to the Finns obeying the rules and just going away and not making a fuss.

**Served by Grumpy**

Buying a pizza in a restaurant: 'I glanced up from the menu to see a grim-faced waitress, whom I'll call Grumpy, standing by our table... our pizzas arrived...when I noticed something disturbing: three sharp pieces of mussel shell were staring at me...I was appalled and expected an apology, a new pizza, a complimentary bottle of champagne and, of course, no charge. When I showed Grumpy the pieces of shell, she just shrugged her shoulders, reluctantly changed the pizza for something else, and offered me free coffee for my inconvenience. Then she had the nerve to charge me full price on the bill. I was angry. Ready to complain to the manager ...but Pekka didn't want me to make a fuss. He asked me to keep silent about the matter. "We may want to come here again," he said.' —Russell Snyder (*The Optimist's Guide to Finland for Business People*, 2003)

From a Finnish reader concerning my comments on customer care: I have the feeling that Helsinki has changed to be slightly better in the last years. I don't know about the rest of the country. My experience is that you get as good service as you care to explicitly request, including quite excellent. The people in the service industry are not ill-meaning but simply don't think thoroughly what service means. Knowing Finnish language helps. So you have quite correct conclusions in your book about this!

Another similar incident I witnessed happened to an Englishman in a supermarket. At the cash desk, he asked whether the shop took VISA. The answer came back, "No". Unfortunately, we then had to wait at the till until the man found enough cash to pay for his items. Actually, the shop took other forms of credit cards and debit cards but not VISA. If the girl behind the counter could not speak English well, she could have pointed out the symbols/logos of the cards they took. But whether she spoke English or not, she was not going to go beyond the obvious question. Her responsibility ended with the answer, "No".

One evening, my Finnish colleague Timo and I were dining out. We both wanted just a light evening meal and decided to stop at a branch of a restaurant chain. He just wanted a plain omelette and ordered it from the waitress, who showed some anxiety about this. After some while, she returned to say that they were unable to cook an omelette because it was not on the menu. We left.

One client travels the world as customer service manager for a Finnish owned multi-national company. He said, for the first edition of this book, that he is appalled at the service levels in his country and was often making comparisons with the Far East and America. He exclaimed, "We put up with anything. We never complain!" He believes that the quality in Finland is perfect but they can't organise service, whilst in Asia they can organise service but the quality is dreadful. In a recent conversation, Timo H. updated his views by saying that service levels have transformed in Helsinki due to more international travel, competition and exposure to other cultures. Helsinki has become more cosmopolitan. He believes that people are starting to become more assertive in what they want and how they want to be treated, which he sees as a good thing. Having returned to Finland last year after living in the States for a few years, he noticed a vast difference from when he left.

**A Finnish Barber**

A foreigners experience in Finland, from Rob J: 'My first visit to a Finnish barber made me nervous. Will they cut too much off and understand me? However, nothing prepared me for what actually happened. He had almost finished, when I asked if he could style my hair with some gel. He replied in English, "Can you do it? I don't want to make my hands sticky."'

## PAYMENT TERMS

The world would be a better place if we could all deal with the Finns. If you send them an invoice which says payment within seven days, you will have your money within seven days. They are prompt payers and always pay to terms, which are normally within 30 days. Okay—there are a very few exceptions. Average payment days in Finland are 24 days.

The Finns are very naïve when it comes to understanding that the rest of the world does not operate in such an honourable way as they do. They are not used to having to chase money and, as they are not used to complaining in their every day lives, some nations really do take the Finns for a ride—but only once.

Although most deals will be signed and sealed officially, you will never need to doubt the word of a Finn. A handshake will seal the deal. The Finns are honest and respect integrity above all else. They will not double deal you. They are frank and open, and appreciate your honesty and frankness. You need not fear laying your cards on the table. But just be aware, that they are good and hard negotiators. After all, they are used to dealing with the Russians!

## CORRUPTION

As previously stated, honesty and integrity are high on the list of Finnish attributes, therefore, corruption is rare. If there is ever the slightest hint of corruption or bribery in government, there will be a huge spread in the daily papers. The Finnish find it difficult to deal with some foreign nations, when everyone in the chain expects to have a 'bung' (a financial payment for their effort). If they had a choice, they would prefer to walk away from these deals. They regard the whole concept as totally dishonest. In a recent survey on comparative corruption levels in countries around the world, Finland took the number one spot as the least corrupt country.

In everyday life, there is no tipping. Tipping is not in the Finnish culture at all. You do not need to tip taxi drivers, waiters or hairdressers. Even the hotel porter does not expect to be tipped. Please do not feel that you are doing them a favour by leaving them a few 'odd coppers' on the side. They genuinely take it as an insult. This is because in an egalitarian society, everyone respects people for the jobs that they do. If their job is to drive a taxi, this is what they are paid to do, and to be civil and polite whilst doing their job is what is expected. They do not need to be tipped, and do not expect it. However some Finns, you will notice, will pay a bill by rounding up the money by a few cents (10p–15p) and will not expect the change.

## MONEY AND BANKING

Finland uses the Euro as their unit of currency. Banks are normally open from 10:00 am–4:30 pm, Monday to Friday, and are not open on Saturdays. Some banks have longer opening hours. Foreign currency can be changed at banks or at cash machines. These have an extensive network and are also in locations with no other banking services. There are cash machines (ATMs) on nearly every street corner and in the smallest of villages. Finnish ATMs (displaying the SOLO symbol) accept foreign bankcards with the symbols Visa, Eurocard, Plus Cirrus and EU. Credit and debit cards are used almost everywhere for everything, even in taxis. The need for cash is much smaller than the need in Britain and elsewhere in Europe. Finns conduct most of their banking transactions using ATMs and BACs.

There are no restrictions on the import and export of currencies between European Union members. However, foreigners from outside the EU cannot take out of the country large amounts of money, and it is therefore advisable for any foreigner to declare any substantial amounts that they are bringing into the country.

Finland leads the world in electronic banking services: Finland was the first country in the world to offer telephone banking in 1982, online share trading in 1988, banking via a mobile phone in 1992, Internet banking in 1996 and banking using a WAP phone in 1999. As a result, only 10 to 15 per cent of all banking transactions in Finland are now done over-the-counter. Finland is still pioneering developments in Internet banking and is well ahead of its continental rivals in terms of customer penetration and the services offered. Finns can do their banking irrespective of time or place with an ordinary phone, personal computer or a wireless terminal such as a laptop computer, GSM or WAP phone. This means that the banks are open 24 hours a day and customers can chose from a variety of services. This is very different from the banking services available in other European countries where Internet banking is only just taking off.

Finland's three biggest banking groups, Merita, Leonia and Okobank, are global pioneers in this field. All services are integrated, for instance users of the Okobank can access

## Business Tips

Things to remember when doing business in Finland:

- Limited companies have the initials OY (always in capital letters) at the end of their name in the same way as we use Ltd.
- A Finn's word and a handshake is as good as a signed contract.
- Be punctual.
- Keep your promise.
- Pay up on time.
- Get to the point and direct speech is welcomed.
- Facts and evidence persuade—keep away from emotion.

WAP services using the same codes that they currently use for GSM services, the Internet, telephone banking and the automatic telephone service. This means that their customers have the opportunity to use those services that suit them best at any given moment. The newest industry buzzword is 'm-banking'. This latest abbreviation stands for 'mobile banking' and they are investing a great deal of money in its development. Although 'wireless' banking services are already in place in Finland using GSM and WAP technology, m-Banking will make use of the new GPRS networks, 3rd Generation mobile phone technology and more sophisticated handsets. It offers much more potential and now the race is on to see who will provide the first services!

## APPLYING FOR A WORK PERMIT

A foreigner wanting paid employment in Finland must usually have a residence permit as an employed person. A person engaged in an independent business or profession in Finland must have a residence permit for a self-employed person. However, there are many exceptions to this rule. For example, citizens of European Union (EU) Member States and equivalent persons do not need a residence permit for an employed person or for a self-employed person. Similar provisions on the right of movement that apply to citizens of EU Member States also apply to citizens of Iceland, Liechtenstein, Norway and Switzerland (http://www.uvi.fi).

## FINDING A JOB

The following information should help you to get started in finding out about jobs and employment opportunities in Finland. Good luck! (Source: The Finnguide Team http://www.finnguide.fi)

**Finland Job Recruitment Agencies**

Below are a few of the recruitment agencies and services operating in Finland:

- http://www.aarresaari.fi—this is a network of Academic Career Services representing 19 Finnish Universities
- http://www.monster.fi
- http://www.mercuri-urval.com
- http://www.proselectum.fi
- http://www.mps.fi. Click 'Työpaikat'
- http://www.eurojobs.com
- http://www.jobsite.co.uk. Search 'Finland'.
- http://europa.eu.int/eures/home.jsp?lang=en
- http://www.cimo.fi
- http://www.cvonline.net Click 'Avoimet työpaikat' (Open vacancies)
- http://www.rekry.com Click 'Uudet työpaikat' (New Jobs)

### The Finnish Labour Administration (Työministeriö)

From the website of the Finnish Labour Administration, you can find some information about working life in Finland. The website is available in Finnish, Swedish and English. The website also contains listings of job vacancies in Finland.

Unfortunately, most of these listings are published in Finnish or Swedish. The Finnish Labour Administration (called Työministeriö in Finnish) can be found at the following URL: http://www.mol.fi.

## Advertised Jobs in the Finnish Media

Many Finnish printed newspapers contain 'employment sections' listing available positions in Finland. One of the main newspapers in Finland is the *Helsingin Sanomat* which publishes an extensive employment section in their Sunday editions (http://www.helsinginsanomat.fi).

## Finnish Company Job And Career Website

Nowadays, most larger companies have an employment section on their websites from where they advertise job vacancies, or invite applicants to send their CVs.

**Useful Job and Career Website**

I recommend that you visit http://www.uranus.fi. This website provides a large amount of information in English which can be very useful to non Finnish speaking people seeking information about employment opportunities in Finland. The website is available in Finnish, Swedish and English .

# FAST FACTS

CHAPTER 10

'The trouble with this world is not
that people know too little,
but that they know too much that ain't so.'
—Mark Twain, *The Innocents Abroad*

## Official Name
Finland

## Capital City
Helsinki

## Population
Approximately 5,223,442 (July 2005) Finland has a Sami (Lapp) population of 6,500. About one million people live in the Helsinki metropolitan area.

## Total Area
338,144 sq km (130,558 sq miles). Finland is the seventh largest country in Europe after Russia, Ukraine, France, Spain, Sweden and Germany.

## Land Border
With Sweden 614 km (381 miles), with Norway 736 km (457 miles) and with Russia 1,340 km (833 miles).

## Other Geographical Facts
188,000 lakes and 179,584 islands, 98,050 of which are in the lakes. Europe's largest archipelago lies off Finland's south-west coast, and the islands of Åland, an autonomous Swedish-speaking province of Finland, are part of this archipelago.

# USEFUL INFORMATION

## Alcoholic Beverages

Alko is a nationwide network of liquor stores with virtual monopoly to sell alcohol. Beer and ciders are also sold in grocery stores. The Alko stores are open—depending on the store—from 9:00 am–8:00 pm, Monday to Friday, 9:00 am–6:00 pm on Saturdays. All stores are closed on Sundays, religious feast days, on Christmas Eve and Easter Saturday.

## Autumn

September–November begins with a short-lived blaze of colour known as *ruska*. The autumnal reds, browns and yellows are especially beautiful on and around the fells of Lapland in September. October sees the first of the snow falling in central Finland; sooner in the north, later in the south.

## Banks

Banks are normally open from 10:00 am–4:30 pm, Monday to Friday. Some banks have longer opening hours. Bank machines have an extensive network, also in locations with no other banking services. Banking machines—ATMs (OTTO)—are all conveniently located.

## Changing Money

Bureaux de Change are available at the airport, the main post office, high street banks or Forex offices. An automatic exchange machine is located at Helsinki airport. Commission rates vary from 1–2.5 per cent. Foreign currency can be changed at banks. Credit cards (Visa, Eurocard, Mastercard, Cirrus, EC) can be used to withdraw cash from cash dispenser with SOLO symbol. Forex is often the easiest, the fastest and the less expensive way to change currency (http://www.forex.fi).

## Chemists

Medicines are sold at pharmacies (*apteekki*). Note that chemists (*kemikaalio*) only sell cosmetics.

## Climate

Four seasons, Midnight Sun, Polar Night, Snow Coverage. See under season: spring, summer, autumn, winter.

## Courier Services

Providers include: TNT (tel: 0800-188-800 or (09) 476-266), DHL (tel: 030-45-345) and World Courier : (09) 8700-3300

## Credit Cards

Most major credit cards and Eurocheque cards are widely accepted and more so in Finland than they are in the USA or the rest of Europe. Pay for taxis and snacks and even small amounts with credit cards instead of cash. Finland is almost a cashless society.

## Currency

Finland is a participant in the European single currency, so its monetary unit is the Euro (€), divided into 100 centii.

## Currency Restrictions

There are no restrictions on the import and export of currencies between European Union members.

## Drink-Driving

Be aware—drunk-driving laws are strict, and acceptable blood alcohol levels are much lower in Finland than elsewhere. Police strictly enforce all traffic laws and institute random roadside breathalyser tests. Drivers who register a .05 or above alcohol content are subject to immediate arrest.

## Economy

Finnish economic growth has proceeded at a faster pace than most OECD countries. Finland's economy has traditionally been based on its most plentiful natural resource: wood. The forest product industries are still important, even if they face increased international competition, but manufacturing industries, engineering and high technology have also played a big economic role in recent decades. The main economic phenomenon of the last two decades has been the rise of telecommunications giant Nokia and the industrial cluster surrounding the IT business.

## Education

That Finnish literacy rates are among the highest—if not the highest—in the world is a tribute to the effectiveness of the Finnish education system. The system begins with pre-school teaching leading to entry to comprehensive school at age seven. This continues through to the ninth grade, after which students can decide to pursue vocational education or secondary education. Upper secondary schools take the students through to the age of 18 or 19, when they matriculate and can then choose to enter higher education, at university or polytechnic.

## Electricity

The electric current in Finland is 220 V (230 V), 50 Hz. Finland has 220 volts and uses the European two pin plugs.

## Emergency

Dial 112 for emergency services in Finland.

## Everyman's Right

Everyman's rights is a concept prevailing in Finland and other Nordic countries. Basically it entitles us to go where we please in the countryside—on land or on water—as long as we don't intrude on people's privacy, cause a nuisance or damage, or leave litter.

## Flag

White cross on a pale blue background.

## Government and Constitution

Independent republic since 1917. The Finnish constitution follows the Western democracy model, with a President elected for six-year terms (for a maximum of two terms), and a 200-member, single-chamber parliament elected every four years by direct elections and on the basis of proportional representation.

## History

The first crusade to Finland was led by the king of Sweden in 1155, starting a union with Sweden that was to last for 600 years. In 1809, Finland was incorporated into the Russian Empire as a Grand Duchy. Swedish laws were retained and the country was allowed to keep its own currency, mail and railway systems. Helsinki became the capital in 1812 (replacing Turku in the south-west). The official national languages were—and still are—Finnish and Swedish. Amid the turmoil of the Russian Revolution, Finland declared its independence in 1917, establishing its present constitution and status as a republic in 1919.

## Internet Services

Free access to Internet is usually offered in libraries (*kirjasto*), reservation recommended. Lots of local cafes offer the service too. (See listing in Resources Guide/Helsinki)

## Language

Finland is officially bilingual: Finnish is the first language of 92 per cent, and Swedish of 5.5 per cent of the population. About 1,700 people in Lapland speak Sami (Lapp) languages. Many people speak English, so tourists do not have much difficulties in communicating.

## Lunch

Cafes, coffee bars and restaurants serve specially-priced meals at lunch-time (11:00 am–2:00 pm).

## Maps

Maps are available in bookstores all over Finland and are free from tourist offices. Maps can also be bought from Genimap Oy, the biggest company in map business in Finland (Tel: 358-201-340-40; Sales@genimap.fi; http://ww.genimap.com)

## Medical Services

In case of emergency, dial 112. Medicines are sold at pharmacies (*apteekki*).

## 24-hour Health Advice Line

Information about health care is available around the clock at tel: 10023. Doctors prepared to do house calls can also be obtained on this number.

## Mobile Phones and Charges

Both the GSM 900 and GSM 1800 networks operate in Helsinki. Visitors from the USA and Canada should obtain a European-standard handset and a SIM card in order to make calls in Finland. All foreign visitors should consult their service provider for details of roaming agreements. Mobile phone hire is available at the airport from AIR Foto tel: (09) 822 099, http://www.airfoto.fi. Example of pre-paid subscription tariff including € 11 talktime is € 17.90; calls 0.16 € /min; SMSs 0.11 € /each; SMSs to foreign country € /each (http://www.sonera.fi/artikkeli/0,3842,l-en_h-10791,00.htm). The better hotels have a mobile telephone charging stand in reception for the convenience of guests, labelled for about half a dozen different makes and models of phone.

## Newspapers

English-language newspapers and journals such as the *International Herald Tribune* and *The Economist* are widely available. Other foreign language newspapers are available in department stores, book stores and R-kiosks. *Helsingin Sanomat* is the largest Finnish-language daily. Available from the Helsinki City Tourist Office: *Helsinki Visitor's Guide* (our own brochure), *Helsinki This Week* (Brochure by Helsinki Expert), and *City in English* (a newspaper).

## Opening Hours

- Shops: The most common opening hours are 9:00 am to 8:00 pm on weekdays and 9:00 am to 3:00 pm on Saturdays.
- Alko Stores: Open from Monday to Thursday from 10:00 am to 5:00 pm, on Fridays from 10:00 am to 6:00 pm and on Saturdays from 9:00 am to 4:00 pm.
- Banks: Banks are open Monday to Friday from 9:00 am to 4:30 pm (office hours may vary regionally).

- Post Offices: Post offices are open Monday to Friday from 9:00 am to 6:00 pm. The Main Post Office is open Monday to Friday from 9:00 am to 8:00 pm.

## Passport

Those arriving in Finland from the Nordic countries and EU countries do not need a passport, (with the exception of Britain); however some identification, e.g. an identity card, is required when entering Finland. People arriving from other countries should contact the Finnish embassy in their home country for detailed information.

## Petrol Stations

Service stations are usually open from 7:00 am to 9:00 pm, and for a shorter time on Sundays. Some stations offer 24-hour sales petrol and many of them have cafés.

## Pharmacies

See information under 'Chemists'.

## Post

Letters within Europe will take two to four days; post to the USA, Canada and Australia may take up to two weeks. Cost: postcard or letter (up to 20gm) to Finland, Europe or other destination € 0.70; info on further tariffs at http://www.posti.fi/english/pricesandinstructions/index.htm.

## Post Offices

Post offices are usually open Monday to Friday from 9:00 am to 6:00 pm. The Main Post Office is open Monday to Friday from 9:00 am to 8:00 pm. There are yellow mail boxes (standing on the ground) for collections daily. Stamps are available at post offices, book and paper shops, R-kiosks, stations and hotels.

## Religion:

Christianity reached Finland about 1,000 years ago, more or less simultaneously from east and west. As a consequence, both the Evangelical-Lutheran and Orthodox churches still have the status of official religions. Some 86 per cent of the population belong to the former and about 1 per cent to the latter, and both faiths are protected under a constitution that guarantees freedom of religion.

## Saunas

Tourists can enjoy a sauna at most hotels, motels, holiday villages and camping sites, where there are separate saunas for men and women. Some hotel saunas are also open to non-residents.

## Shops

Retail shops are open Monday to Friday from 7:00 am to 9:00 pm and on Saturdays from 7:00 am to 6:00 pm. Smaller grocery stores may be open also on Sundays from 12:00 pm to 9:00 pm. Other retail outlets may be open on Sundays from 12:00 pm to 9:00 pm in May, June, July, August, November and December. At other times, they are closed on Sundays.

## Spring

March–May is short and very sweet, an explosion of growth and almost tangible optimism after the long winter. In Helsinki and the south, the snow and ice starts melting midway through March, while in the north it's more stubborn and can linger right into May.

## Summer

June–August is Finland at its magical best, with long light-filled days. The best weather normally follows the Midsummer period, with temperatures well up in the 20s and even 30s possible in July and August. Visitors might find it hard to sleep in the summer months, especially in the north, when the sun stays above the horizon for several weeks.

## Taxis

Taxis can be obtained by telephone (see telephone directory under *Taksi*) or from taxi ranks. All taxis have an illuminated yellow sign *taksi*/taxi. When the sign is lit, the taxi is vacant.

## Telephones

Nowadays, there are not many public telephones left and it is sometimes difficult to find international telephone cards. Often the simplest way to make a phone call (especially to abroad) is to find a Tele Center. All public telephones accept phone cards and you can buy pre-paid cards for mobile phones for example in kiosks called R-kioski that can be found everywhere in the city. Most hotel rooms have telephone sockets for modem dialling to the Internet.

## Telephone Country Codes

- City code: 09 (when dialling from outside Finland, the initial zero is dropped)
- Calls from Finland: dial the international prefix (00, 990, 994 or 999), the country code, the trunk code and the subscriber's number. Calls to Finland: dial the international prefix of the country you call from, the country code to Finland (358), the trunk code without the prefix 0 and the subscriber's number.
- Directory enquiries (in English): 118 or 020-202
- International directory enquiries: 020-222
- Operator (in English): 118
- International operator: 020-222

## Television and Radio

Two national channels, TV1 and TV2, as well as two commercial channels, MTV3 and Nelonen, broadcast English-language programmes from Britain and the USA; otherwise programmes are in Finnish or Swedish. There are four national radio stations (http://www.yle.fi/rfinland). In Helsinki, Capital FM (103.7MHz) broadcasts English programmes such as BBC World News, Voice of America and Radio Australia. BBC World Service and Voice of America frequencies are correct at the time of going to press, but do change.

- BBC: MHz 17.64 12.10 9.410 6.195
- Voice of America: MHz 11.97 9.760 6.040 0.792

Information about the frequencies etc. from YLE: http://www.yle.fi/fbc/thisyle.shtml

## Time Zone

Time in Finland is 2 hours ahead of Greenwich Mean Time (GMT). The time difference between Eastern U.S. Standard Time and Finnish Standard Time is 7 hours. Daylight Saving Time (DST) is in effect during the winter as in the rest of the European Union. Finland is always one hour ahead of Central European Time (CET) and two hours ahead of time in the UK and Ireland.

## Tipping

Tips are not expected in Finland at restaurants, cafés or coffee bars because service is included in the price.

## Train Service

Passenger trains in Finland have at their disposal 4,000 km of tracks. The network interconnects the major Finnish cities. The most important sections of line are electrified.

## Traveller's Cheques

Travellers cheques such as American Express and Thomas Cook cheques are accepted. Some banks charge as much as € 6 per transaction to exchange travellers cheques, while independent facilities such as Forex charge € 2 per cheque. Euro travellers cheques are not widely accepted and you are likely to have to pay commission per cheque cashed rather than for the amount. It is more advisable to take Euro's cash.

## Weights and Measures

Finland uses the Metric system of measurement and Centigrade for temperature. Clothes and shoes are in European sizing.

## Winter

December–February, there is nearly always plenty of snow in eastern and northern Finland even if the winter is unusually warm. The snow cover in coastal regions may sometimes be scant. The extra long season in northern Finland begins in November and lasts at least until May. In the inland regions of southern and central Finland, the snow settles at the beginning of December and melts in open places in mid or late April, and in the forests (65 per cent of the total land area) at the beginning of May.

# CULTURE QUIZ

## SITUATION 1

You are giving a business presentation to a group of Finns. This is the first time you have met a group of Finns. The presentation seems to go well and at the end of the presentation, you stop to ask if anyone has any questions. There is total silence. No one responds. Not a single question is asked. Do you......?

- Ⓐ Die on the spot and run out of the room, thinking you have been a disaster.
- Ⓑ Patiently wait a few moments, hand out your business card, then invite people to contact you if they would like further information.
- Ⓒ Repeat your question and tell them that they really must have things to ask.

### Comments

Finns are very reserved. They do not like to stand out from the crowd by speaking up. Most probably your audience were fascinated by your presentation, have lots of questions but are afraid to ask. By handing them your business card, you are enabling them to phone you to talk on a one-to-one basis about your presentation. Answer Ⓑ. Remember you are not a disaster!

## SITUATION 2

You are at a petrol station wanting to fill your car up. You arrive at the pump, insert the nozzle into your car, squeeze the handle, but nothing happens. Do you...?

- Ⓐ Look pleadingly at the attendant in the garage shop.
- Ⓑ Decide the stupid thing must be broken and drive to another pump.
- Ⓒ Remember that technology rules in Finland and you must be to blame.

## Comments

Finnish petrol pumps accept payment and pump petrol all in one operation. When filling your car up, you either insert your credit card, insert cash or use your mobile phone to key in your transaction. After that, the pump will dispense the petrol (and give you back any change remaining from your cash deposit)! Answer Ⓒ. Technology rules in Finland.

## SITUATION 3

When visiting a Finnish person's home, it is correct and polite:

Ⓐ Not to take your shoes off.
Ⓑ To take your shoes off.
Ⓒ To take your shoes and socks off.

## Comments

The Finns keep their shoes for outdoor wear and can often be seen walking around in their stocking feet or in sandals, even at the office. Answer Ⓑ. You should at least offer to take your shoes off.

## SITUATION 4

Having a sauna in a traditional Finnish way may mean which of the following?

Ⓐ You will go ice swimming (frozen lake, a hole in the ice and off you go), smeared with honey, and whipped with birch twigs.
Ⓑ A relaxing snooze in the heat, modestly attired in your swim suit.
Ⓒ An opportunity to gather naked, in a warm place, to meet members of the opposite sex!

## Comments

The traditional manner in which to take a sauna generally means women and men go separately. It is not customary to keep your bathing costume on in the sauna as this is thought to be unhealthy. After a short while in the sauna, a Finn will either plunge into a cold swimming pool, lake or have a shower and then return to the sauna (even in the middle of winter). Answer Ⓐ. It is thought to be very therapeutic to smear yourself with honey and be lightly whipped with birch twigs in order to stimulate the circulation. The cold water helps this as well.

## SITUATION 5

You are spending the weekend in Helsinki. Your Finnish friend knows you will be alone, so you are invited round for coffee. How do you behave?

- Ⓐ You smarten yourself up, ensure you don't arrive dead on time (the Finns work on –ish time, don't they?) and bring a small gift with you.
- Ⓑ You dress up, arrive dead on time, but come empty-handed as you are only invited round for coffee.
- Ⓒ You don't dress up, arrive dead on time and bring the hostess a posy of flowers.

### Comments

It will be rare to be asked to a dinner party, but Finns more often entertain by asking people around for coffee. Traditionally this will be served with seven varieties of cakes/cookies. Never be late. Even if you think you will be 10 minutes late, it is polite to give your host a call. The Finns dress casually, so you will want to smarten up without getting too dressed up. Answer Ⓒ. Arrive with a posy of flowers for the invite to coffee, or for a dinner party you should bring flowers and/or wine.

## SITUATION 6

You have gone to a summer shindig in the middle of nowhere and need to get home. You phone a local taxi firm to pick you up to take you back to the city. However, you realise you probably haven't got enough cash to cover the fare. Do you ....?

**A** Haggle and agree the fare with the taxi driver before you set off.
**B** Think he is a rural peasant and will probably charge you twice as much as he would a Finn, so on arrival start to negotiate like mad.
**C** Trust that he is honourable, enquire the price of the fare, ask about a discount and not worry because you can pay by credit card.

## Comments

Taxis have impressive communications systems. Wherever you are in Finland, a taxi driver can enquire the cost of a journey to a specific location and a computer will give him the exact fare. Payment by credit card can be made through the remote electronic metre installed in the car. Answer **C**. Taxi drivers are trustworthy and do not expect a tip.

## SITUATION 7

You are with a group of a dozen people at dinner. You have been served, along with the people immediately around you. Should you ...?

**A** Start eating so that your dinner doesn't get cold.
**B** Wait for everyone to be served.
**C** Start eating as soon as half the people have been served.

## Comments

Whatever traditional etiquette may have said, it is common to start eating as soon as four people at the table have been served. Answer **A**.

## SITUATION 8

Drinking a toast with Finnish white wine (*koskenkorva*) usually involves:

**A** Knocking the drink back in one gulp and throwing your glass into the fireplace.

**B** Taking polite sips, remembering that you are drinking neat vodka!
**C** Knocking the drink back in one gulp, exclaiming "*Kiipis*!"

## Comments

*Koskenkorva* is neat vodka and the Finns are proud of the fact that it can be lethal. However, when taking a toast with this Finnish white wine, knock it back in one go. Answer **C**. *Kiipis*, pronounced 'key-piss' means 'cheers' or 'bottoms-up'.

## SITUATION 9

When having a conversation with a Finn, an excellent topic to discuss would be:

**A** Past times, especially history of the war with Russia.
**B** About Sweden beating Finland at ice hockey.
**C** About the unbelievable success of Nokia mobile phones—good for Finland!

## Comments

Whilst the Finns are very proud of not being beaten in the World War II and are very keen on sport, the perfect topic of conversation is their global dominance of the mobile phone industry! Answer **C**. It is almost a status symbol in Finland to have the latest Nokia phone.

## SITUATION 10

You are at the airport and have been called for boarding. Everyone has their boarding ticket and, logically, has a seat on the plane. There is a large group of people huddled around the boarding gate. Do you .....?

**A** Find the end of the queue and wait your turn to get on the plane.
**B** Just push your way in where you can.
**C** Remember there is no seat allocation on domestic flights, so it is everyone for themselves, and you owe it to yourself to get on the plane as soon as you can.

## Comments

There is no seat allocation on domestic flights, but the Finns do queue in an orderly fashion. Jumping the queue will bring you disapproving looks. Answer Ⓐ. In many places, there is a ticketing system to ensure people are served in order—at the post office, in banks, chemists, supermarkets and travel agencies—but not at the airport; it is a free for all. People push in politely!

# DO'S AND DON'TS

## DO'S

- Keep your promises—the Finns keep their promises and naturally assume you will keep yours.
- Take note that Finnish people may seem very naïve (they are extremely honest), but they are not gullible. If you cross them once, you have crossed them for life. They will never trust you again.
- Shaking someone's hand on a deal is as good as signing a contract.
- Remember that the Finns dress far more casually than most Europeans.
- Take the nearest seat to the door in the sauna if you are unused to it, so you can get out without disturbing others.
- Remember the Finns might well want to test you by keeping the sauna very hot!
- Try the local cuisine (as my Finnish friends say, "It isn't dangerous!").
- Be prepared to drink lots and lots of coffee.
- Do use simple expressions and short sentences (see note on the opposite page about irony).
- Do remember that Finnish people have been taught from an early age that silence is golden.
- Remember that Finnish people are very unused to small talk. They aren't rude, but can sometimes come across as such.
- Do bring up Santa Claus and Nokia in your conversations. The Finns are extremely proud of these two home-grown products.
- Remember that the Finns are very proud that they fought off their aggressors in World War II and remained independent and unoccupied. However, they are a little ashamed that they had to bow to the might of Russia during the 1950s, 1960s and 1970s.
- Do appreciate what a difficult struggle Finland has had, to be its own country, and that it is still relatively young (90 years).

- Remember that Finland was virtually a closed country until it joined the EU in the mid-1990s.
- Make jokes about the Swedes. The Finns have a love-hate relationship with them and traditionally they are the butt of Finnish humour.
- You can drink one beer only and still drive (the limit is 0.5 per cent).
- Be prepared for the cold. The temperature will drop to –30°C at least once each winter.
- Do remember that winter tires are compulsory for driving during the cold months. Even though you think the Finns drive like maniacs on icy roads, they are used to it.
- Take into account that the culture in the southern part of Finland (Helsinki-Turku-Tampere-triangle) is a lot more urban and cosmopolitan than the culture in the other parts of Finland.
- Remember that Finland belongs to Euro zone.
- Note: nearly all Finns studied English for several years at school so their understanding of English is generally a lot better than you might think at first. First impressions are distorted by the fact that, in the beginning, many of them find speaking English uncomfortable.
- Note: many Finns joke about themselves in self-ironic jokes in which someone shows that mistakes can happen to herself/himself, too.
- Remember that ice-hockey is a very popular sport in Finland. Especially among males, it is quite common to discuss ice-hockey during business negotiations.
- Remember that the scale of things in Finland is smaller than many other European countries, the population being only some 5 million people.
- Do remember that Finns are sport fanatics. Get to know which Finn is famous at the moment—always a racing driver!
- Be aware of the strong Finnish wholesalers and their high margins. If they don't let you into the market, you won't get in!
- Do remember that Finnish women are quite successful and powerful in business and in politics. However, Finland is a very 'macho' country in attitude towards women.

- Finland may be the number one at Internet connections but newspapers, magazines and TV are still number one when introducing new products into the Finnish market. TV commercials have a great impact on sales.

## DON'TS

- Don't assume that because your Finnish colleague speaks good English, your meanings/message have been interpreted as you wanted them to be understood.
- Don't be late for meetings—give a call if you are going to be late.
- Don't dress too formally for business meetings (suits are a rarity in Finland).
- Be careful drinking Finnish 'white wine'(vodka) called *Koskinkorva*.
- Don't wear your swimming costume in the sauna.
- Don't use "Would you....?", "Could you....?" etc., when asking someone to do something. They don't understand this is a command!
- Don't take any personal slight when the Finns speak very directly. When they ask you to do something, it can sound like a command (see above). They say what they want and they believe what you say.
- Don't use British 'understatement' or irony in your speech. This is guaranteed to be misunderstood.
- Don't speak unless you have something important to contribute. Remember that silence is valued.
- Don't be concerned if strangers do not return your big smile. The Finns are unused to grinning foreigners, but they will eventually give you a quick nod.
- Don't think because everyone looks miserable that they are miserable! Finnish people are unaccustomed to walking around smiling.
- Don't assume that silence means agreement. Usually it means the opposite—but they won't say anything because they don't want to offend you.
- Don't judge Finns by their dress, manners or etiquette. They have low self-confidence in this respect, being unsure of how to dress or how to behave outside their own

environment. However, they are always perfectly polite and anxious to please.

- Don't be surprised at how much the Finns use their mobile phones. Text messaging is very popular and they are all Olympic champions at it. Also, vending machines can be operated by them, along with petrol pumps and the car wash.
- Don't tip taxi drivers or waitresses, etc.
- Don't define distances in terms of time—use km. It is 400 km from Kuopio to Helsinki (about four hours driving time). In the UK, we would say that we lived about two hours away from London by train/car.
- Don't drive on the left in Finland.
- Don't mention Finland and Russia in the same breath. The Finns hate being associated with the Russians, for whom they have a great loathing and distrust.
- Don't be noisy in public places—and don't let your children run around screaming and shouting.
- Don´t think that the Finns being quiet in a conversation means that they are impolite or bored—normally it is just that most of the Finns are not accustomed to small talk.
- If you visit Finland in the winter, don´t think that the weather is always as cold. The changes between seasons are great and the temperature can vary a lot in different parts of the country.
- Don't cross the street against a red light. Finnish mothers teach their children to wait until the light turns green.
- Don't expect Finnish companies to answer business letters or faxes. Send an SMS (text message) on the mobile phone.
- Don't think that young Finns are as silent and shy as the old generation. The youngsters have grown up with CNN, MTV and Interrail and quite a few have spent their summers or a whole year in the UK or in the US.

# GLOSSARY

## GENERAL GREETINGS AND PHRASES

| English | Finnish |
|---|---|
| Good morning | *Hyvää huomenta* |
| How do you do? | *Paivää* |
| Good evening/Goodbye | *Hyvää iltaa/Näkemiïn* |
| Yes, No | *Kyllä, Ei* |
| Thank you, Hello | *Kiitos, Hei!* |
| Cheap, expensive | *Halpa, kallis* |
| Cold, warm | *Kylmä, lämmin* |
| More, less | *Enemmän, vähemmän* |
| Mr, Mrs, husband, wife | *Herra, rouva, mies, vaimo* |
| Woman, man, boy, girl | *Nainen, mies, poika, tyttö* |
| Where, there, when, who | *Missä, tuolla, millain, kuka* |
| I do not understand | *En ymmärrä* |
| How much is it? | *Paljonko se maksaa?* |
| I will buy it | *Ostan sen* |
| Does anyone speak English? | *Puhuuko kukaan englantia?* |
| I come from England. | *Olen kotoisin Englannista* |
| One, two, three four, five | *yksi, kaksi, kolme, neljä, viisi* |
| Six, seven, eight | *kuusi, seitsemän, kahdeksan* |
| Nine, ten | *yhdeksän, kymmenen* |
| Twelve, fifteen | *kaksitoista, viisitoista* |
| Twenty, fifty | *kaksikymmentä, viisikymmentä* |
| Hundred, five hundred | *sata, viisi sataa* |
| Thousand, five thousand | *tuhat, viisi tuhatta* |
| Ten thousand | *kymmennen tuhatta* |
| Fifty thousand | *viisikymmentä tuhatta* |
| Hundred thousand, million | *sata tuhatta, miljoona* |

| English | Finnish |
|---|---|
| At two o'clock | *Kello kahdelta* |
| Tomorrow | *Huomenna* |
| How long do I have to wait? | *Kauanko minun pitää odottaa?* |
| Arrival time | *Saapumisaika* |
| Departure time | *Lähtöaika* |

## EATING OUT

| English | Finnish |
|---|---|
| Please bring me the menu | *Saanko ruokalistan* |
| Please bring me the bill | *Saanko laskun* |
| Receipt, extra chair | *Kuitin, lisätuolin* |
| Do you have free tables? | *Onko teilla vapaita pöytia?* |
| Where is the toilet? | *Missä on WC?* |
| I would like to order local specialities | *Haluaisin tilata paikallisia ruokia* |
| Bring me something good you have ready | *Tuokaa minulle jotain hyvää mitä teillä on valmiina* |
| Restaurant, fast food | *Ravintola, pikaruoka* |
| Coffee, tea, orange juice | *Kahvi, tee, tuoremehu* |
| Beer, wine, milk, water, vodka | *Olut, viini, maito, vesi, koskenkorva* |
| Bread, cheese, butter | *Leipä, juusto, voi* |
| Salt, sugar, pepper | *Suola, sokeri, pippuri* |
| Ketchup, mustard | *Ketsuppi, sinappi* |
| Salad, soup, vegetables | *Salaatti, keitto, vihannekset* |
| Potatoes, chips | *Peruna, ranskalaiset perunat* |
| Meat, beefsteak | *Liha, pihvi* |
| Mutton, veal, pork, sausage, fish | *Lammas, vasikka, sika, makkara kala* |
| Boiled, fried | *Keitetty, paistettu* |
| Baked, grilled | *Leivottu, grillattu* |
| Dessert, fruit | *Jälkiruoka, hedelmat* |
| Cigarettes, ashtray | *Savukkeet, tuhkakuppi* |

## TRAVEL AND DIRECTIONS

| English | Finnish |
|---|---|
| Left, right, straight | *Vasen, oikea, suoraan* |
| Where is …? | *Missä on…?* |
| How far is …? | *Kuinka kaukana on …?* |
| Could you tell me the way to… | *Voisitteko neuvoa tien* |
| Town centre | *Keskusta* |
| Town hall | *Kaupungintalo* |
| Indoor market | *Kauppahalli* |
| Market square | *Kauppatori* |
| Museum | *Museo* |
| Art gallery | *Taide Galleria* |
| Theatre | *Teatteri* |
| Post office, railway station | *Posti, rautatieasema* |
| Bus station | *Linja-autosema* |
| Police, harbour, airport | *Poliisi, atama, lentokenttä* |
| Customs, passport | *Tulli, passi* |
| Car documents | *Autopaperit* |
| Car, bus, truck | *Auto, linja-auto, rekka* |
| Train, aeroplane | *Juna, lentokone* |
| Boat, ship, ferry | *Vene, laiva, lautta* |
| Rail, track | *Rautatie* |
| Hill | *Tunturi, Kukkula* |
| Mountain | *Vuori* |
| Lake | *Jarvi* |
| River | *Joki* |
| Island | *Saari* |
| Park | *Puisto* |
| Road | *Tie* |
| Street | *Katu* |
| House | *Talo* |
| Church | *Kirkko* |
| Castle | *Linna* |

| English | Finnish |
|---|---|
| Town | *Kaupunki* |
| Village | *Kyla* |
| Hotel, camping site, cottage | *Hotelli, leirintäalue, mökki* |
| Room for one/two nights | *Huone yhdelle/kaski yotä* |
| For two/four persons | *Kahdelle/neljälle* |
| Bathroom, shower, TV | *Kylpyhuone, suihku, TV* |
| Floor, room, lift, stairs | *Kerros, huone, hiss, portaat* |
| Guarded parking space | *Vartioitu, parkkipaikka* |
| Breakfast, lunch, bar | *Aamiainen, lounas, baari* |

## SIGNS

| English | Finnish |
|---|---|
| Entrance | *Sis äänkäynti* |
| Toilet | *WC* |
| Ladies | *Naistenhuone/naiset* |
| Gents | *Miestenhuone/miehet* |
| Arrival | *Saapuminen* |
| Arrivals | *Saapuvat* |
| Departure | *Lähtöminen* |
| Departures | *Lähtevät* |

## HEALTH

| English | Finnish |
|---|---|
| Doctor | *Lääkari* |
| Hospital | *Sairaala* |
| Accident and Emergency | *Ensiapu* |
| Pharmacy | *Apteekki* |
| Medicine | *Lääke* |
| Ill | *Sairas* |
| Sick (nausea) | *Pahoinvoiva, Huonovointinen* |
| Pain | *Kipu* |

| English | Finnish |
|---|---|
| Headache | *Päänsärky* |
| Stomachache | *Vatsakipu* |
| Body | *Keho* |
| Arm | *Käsi Varsi* |
| Hand | *Käsi* |
| Leg/Foot | *Jalka* |
| Neck | *Niska* |
| Head | *Pää* |
| Eyes | *Silmät* |
| Ears | *Korvat* |
| Nose | *Nenä* |
| Throat | *Kurkku* |
| Sore throat | *Kurkkukipu* |
| Sore | *Kipea* |
| Itch | *Kutina* |
| Rash | *Ihottuma* |
| Spots | *Näppylät* |
| Skin | *Iho* |
| Sunburn | *Auringossa Palanut* |
| Wound | *Vamma* |
| Cut | *Haava* |
| Stitches | *Tikit* |
| Plaster | *Kipsi* |
| Antiseptic (cream) | *Antiseptinen (voide)* |
| Disinfectant | *Desinfiointiaine* |

## BUSINESS

| English | Finnish |
|---|---|
| Meeting | *Kokous* |
| Appointment | *Tapaaminen* |
| Contract | *Sopimus* |
| Negotiation | *Neuvottelu* |

| English | Finnish |
|---|---|
| At what time? | *Mihin aikaan?* |
| | *Milloin?* |
| | *Koska?* |
| Turnover | *Liikevaihto* |
| Profit | *Voitto* |
| Bank | *Pankki* |
| Post Office | *Posti* |
| Headquarters | *Pääkonttori* |
| Owner/manager | *Omistaja/Johtaja* |
| Managing Director | *Toimitusjohtaja* |
| Finance Director | *Talousjohtaja* |
| Phone | *Puhelin* |
| Mobile phone | *Kännykkä* |
| Address | *Osoite* |
| Telephone number | *Puhelin-numero* |
| Contact | *Yhteyshenkilo* |
| Name | *Nimi* |
| Expensive | *Kallis* |
| Cheap | *Halpa* |
| Value for money | *Vastinetta Rahoille* |
| How much? | *Kuinka Paljon?* |
| How many? | *Monta?* |
| Good quality | *Hyvä Laatu* |
| Reliable | *Luotettava* |
| Supplier | *Toimittaja* |
| Customer | *Asiakas* |
| Manufacturer | *Valmistaja* |
| Wholesaler | *Tukkumyyjä* |

# RESOURCE GUIDE

## GETTING TO KNOW HELSINKI:

Available from the City Tourist Office:

- *Helsinki Visitors' Guide* (its own brochure)
- *Helsinki This Week* (brochure by Helsinki Expert)
- *City in English* (a newspaper)

They also have lots of other information in English concerning Helsinki.

Below is a list of the most popular annual events:

- New Year's Eve, 31 December, Senate Square
- May Day Eve and May Day, 30 April and 1 May (Student and national celebrations, including traditional picnics in Kaivopuisto Park on May Day)
- Sailing Season Opening, early May
- Tuska Festival at Kaisaniemi Park, (the biggest heavy metal event in the Nordic Region), June
- Midsummer at Seurasaari (midsummer festival with bonfires), June
- The Provincial Event, June, Senate Square
- Helsinki Day (Helsinki's birthday events throughout the city center), June
- Jazz Espa at Esplanade park (jazz concerts on the Espa stage daily 4:00 pm–6:00 pm), July
- Helsinki Cup (international junior soccer tournament), July
- Helsinki City Marathon, August
- Viapori Jazz at Suomenlinna, August
- Vantaa Baroque Week, early August
- Night of the Arts, all around the city centre (cultural happenings fill the streets of Helsinki late into the evening), August
- Helsinki Festival (festival of dance, music, theatre), end of August–September
- The Baltic Herring Market, October
- Opening of the Christmas Lights at Aleksanterinkatu, November

- Finnish Independence Day (ceremonial events and festivities), 6 December
- Lucia Parade from Helsinki Cathedral to Finlandia Hall, 13 December
- Christmas markets on December: St. Thomas Christmas Market at Esplanade Park and Women's Christmas Market at Wanha Satama

For up to date information on events in Helsinki and in Finland, visit:

- http://www.visithelsinki.fi
- http://www.visitfinland.com
- http://www.festivals.fi
- http://www.kulttuuri.net

## GETTING TO HELSINKI—BY AIR:

- Helsinki-Vantaa International Airport (HEL)
  Tel: (09) 82771 or (09) 61511
  Fax (09) 8277-2099.
  Website: http://www.finavia.fi
  The airport, with two linked terminals for national and international traffic, is located in Vantaa, 19 km (about 12 miles) from the city centre.
- Major airlines: More than 25 airlines fly into Helsinki from all major European cities, including a daily service from New York, non-stop flights from Miami, San Francisco and Toronto, and new direct flights from Asia. The national airline is Finnair (Tel: 600-140-140; Email: information@finnair.fi; Website: http://www.finnair.fi).
- Approximate flight times to Helsinki: From London is 2 hours 50 minutes; from New York is 8 hours; from Los Angeles is 17 hours 15 minutes; from Toronto is 8 hours 40 minutes; and from Sydney is 27 hours 30 minutes (two stopovers).
- Transport to the city: Bus 615 goes to Rautatientori (Railway Square) every 20–30 minutes (€ 3.60); while a Finnair bus goes to the centre with various stops (€ 5.20). Standard taxis charge about € 25–30, while shared taxis, run by Yellow Line, cost between € 22–30; (Tel: 0600-555-555).

## GETTING AROUND HELSINKI

### Public Transport

Helsingin Kaupungin Liikennelaitos (HKL)/Helsinki City Transport (Tel: (09) 010-0111; Website: http://www.hel.fi/hkl) operates the metro, local trams, buses and the ferry to Suomenlinna Island Fortress. A ticket for a single journey costs € 2.20 when purchased on board, € 2 when purchased beforehand. Tickets solely for trams are cheaper at € 2 (on board) or € 1.80 (pre-purchased). Transfers are allowed for single and multi-trip tickets within one hour of the time stamped on the ticket when initially boarding. Tickets can be purchased beforehand from ticket machines found in metro stations, some tram stations and the departure point of Suomenlinna ferry. Buses and trams run 5:45 am–12.00 am. There are also special night buses that operate through the night on Friday–Saturday and Saturday–Sunday nights, price € 3.50, departure point Railway Station.

To find out about the prices for all the ticket types, visit: http://www.hel.fi/wps/portal/HKL_en/Artikkeli?WCM_GLOBAL_CONTEXT = /en/Helsinki + City + Transport/Tickets/Ticket + fares + for + Helsinki + local + transport

### Passes

The Helsinki City Transport Tourist Ticket allows unlimited travel on all buses, trams, metro and local trains in Helsinki (plus the Suomenlinna ferry; see the Sightseeing section for details). Prices: one day—€ 6 adults, € 3 children; three days—€ 12 adults, € 6 children; five days—€ 18 adults, € 9 children. Can be bought from Helsinki City Tourist Information, HKL office at the Railway Station and on board (trams and busses, only one day).

### The Helsinki Card

A handy and economical way of getting around the city and getting to know its numerous attractions. A transport and entrance ticket all in one. The card is accompanied by a guidebook. Unlimited free travel on public transport and free entrance to the major sights of Helsinki (also free sightseeing bus tour around the city by Helsinki Expert). 24-hour pass at

€ 33, 48-hour at € 43 and 72-hour at € 53 (children's prices: € 11/ € 14/ € 17). For more information, visit Helsinki Expert: http://www.helsinkiexpert.fi/index_english.html.

## Taxis

Most taxis are Mercedes. They can be hailed on the street or booked by telephone from Helsinki Taxi Centre (Tel: (09) 700-700). A taxi is available for hire if the yellow 'TAXI' sign is lit. Tipping is not required.

## Limousines

Providers include Limousine Service Helsinki (Tuulimyllyntie 7; Tel: (09) 2797-800; Fax: (09) 2797-8027). For more information and rates for limousine service, visit: http://www.limousineservice.fi/index_eng.php

## Driving in the City

As the public transport system is excellent and most of central Helsinki is accessible on foot, it is not necessary to take a car into Helsinki city centre. The city is divided into three parking zones, of which Zone I (I-vyöhyke) is the most central, and accordingly the most expensive. Parking is subject to a charge in all zones from Monday to Friday from 9:00 am to 7:00 pm. With a few exceptions, parking is free after 7:00 pm. On Saturdays, parking is usually subject to a charge in Zone 1. The chargeable parking hours are marked on each ticket machine and parking meter. Parking meters take ordinary coins or parking cards, which can be purchased in advance from R-kioski and service stations. The current fees are:

- Zone 1: € 3.00/hour
- Zone 2: € 1.60/hour
- Zone 3: € 0.80/hour

## Car Hire

A credit card is usually required as a deposit. The minimum age for car hire varies from 19–21 and extra charges are made for additional drivers. One year's driving experience is required. Car hire is available at the airport, railway station, major hotels and tourist offices. Operators include:

- Budget
  Malminkatu 24
  Tel: (09) 686-6500; Fax: (09) 685-3350
- Europcar InterRent
  Radisson SAS Hesperia Hotel
  Tel: (09) 4780-2220; Fax: (09) 4780-2222
- Hertz
  Mannerheimintie 44
  Tel: (020) 555-2300

### Bicycle Hire

Owing to Helsinki's flat terrain, bicycles are a popular way of getting around and the lanes run concurrently with footpaths. It should be noted that all bike traffic lights must be obeyed to avoid a fine. Here are some current bicycle hiring companies:

- Greenbike
  Website: http://www.greenbike.fi/vuokraus_eng.html
- Töölönlahden ulkoilukeskus (Nordic Fitness Sports Park)
  Website: http://www.ulos.fi/toolo
- Ecobike
  Website: http://www.ecobike.fi/index.en.html

### Boat Hire

See below for complete list of hirers of canoes, kayaks, etc.

## CANOE RENTAL, KAYAKS, PADDLING COURSES AND SAFARIS

- Bear & Water
  Keilaranta 11, Espoo
  Tel: (09) 455-6066 (shop), (09) 455-6141 (rental)
  Website: http://www.bearwater.fi
  Prices from €14 per 2 hours.
- Canoe Rent Center
  PL 309, 00151 Helsinki
  Tel: (050) 585-6000
  Email: markku.rajala@canoerentcenter-finland.fi
  Website: http://www.canoerentcenter-finland.fi

Canoe Safaris in Southern Finland. Prices: € 30/day, € 50/weekend, € 100/week.

- Helsingin Melontakeskus
  Rajasaarenpenger 8, Helsinki
  Tel: (09) 436-2500
  Email: myynti@helsinginmelontakeskus.fi
  Website: http://www.helsinginmelontakeskus.fi
  Office open Mon–Fri, 10:00 am–3:00 pm, paddling safaris and event services; prices from € 10/hour.
- Rastilan leirintäalue /Rastila camping
  Helsinki, Karavaanikatu 4
  Tel: (09) 310-78517
  Email: rastilacamping@hel.fi
  Website: http://www.hel.fi/rastila
  Kayak rental during the summer. Kayak for one: € 5/hour, € 25/24 hours + deposit; kayak for two: € 9/hour, € 40/day + deposit.
- Töölönlahden Venevuokraamo
  Helsinki, Behind Finlandia Hall at Töölö Bay
  Tel: (041) 530-9240
  Season starts 15 May 2007; rowing boats and pedal boats.
- Welhonpesä oy
  Kauppakuja 10, 01801 Klaukkala
  Tel: (09) 879-8886, (040) 544-2501
  Email: welho@nettilinja.fi
  Website: http://www.welhonpesa.fi
  Canoes and kayaks for rent, paddling courses and safaris.
  Opening hours: Mon–Fri 10:00 am–5:00 pm,
  Sat 10:00 am–2:00 pm.

## EATING AND DRINKING

### Restaurants

For information on restaurants, visit http://www.eat.fi—a dedicated website in English—or http://www.visithelsinki.fi (see the 'Helsinki menu'). Pick up *Helsinki This Week*, the free English-language magazine which provides information about restaurants and events. See also Chapter 6 on Food & Entertaining for selected restaurant listings.

## WHAT TO SEE AND DO IN HELSINKI

- Helsinki Expert Sightseeing—Sightseeing trip aboard deluxe coach showing you the top sights of the capital. Voice-overs in ten languages and information given in small, easily absorbable chunks. For updated information on Helsinki Expert's tours, see: http://www.helsinkiexpert.fi/sightseeing/

In addition to the sightseeing bus, during the summer there are different sightseeing tours by boat around the coast of Helsinki and the nearest islands. The companies include:

- Sun lines
  http://www.sunlines.fi/web/index.php?id = 31
- Royal line
  http://www.royalline.fi/english/english.html
- IHA-lines
  http://www.ihalines.fi

### Attractions

You can check out the main attractions at: http://www.visithelsinki.fi. Definitely one of the most popular attractions is Suomenlinna fortress island (see below under Museums).

- Korkeasaari
  Helsinki Zoo is located on the picturesque island of Korkeasaari. Ferries from the Market Square and Hakaniemi (ferries during the summer, during the winter reachable by public transportation: http://www.korkeasaari.fi/englanti/sub/tietoa_kavijalle.html).
- Senate Square
  Surrounded by neo-classic buildings, the square represents the soul of the city. Here you can find the grand Cathedral.
- Sibelius Monument
  Created in honour of Finland's most famous composer and designed by Eija Hiltunen. Set in beautiful parkland.
- Temppeliaukio Church
  This church has been carved inside a solid rock face and has rough granite walls and a rolled copper roof. It represents its own work of art. Go here to listen to many concerts held throughout the year.

- Upenski Cathedral
  This impressive, red-brick structure with 13 golden cupolas is located near the harbour. It is the largest Orthodox church in Western Europe. It is a must to see the interior, which is vividly and ornately decorated with exquisite icons, paintings and chandeliers.

## MUSEUMS

- Ateneum
  The Finnish National Gallery is the oldest art museum in Finland.
- Finnish Museum of Natural History
  Look for the moose standing at the entrance. Fascinating collection of skeletons and fossils of mammals, reptiles and birds. Hands-on displays for children.
- Kiasma
  The Museum of Contemporary Art is housed in a fascinating building, designed by world famous architect Steven Holl. The museum is famed as much for its building and the aesthetic qualities of the interior design as for its contents. Café Kiasma on the ground floor is worth a visit.
- National Museum
  Set in a castle-style building, the National Museum houses an interesting collection of Finnish history from pre-historic to modern times.
- Seurasaari Open-Air Museum
  Large, spacious outdoor museum with folk buildings from different parts of Finland dating back to 17th century. Showing traditional rural life, also great for walks, picnics, even swimming at one or two beaches. Open May till end September.
- Sports Museum of Finland
  Located in the Olympic Stadium, specialising in Finnish sport and physical culture. History of Olympic Games and memories of the champions.
- Suomelinna Island Fortress
  This is included in UNESCO's World Heritage Sites. It is an ancient sea fortress and is the largest in Scandinavia.

Still inhabited and serviced by ferries from Market Square (Helsinki harbour), the island is both picturesque and awesome. Museums, visitor centre, church and cafes to visit. Great walks, caves, cliffs, and beach (of sorts), comes complete with canons! More info at: http://www.suomenlinna.fi/index.php?lang=eng

- Other popular museums: design museum, Arabia museum, Helsinki city museum, Amos Andersson museum, etc.
- Outside Helsinki, but near: for example Hvitträsk, Gallen-Kallela museum, Ainola, Heureka (not actually a museum but a science park, especially interesting for children: http://www.heureka.fi/portal/englanti).

## MARKETS

- Hakaniemi Market

  In striking contrast to Market Square, this market is located in the heart of working-class Helsinki. Colourful stalls and an abundance of fresh produce. There is also Hakaniemi market hall, next to the Hakaniemi market square.
- Hietalahti Flea Market

  From junk to gems, this is the best place to find anything—fresh produce, flowers and refreshments. There is also a market hall, which sells art and antiques, next to the Hietalahti market square (Hietalahti Antique and Art Hall).
- Market Square and Old Market Hall

  Bordered by the harbour, the market square is surrounded by interesting and picturesque examples of architecture. The Market Hall, which is located nearby, is a quaint old building and the purchase of local delicacies is a must! Sells everything from flowers to Lapp hunting knives.

## BEACHES

- Hietaniemi

  Sometimes referred to locally as Hietsu, Hietaniemi is the most obvious choice for the inhabitants of Helsinki. Swimming, sun worshipping, and modest refreshments. Bad parking, so taking the bus or walking is advisable.
- Pihlajasaari

  The perfect escape. Until recently, Helsinki's best-kept

secret. Nice beachfront, lots of sand, plenty of trees, rocks, boats and refreshments.

- Uunisaari
  A small island located 5 minutes by boat from the shores of the town. Boats from the Kompassi pier on Merisatamaranta. Café/restaurant, terrace, even a sauna (must be pre-booked).

## POOLS

- Yrjönkatu Swimming Hall
  Yrjönkatu 21 b, 00120 Helsinki
  Tel: (09) 310-87401
  A very popular swimming hall right in the city centre. For decades it was the only public indoor pool in Finland. Yrjönkatu Swimming Hall is an impressive example of 1920s classicism and it is an important building historically as well as architecturally. Over the decades, the hall has retained its original appearance. There are separate times for women and men. Customers may swim with or without a bathing suit. Bathing suits have been allowed since September 2001.
- Makelanrinne Swimming Centre
  Has Olympic-sized pool, diving tower, kiddy pools, whirlpools, sauna, steam sauna, solarium, hydrobic and a gym.
- Swimming Stadium
  Popular outdoor pool (Olympic proportions) set in expansive grounds. Open May to end September.
- Itakeskus Swimming Hall
  A tropical oasis features several pools, seven saunas, massage, solarium and gym. Situated entirely underground.

## SHOPPING

- Department Stores
  Stockmann is the biggest and perhaps the most exclusive in the Nordic countries; Sokos is a comprehensive store which has just been completely renovated; Anttila Kodin Ykkonen offers a wide selection of household goods and home furnishings.

- Shopping Centres
  Forum is arguably the biggest and most varied in the city centre; Itakeskus is 10 minutes away by metro from the city centre and the largest shopping centre in the Nordic countries, with 190 shops, restaurants and other services; Kluuvi has around 30 shops and restaurants; Kamp Gallery has around 50 shops and restaurants, featuring elegant shopping gallery on three floors; The Kiseleff Bazaar is a treasure trove for tourists, full of Finnish handicrafts, giftware and fashion. Located on Senate Square. There is a brand new big shopping centre, Kamppi, right in the city centre (the main bus station is in the same building, downstairs). It advertises as 'six floors of shops, services, leisure and entertainment' (http://www.kamppi.fi/english/index.html).
- Music
  Fuga for classical; Digelius for jazz, world, ethno; Free Record Shop for various music.
- Clothing Stores
  Finnish clothing stores especially in Pohjoisesplanadi and Design district (see below), international brands and chain stores (H&M etc.) especially on Aleksanterinkatu and shopping centres.
- Interesting Shopping Streets
  Fredrikinkatu, Korkeavuorenkatu and Iso Roobertinkatu all near the main shopping area, having numerous and varied small shops with a character of their own. There is also the Design District, with lots of small design shops where you can find Finnish design products and really original works.

## THE ARTS, THEATRES AND CINEMAS

- Finnish National Opera
  Helsinginkatu 58
  Tel: (09) 4030-2211
  Opera and Ballet
- National Theatre
  Railway Square.
  Tel: (09) 1733-1331

The biggest and oldest Finnish-language theatre in Finland. Four stages, offering about 20 plays, including children's theatre. Performances in Finnish.

- Helsinki City Theatre
  Elaintarhantie 5
  Tel: (09) 394-0422
  Drama, music theatre and dance theatre.
- Swedish Theatre
  Erottaja
  Tel: (09) 6162-1411
  Performances in Swedish.
- Dance Theatre Hurjaruuth
  Cable Factory, Tallberginkatu 1 A, 2nd floor
  Tel: (09) 565-7250
- Zodiak
  The Centre for New Dance
  Cable Factory, Tallberginkatu 1 B
  Tel: (09) 694-4948
- Cinemas
  Information about films showing is available from hotels, daily papers and cinemas. Box offices open 30 mins to an hour before the first showing of the day. Films are shown in their original language, with subtitles in Finnish. Cinemas include Kinopalatsi (10 screens), Kaisaniemenkatu 2B, or Tennispalatsi (14 screens), Salomonkatu 15, (both are now owned by Finnkino, Tel: 0600-007-007).

## MEDICAL SERVICES

- Emergencies: Helsinki University Central Hospital
  Toolo Hospital for serious accidents at Topeliuksenkatu 5, Tel: 4711 and Meilahti Hospital for medicine and surgery at Haartmaninkatu 4, Tel: 4711. Contact details for other hospitals and health centres are available in every hotel. For non-emergency visits, especially for foreigners, go to Mehiläinen Clinic: http://www.mehilainen.fi
- Emergency Dental Care
  Ympyratalo Dental Clinic at Siltasaarenkatu 18a, Tel: (09) 709-6611. Dental Clinic Oral (on duty 24h): http://www.hammassairaala.fi (especially for foreigners).

- Pharmacy
  Look for the sign 'Apteekki'. Yliopiston Apteekki at Mannerheimintie 96 is open 24 hours a day.

## INTERNET ACCESS IN HELSINKI

### Free Public Internet access/WLAN

Tip! free WLAN (wireless internet connection) in some areas eg. the Esplanade park (OpenEspa).

- Cafe Engel
  Aleksanterinkatu 26
  Tel: (09) 652-776
  Mon–Fri 8:00 am–10:00 pm, Sat 9:00 am–10:00 pm, Sun 10:00 am–10:00 pm. Free WLAN in the backroom.
- Cafe Carusel
  Merisatamanranta 10
  Tel: (09) 622-4522
  Mon–Sun 10:00 am–10:00 pm
  Two terminals for customers, WLAN
- Cafe Carusel Carusel-Esplanad Bar & Cafe
  Eteläesplanadi 2
  Mon 8:15 am–5:00 pm, Tue–Fri 8:15 am–10:00 pm
  Sat 9:00 am–10:00 pm, Sun 11:00 am–5:00 pm
  Free WLAN.
- Cafe Ursula
  Ehrenströmintie 3
  Tel: (09) 652-817
  Monday–Sunday 9:00 am–8:00 pm
  Free WLAN
- Cafe Ursula/Aleksi 13
  Aleksanterinkatu 13, 5th floor
  Mon–Fri 9:00 am–9:00 pm, Sat 9:00 am–6:00 pm
  Free WLAN
- Cafe Kiasma
  Mannerheiminaukio 2
  Tel: (09) 1733-6504
  In summer: Tue–Sat 10:00 am–10:00 pm
  Sun 10:00 am–6:00 pm
  Free WLAN in parts of the cafe

- Cafe Java
  Mannerheimintie 22-24
  Tel: (09) 640-065
  Mon–Thu 8:00 am–11:30 pm, Fri 8:00 am–1:30 am,
  Sat 9:00 am–1:30 am, Sun 11:00 am–11:30 pm. Free WLAN
- DTM Café
  Iso Roobertinkatu 28
  Tel: (09) 676-315
  Mon–Sat 9:00 am–4:00 am, Sun 12:00 pm–4:00 am
  Three terminals for customers.
- Parliament Visitor Center
  Arkadiankatu 3
  Tel: (09) 432-2198
  Mon–Thu 10:00 am–6:00 pm, Fri 10:00 am–4:00 pm
  Six terminals
- Helsinki City Tourist Office
  Pohjoisesplanadi 19
  Tel: (09) 169-3757
  In summer: Mon–Fri 9:00 am–8:00 pm
  Sat–Sun 9:00 am–6:00 pm.
  In winter: Mon–Fri 9:00 am–6:00 pm
  Sat–Sun 10:00 am–4:00 pm
  Three terminals, WLAN
- Café Soihtu
  Aurorankatu 13 B 16
  Tel: (045) 652-0787
  Mon–Fri 11:00 am–9:00 pm, Sat 1:00 pm–9:00 pm
  Sun 1:00 pm–6:00 pm
  Two terminals for customers, WLAN.
- Meetingpoint@Lasipalatsi
  Lasipalatsi, Mannerheimintie 22-24
  Tel: (09) 3108-5900
  Mon–Fri 11:00 am–6:00 pm
  13 terminals, WLAN
- Compass Youth Information Center
  Lasipalatsi, Mannerheimintie 22-24
  Tel: (09) 3108-0080
  Mon, Wed, Thu 12:00 pm–7:00 pm
  Tue, Fri 12:00 pm–4:00 pm

Seven terminals, max. 30 minutes
Note please! Age limit under 26 years

- Kontupiste Information Center
  Keinulaudankuja 4B, (Kontula Shopping Center)
  Tel: (09) 340-2104
  Mon–Fri 10:00 am–6:00 pm, Sat 10:00 am–5:00 pm
  11 terminals, max 30 minutes
- Kämp Gallery
  Kluuvikatu 4, 2nd floor
  Mon–Sat 8:00 am–9:00 pm
  Sun 8:00 am–9:00 pm (ony in the summer)
  A free terminal
- Luckan Information Center
  Simonkatu 8
  Tel: (09) 6813-4510
  Mon 10:00 am–4:00 pm, Tue 12:00 pm–8:00 pm,
  Wed–Fri 12:00 pm –4:00 pm, Sat 12:00 pm–3:00 pm
  Free 30 min/person/day
- Nordic Institute in Finland
  Kaisaniemenkatu 9
  Tel: (09) 1800-380
  Mon, Tue, Thu 10:00 am–5:00 pm
  Wed 10:00 am–8:00 pm, Fri 10:00 am–4:00 pm
  Four terminals.
- Restaurant Rytmi
  Toinen Linja 2
  Tel: (09) 7231-5550
  Mon–Sat 11:00 am–2:00 am
  A free terminal for customers, free WLAN
- Restaurant Toveri
  Castreninkatu 3
  Tel: (09) 753-3862
  Mon–Thu 4:00 pm–2:00 am, Fri–Sat 3:00 pm–2:00 am
  A free terminal for customers

**Robert's Coffee Cafes:**

- City-Käytävä
  Aleksanterinkatu 21
  Tel: (09) 6227-1960

Mon–Fri 7:00 am–8:00 pm, Sat 10:00 am–4:00 pm
Two terminals for customers for 15 min.

- Forum
  Mannerheimintie 20 B
  Tel: (041) 445-4904
  Mon–Fri 7:00 am–8:00 pm, Sat 10:00 am–6:00 pm
  Four terminals for customers for 15 min.
- Kluuvi
  Kluuvikatu 7
  Tel: (09) 6871-0570
  Mon–Fri 7:30 am–9:00 pm, Sat 10:00 am–8:00 pm,
  Sun 12:00 pm–6:00 pm
  Two terminals for customers for 15 min.
- Netcup
  Stockmann, Aleksanterinkatu 52
  Tel: (09) 121-3759
  Mon–Fri 9:00 am–9:00 pm, Sat 9:00 am–6:00 pm
  Two terminals for customers for 15 min.
- Olympia Terminal
  Olympiaranta 1
  Tel: (09) 662-958
  Mon–Sun 9:00 am–7:00 pm
  One terminal for customers for 15 min.

**Wayne's Coffee Cafes:**

- Aleksanterinkatu 11
  Tel: (09) 679-725
  Mon–Sat 10:00 am–9:00 pm, Sun 12:00 pm–7:00 pm
  Two terminals, WLAN.
- Kaisaniemenkatu 3
  Tel: (040) 413-5401
  Mon–Fri 8:00 am–9:00 pm
  Sat 10:00 am–9:00 pm, Sun 12:00 pm–9:00 pm
  One terminal, WLAN
- Yrjönkatu 30
  Tel: (09) 6227-1965
  Mon–Fri, 8:30 am–6:00 pm, Sat 10:00 am–6:00 pm
  One terminal, WLAN

## Internet Cafés, Call Centres, WLAN with a Fee

- Café Senaatti
  Kiseleff House, Aleksanterinkatu 28
  Tel: (09) 602-462
  Mon–Fri 10:00 am–6:00 pm, Sat 10:00 am–4:00 pm
  One terminal € 1/15 min, possibility to print b/w € 0.20/A4, WLAN

**Call Centres**

4–5 terminals, € 1/30min. Also (international) phonecalls, faxing, copying, burning CDs, scanning and printing.

- Kaisaniemi
  Vuorikatu 8
  Tel: (09) 670-612
  Mon–Sat 9:00 am–9:00 pm, Sun 12:00 pm–8:00 pm
- Hakaniemi
  Näkinuja 4
  Tel: (09) 2722-550
  Mon–Sat 11:00 am–10:00 pm
- Sörnäinen
  Hämeentie 23
  Tel: (09) 685-2995
  Mon–Sat 11:00 am–10:00 pm
- Gaming Café Level 7
  Vilhonkatu 5b
  Tel: (09) 673-327
  Mon–Sun 1:00 pm–10:00 pm
  30 terminals at € 4/h (members € 3/h).
- JohtoCafe
  Kamppi Centre, Urho Kekkosenkatu 1
  Tel: (050) 597-5928, (09) 5840-0607
  Mo–Fri 9:00 am–9:00 pm, Sat 9:00 am–6:00 pm
  Sun 12:00 pm–6:00 pm (in summer only),
  18 terminals € 2/½h, € 3.5/1h, free WLAN for the customers.
- mbar
  Lasipalatsi, Mannerheimintie 22-24
  Tel: (09) 6124-5420
  Mon–Tue 9:00 am–12:00 am, Wed–Thu 9:00 am–2:00 am

Fri–Sat 9:00 am–3:00 am, Sun 12:00 pm–12:00 am, 13 terminals (€ 2/20min, € 3/30min, € 5/1h), WLAN, possibility to use USB memory-cards.

- Osuma Center
  Porthaninkatu 6
  Tel: (09) 694-1706
  Mon–Fri 8:30 am–9:00 pm, Sat–Sun 10:00 am–7:00 pm
  22 terminals, € 1/h, printing € 0.4/page.
- Ravintola Kola
  Helsinginkatu 13
  Tel: (09) 694-8983
  Mon–Sun 12:00 pm–2:00 am
  One terminal, € 1/ ½h.

## Public Libraries

At least one terminal/library, all together over 200 terminals. Note: A library card is needed at public libraries (except Library 10)

- Rikhardinkatu Library
  Rikhardinkatu 3
  Tel: (09) 3108-5013
  Mon–Thu 10:00 am–8:00 pm, Fri–Sat 10:00 am–4:00 pm
  Ten terminals without reservation, 30 minutes, also possibility to make a reservation for a longer time. A library card is needed.
- Library 10
  Main Post Building, Elielinaukio 2 G
  Tel: (09) 3108-5000
  Mon–Thu 10:00 am–10:00 pm, Fri 10 am–6:00 pm, Sat–Sun 12:00 pm–6:00 pm
  34 terminals, of which 22 units can be reserved for 30 minutes to three hours, 12 units for 30 minutes without prior reservation. Possibility to print in b/w or colour, € 0.20/A4. A termial for disabled persons for 30 minutes to three hours. WLAN.
- Parliament Library
  Aurorankatu 6
  Tel: (09) 432-3423
  Mon 9:00 am–6:00 pm, Tue–Thu 9:00 am–8:00 pm,

Fri 9:00 am–6:00 pm, Sat 9:00 am–3:00 pm
19 terminals.

## USEFUL CONTACTS

- Helsinki Expert
  http://www.helsinkiexpert.fi
  http://www.helsinkiexpert.fi/aboutus/yhteystiedot.html
  For useful up-to-the-minute advice and sightseeing and tours, accommodation booking and guide services.
- City of Helsinki Tourist Office
  Pohjoisesplanadi 19, 00100 Helsinki
  Tel: (09) 3101-3300
  Fax: (09) 3101-3301
  Email: tourist.info@hel.fi
  Website: http://www.hel.fi/tourism
- Finland Tourist Information:
  Finnish Tourist Board (UK)
  PO Box 33213, London SW6 8JX
  Tel: (020) 7365-2512 (consumer information)
  Email: finlandinfo@mek.fi
  Website: http://www.visitfinland.com/uk
- British Embassy
  Itäinen Puistotie 17, 00140 Helsinki
  Tel: (09) 2286-5100
  Fax: (09) 2286-5262
  Email: mailbox@ukembassy.fi
  Website: http://www.ukembassy.fi
- Finnish Embassy (UK)
  38 Chesham Place, London SW1X 8HW
  Tel: (020) 7838-6200
  Fax: (020) 7235-3680
  Website: http://www.finemb.org.fi

## BUSINESS SERVICES

- For more information: http://www.hel2.fi/convention/EN/ (professional congress organisers).
- Convention and Meeting Planners
  Helsinki-Finland Congress Bureau
  Fabiankatu 4b, 00130 Helsinki

Tel: (09) 668-9540
Fax: (09) 6689-5410
Email: hfcb@hfcb
Website: http://www.hfcb.fi

- Finland Travel Bureau Ltd
PO BOX 319, 00101 Helsinki
Tel: (09) 18-261
Fax: (09) 622-1524
Email: groups.incoming@smt.fi
Website: http://www.smt.fi
- Finland Travel Marketing
Sibeliusaukio, 004400 Järvenpää
Tel: (09) 2790-970
Fax: (09) 2712-843
Email: rauno.pusa@ftm.inet.fi
Website: http://www.finland-tm.com
- Bennett BTI Nordic
Congress Service, PO Box 1149, 00101 Helsinki
Tel: (09) 685-850
Fax: (09) 6858-5280
Email: helsinki.incoming@bennettbti.com
Website: http://www.bennettbti.com
- Congrex Blue & White Conferences
PO Box 81, Sulkapolku 3, 00371 Helsinki
Tel: (09) 560-7500
Fax: (09) 5607-5020
Website: http://www.congrex.com
- Convenio Ltd
Ilmarinkatu 10c, 00101 Helsinki
Tel: (09) 241-0424
Fax: (09) 241-0425
Email: convenio@pp.kolumbus.fi
Website: http://www.convenio.fi
- Marina Conventure
Pajalahdentie 9, 00200 Helsinki
Tel: (09) 682-2306
Fax: (09) 682-2307
Email: marina@marinaconventure.fi

- TSG Congress
  Kaisaniemenkatu 3b, 00100 Helsinki
  Tel: (09) 628-044
  Fax: (09) 667-675
  Email: info@tsgcongress.fi

## CONGRESS AND MEETING VENUES

- http://www.hel2.fi/convention/EN/ (conference facilities)
- Finlandia Hall
  Mannerheimintie 13e, 00100 Helsinki
  Tel: (09) 40-241
  Fax: (09) 446-259
  Email: finlandiahall@fin.hel.fi
  Website: http://finlandia.hel.fi
  The hall is in Hesperia Park, within walking distance of the larger hotels. It has capacity for up to 2,000 people and seating in the main auditorium for up to 1,700.
- Helsinki Fair Centre
  PO Box 21, 00521 Helsinki
  Tel: (09) 15-091
  Fax: (09) 142-358
  Email: info@finnexpo.fi
  Website: http://www.finnexpo.fi
  The centre has several restaurants, cafés and private dining rooms, with total seating for up to 2,940.
- Marina Congress Center
  Katajanokanlaituri 6, 00160 Helsinki
  Tel: (09) 16-661
  Fax: (09) 629-334
  Email: grandmarina@scandic-hotels.com
  Website: http://www.scandic-hotels.com
  Five meeting rooms, seven conference halls for 150-2,000 guests. Video monitoring system, closed-circuit TV system, teleconferencing facilities, permanent TV and radio cables for mobile broadcasting units.
- Paasitorni Conference Centre
  Pastorni, Paasivuorenkatu 5a, 00530 Helsinki
  Tel: (09) 708-9611
  Fax: (09) 708-965

Email: myynti@paasitorni.fi
Website: http://www.paasitorni.com
This centre has large conference halls and room for up to 2,000 banqueting guests.

- Radisson SAS Royal Hotel Helsinki
Runeberginkatu 2, 00100 Helsinki
Tel: (09) 69-580
Fax: (09) 6958-7100
Email: info@helzh.rd.sas.com
Website: http://www.radisson.com
Five meeting rooms, five conference rooms for 150-1,000 guests. 262 hotel rooms including eight suites.
- Strand Inter-Continental Helsinki
John Stenbergin ranta 4, 00530 Helsinki
Tel: (09) 39-351
Fax: (09) 393-5255
Email: strand@interconti.com
Website: http://www.interconti.com
Four meeting rooms, two conference rooms for up to 800 guests. 200 hotel rooms including eight suites, four saunas, swimming pool, 24-hour room service and airline check-in.

## EMBASSIES

| Embassies | Address | Telephone |
|---|---|---|
| Argentina | Bulevardi 5 A 11 | (09) 607-630 |
| Austria | Keskuskatu 1 A | (09) 171-322 |
| Belgium | Kalliolinnantie 5 | (09) 170-412 |
| Canada | Pohjoiseplanadi 25 B | (09) 171-141 |
| Chile | Erottajankatu 11 | (09) 612-6780 |
| China | Vanha Kelkkamaki 9-11 | (09) 228-9010 |
| Czech Republic | Armfeltintie 14 | (09) 171-169 |
| Denmark | Keskuskatu 1 A | (09) 684-1050 |

| Embassies | Address | Telephone |
|---|---|---|
| Estonia | Itainen Puistotie 10 | (09) 622-0288 |
| Fed. Rep. Germany | Krogiuksentie 4 B | (09) 458-580 |
| France | Itainen Puistotie 13 | (09) 618-780 |
| Great Britain | Itainen Puistotie 17 | (09) 2286-5100 |
| Greece | Maneesikatu 2 A 4 | (09) 278-1100 |
| Hungary | Kuusisaarenkuja 6 | (09) 484-144 |
| Iceland | Pohjoiseplanadi 27 C, 2nd floor | (09) 612-2460 |
| India | Satamakatu 2 A 8 | (09) 608-927 |
| Ireland | Erottajankatu 7 A | (09) 646-006 |
| Israel | Vironkatu 5 A | (09) 135-6177 |
| Italy | Itainen Puistotie 4 | (09) 681-1280 |
| Japan | Etelaranta 8, 4th floor | (09) 686-0200 |
| Mexico | Simonkatu 12 A, 7th floor | (09) 5860-4322 |
| Netherlands | Erottajankatu 19 B | (09) 661-737 |
| Norway | Rehbinderintie 17 | (09) 686-0180 |
| Poland | Armas Lindgrenin tie 21 | (09) 684-8077 |
| Portugal | Itainen Puistotie 11 B | (09) 682-4370 |
| Russian Federation | Tehtaankatu 1 B | (09) 661-876 |
| South Africa | Rahapajankatu 1 A 5 | (09) 6860-3100 |
| Spain | Kalliolinnantie 6 | (09) 687-7080 |
| Sweden | Pohjoisesplanadi 7 B | (09) 651-255 |
| Switzerland | Uudenmaankatu 16 A | (09) 649-422 |
| Turkey | Puistokatu 1 b A 3 | (09) 681-1030 |

| Embassies | Address | Telephone |
|---|---|---|
| United States of America | Itainen Puistotie 14 A | (09) 171-931 |
| Venezuela | Bulevardi 1 A 62 | (09) 641-522 |
| Yugoslavia | Kulosaarentie 36 | (09) 684-7466 |

N.B: for up-to-date information on the embassies, check *Helsinki This Week*.

# FURTHER READING

*A Short History of Finland*. Fred Singleton. Cambridge: Cambridge University Press, 1989.

*A Survival Guide to Finnish Cuisine for Business People*. Hese Hyvärinen, Marja Nurmelin and Timo Mäkelä. Yrityskirjat OY, 2000.

*A History of Finland*. John Wuorinen. New York: Columbia University Press, 1965.

*Finland, World Bibliographical Series, Vol.31*. J E O Screen. Oxford: Clio Press, 1981.

*Finland and Europe: International Crises during the Period of Autonomy, 1808-1914*. J Paasivirta. London: Hurst, 1981.

*Finland in the 20th Century*. D G Kirby. London: Hurst, 1979.

*Four Finns; Political Profiles: Mannerheim, Tanner, Stahlberg, Paasikivi*. M Rintala. Berkeley: University of California Press, 1969.

*Folklore and Nationalism in Modern Finland*. W A Wilson. Bloomington: Indiana University Press, 1976.

*The Kalevala or Poems of the Kalevala District*. F P Magoun. Harvard University Press, 1963, reprinted 1985.

*Finland: Cultural Lone Wolf*. R D Lewis. Intercultural Press, 2005.

*From Finland With Love*. R Roman Schatz. Johnny Kniga, 2005.

*Finland*. Lonely Planet Publications. Victoria, Australia: Lonely Planet Publications Pty Ltd., 1999.

*Finland.* Insight Guides. APA Publications (HK) Ltd, 1996.

*The Lighter Side of Finland: For Businessmen.* R Snyder. Finland: Yrityskirjat OY, 1996.

*The Optimist's Guide To Finland For Business People.* R Snyder. Finland: Yrityskirjat OY, 2003.

*Sauna, Sisu and Sibelius: A Survival Guide to Finnish for Business People.* M Dahlgren and M Nurmelin. Finland: Yrityskirjat OY, 1999.

*The Birth of the Kalevala.* A Asplund and U Lipponen. Helsinki: Finnish Literature Society, 1985.

*The Kalevala* (1835). E Lonnrot. London: translated by Kirby, Atholone Press, 1985.

Folklore and the Development of National Identity in Finland. T K Ramnarine. Europa, number 1 article 6, 1996.

*A Short Introduction to the Finnish Language.* J Korpela. http://www.hut.fi/~jkorpela/Finnish 08.09.1998.

*Finnish Folklore Research 1828-1918.* J Hautala. Helsinki: Finnish Society of Sciences, 1968.

'A Hundred Years of Finnish Folklore Research: A Reappraisal', in *Folklore* 1979: 141-152. L Honko.

## From Publisher Yrityskirjat OY of Finland

- Faces of Finland
  ISBN: 952-9660-71-5
- Finland in a Small Book
  ISBN: 952-9660-53-7
- Finnish Elements of Strength
  ISBN: 952-9660-54-5
- The Best of Helsinki
  ISBN: 952-9660-50-2

- A Survival Guide to Finnish Sauna Sisu & Sibelius
  ISBN: 952-9660-18-9
- A Survival Guide to The Finnish Sauna for Businesspeople
  ISBN: 952-9660-37-5
- Four Moods of Finland
  ISBN: 952-9660-37-5

# ABOUT THE AUTHOR

Dr Deborah Swallow is a cross-cultural communications consultant and trainer and has worked in private, voluntary and public (mainly overseas governments) sectors across 19 countries. She has worked with business leaders and diplomats around the world; devised, written and delivered Good Governance seminars; helped to develop frameworks for accountability and transparency; created sets of good practice examples; and spoken to businesses about the challenges of globalisation. Deborah won the UK National Training Award as an individual in 1999, the highest accolade in the business.

She openly acknowledges that coming to Finland changed her life and her value-set. As a consequence, today she passionately believes in responsible business solutions as drivers of success. Her mission is to promote organisations with a values-driven ethos for environmentally sustainable development and poverty alleviation, through encouraging business leaders to adopt ethical business practices.

Deborah is a sought after conference speaker, consultant and trainer and lives in the south-east of England.

# INDEX


A
accommodation 116–121
alcohol 108–109
alternative lifestyles 101–102

B
banking 239–241
bilingualism 57–58
business 223–235
  consensus 232–233
  decisions and actions 231–232
  getting down to business 227–229
  letter and emails 234–235
  meetings and appointments 229–230
  negotiations 230
  presentations 233–234
  the Finnish handshake 226–227

C
cinema 186
classless society 67–71
cleanliness 6–7
climate 20–26
coffee 153–154
conformity 2–3
corruption 238–239
credit cards 247
currency 247
customer care 7–9

D
dancing 107–108, 182–183
daylight hours 10
debt 65–66
divorce 85–89
domestic help 121–122
dress code 92–97

E
economy 41–49
education 79–80, 122–126
  language lessons 124–126
  pre-school 122–123
  school 123
  university 123–124
electricity 63–64

F
family 85–89
Finnish heros 164–169
flirting 106–107
flooring 118
food 139–162
  buying food 160–162
  cafés 154–155
  eating out 150–153
  Lappish food 144–145
  restaurants 155–160
  special occasions 149–150
  the cuisine 140–144
  typical Finnish dishes 145–148

G
geography 16–20
government 49–52

H
Helsinki 199–201
Helsinki Airport 188, 189
history 26–39
holidays 170–175
hotels 191–195
humour 104–106

I
imports 133–135
  importing animals 134
  importing food 133–134
  import prohibitions 134–135
Internet 121

J
jobs 242–243

K
Karelia 198
Kuopio 204–206

L
Lake District 198
language 208–221
  Finnish folklore 219–220
  Finnish sayings 220–221
  learning the language 213–216
  the literature 216–219
Lapland 195–197

M
makkara 142, 143
maps 249
marriage 85–89
medical facilities 126
military 52–53
mobile phones 4–5, 250
music 180–182

N
newspapers 250

O
opening hours 250–251

P
passport 251
payment terms 238
personal space 71–73
physical characteristics 56–57
population 55–56
punctuality 63

R
regional differences 113–114
reliability 67
religion 76–79, 126–127

S
Sami 15, 27, 55, 56, 70, 185, 195, 245, 249
Santa Claus 175–180
sauna 109–113
scandal 100–101
shopping 135–137
silence 102–104
smoking 108–109
Southern Finland 198–199
sports 183–186

T
Tampere 203–204
Tarja Halonen 89–90
technology 5–6
telephone 121
telephone codes 253
television 120–121
time zone 254
tipping 254
tolerance 97–100
traffic 9–10
tranquility 2–3
transportation 127–133
  buses 127–128
  cars and bicycles 130–132
  railways 128–130
  taxis 127
  traffic 132–133
travel 186–191
traveller's cheques 254
Turku 201–202

V
values 60–67
visas 188

W
windows 118–119
women 80–85
work permit 241–242
World War I 33
World War II 35

## Titles in the CULTURESHOCK! series: